MODERN BRITISH HISTORY ★ A Garland Series

Edited by
PETER STANSKY and
LESLIE HUME

NATIONAL HEALTH INSURANCE AND THE MEDICAL PROFESSION IN BRITAIN, 1913–1939

Norman R. Eder

Garland Publishing, Inc.
New York & London ★ 1982

Library of Congress Cataloging in Publication Data

Eder, Norman R.
National health insurance and the medical profession in Britain, 1913–1939.

(Modern British history)
Bibliography: p.
Includes index.
1. Insurance, Health—Great Britain—History—20th century. 2. Physicians—Great Britain—History—20th century. I. Title. II. Series.
HD7102.G7E3 1982 368.4′2′00941 81-48358
ISBN 0-8240-5154-8

All volumes in this series are printed on acid-free, 250-year-life paper.
Printed in the United States of America

ACKNOWLEDGMENT

This work was completed during five years of study at the University of Illinois at Chicago Circle and was made possible by the financial support of the State of Illinois. I would also like to acknowledge the ever present aid of the Newberry Library and its cast of characters.

The bulk of the research for this project would have been impossible without the interest of Dr. John Marks, who persuaded the British Medical Association to allow me free access to its archives. I would also like to thank Drs. Ernest Colin-Russ, Frank Gray and Solomen Wand who agreed to speak to me about their medical careers and for adding a personal touch to the historical record. In addition, I also wish to thank the library staffs of the Department of Health and Social Security (Elephant and Castle & John Adam Street), the Public Record Office, the British Library and the Wellcome Institute for their invaluable assistance. A special note of appreciation is also due to Professor Maurice Bruce, whose stream of letters and day trips to London provided a wealth of intellectual and moral support throughout a wet and chilly English summer.

My work, however, would never have been completed without the kindness, insight and scotch of Professor Bentley B. Gilbert. The door to his office and home were always open and his influence as a mentor will always be keenly appreciated. I would also like to thank the members of my committee, Drs. James Sack, Marion Miller, William Hoisington and Carolyn Edie for their well placed criticism and suggestions. Most importantly, I owe an enormous debt to Sharon Eder. She not only typed the manuscript but she provided unequalled criticism and encouragement. She deserves much more than a simple thank you.

TABLE OF CONTENTS

INTRODUCTION

Health and health services have in the twentieth century become topics of major concern in both industrialized and developing nations. In keeping with this international interest social scientists have rushed to analyze the nature of medical care, health institutions and the delivery of medical services in modern societies. Health services research, though, has been dominated by entirely contemporary minded disciplines. Historians of medicine have played almost no role in the effort to understand the nature of health care, health administration or their broad social implications. By choice or design, the history of medicine has been kept within rather traditional boundaries. Medical biographies, the examination of scientific advancement and the history of public health measures have largely defined the field. To be sure, this approach has been valuable but it has also produced a narrow and often isolated area of historical study.[1] Some historians of medicine have recently moved to break through this isolation and expand the scope of medical history towards a broader synthesis of what has been called the social history of medicine.[2]

The first pioneering work in the social history of medicine was completed by American scholars, yet in the past ten years historians in Britain have produced some of the most important studies.[3] The appearance of books dealing with medical institutions in Britain, the cholera epidemics, polular medicine, the Victorian medical profession in London and nineteenth century health care from the perspective of patients illustrates the fertility and breadth of the subject area.[4] This examination of the politics, administration and medical work of the national health insurance act's medical service from the viewpoint of the medical profession is squarely within this new approach to the history of medicine and medical care. Unlike the older brand of medical history, it shares with recent work in the field a concern for the history of health care at the point of delivery and the interplay between medicine and society. This examination of national health insurance in Britain, however, does offer something new to the social history of medicine. It extends the boundaries of the emerging field beyond the nineteenth century into the complexities of twentieth century British politics, social administration and medicine.

Even at its most basic level the internal dynamics of providing medical attention are far from easy to describe and define. Medicine entails more than the application of medical science, money and the skill of the practitioner. Fundamental emotions concerning life, death and well-being are interwoven throughout the fabric of medical work. Reflecting this balance of science, art and human emotion, medical practice has historically been based upon the social and economic relationships between individual doctors and their patients. Fees were linked directly to service and should the patient become dissatisfied with one practitioner another could always be found. In the twentieth century, however, this pattern of medical attendance has been the target of widespread criticism as modern societies have brought medical care within the scope of state sponsored social services.

In Britain medical care became part of public policy in 1911, when David Lloyd George succeeded in guiding the national insurance act through Parliament.[5] The act, though, was more than a partisan program of reform. It symbolized a deep-seated change in the manner in which Britons of all parties had come to view poverty and society's poor. For the mid-Victorians, destitution was a disgrace suffered by those who had failed to measure up to the test of social competition. Poverty was the fault of the poor and the New Poor Law of 1834 was a reflection of Victorian society's desire to protect itself from the undeserving. Nonetheless by the 1880s English society was being made acutely aware of the plight of its industrial and rural poor.

A new breed of social commentator began to apply their skills of scientific observation and quantitative measurement to the physical environment of Britain. Through statistics they laid bare the conditions of work of factory operatives, miners and the children of the laboring classes. The most notable of these writers was Charles Booth. In his *Life and Labour of the People of London* he described in vivid detail the horrors of late nineteenth century London life for the impoverished. Booth and his research team, which included Beatrice Potter, found that in East London fully 35% of the population lived in adject poverty and that more than half of those interviewed belonged to families with incomes of less than 18s. per week in 1887. The food consumed by the poor was tainted and tuberculosis and chronic bronchitis were shown by Booth to be rampant among the 900,000 persons crowded into Britain's capital city.

Charles Booth was certainly not the first to apply statistical measurement to health and environmental problems. But unlike the sanitarians, William Farr, Florence Nightengale, Edwin Chadwick and Sir John Simon, Booth and those who followed him argued for far more than public cleanliness. Their sociological science sought to define, identify and then eliminate poverty. It was a popular movement that struck a responsive chord among a new middle class generation that was genuinely shocked by the human tragedy that had been revealed by Booth's studies. In large numbers young men and women began to flock to settlement houses and soup kitchens in England's industrial slums. Whereas their parents had been content to live in quiet ignorance of the great mass of the poor, the late Victorian generation volunteered in baby saving campaigns, attended public lectures and openly promoted socialist measures of reform in order to improve the condition of the poor.

The impact of the growing concern for the impoverished in English society was dramatic, if subtle. By the early twentieth century pauperism and become poverty and illness and disease had been redefined in the public mind from a personal misfortune to an acknowledged social disgrace. Poverty was now the fault of society rather than the responsibility of those in distress. Still, the growing concern for the condition of the poor lacked a political focus. As a result the new interest in social investigation, so avidly promoted by reformers, remained largely a matter of personal rather than national attention. This, though, was dramatically altered by the shocking revelations of the Boer War.

Widespread sickness, physical disability and illiteracy were uncovered among those volunteering for service in the South African war. In East London, the very area that Booth had studied, eleven out of twelve men were rejected for military service by the army's doctors in 1900. Clearly the physical results of poverty could no longer be ignored or left to the Poor Law Guardians, philanthropists and social statisticians. The very heart of the empire was threatened and with it the British imperial position in an increasingly hostile world. England needed vigorous and healthy citizens if she was to remain productive at home and strong abroad.

The press gave wide coverage to the problem of national efficiency and in the years following the Boer War local authorities and the central government stepped up their public health activities. By the time the Liberal party came to power in

January 1906 the issue of the nation's vitality had received such wide attention that nearly all of the leaders of the party were committed to some measure of social reform. For the liberal politicians, though, easing the burden of poverty was far more than a moral imperative. Reform was also a political necessity. Not only was the empire threatened by the waste of the nation's human resources but the enfranchised masses presented fertile soil for socialists, trade unionism and the young but vocal Labour party. In order to protect the Liberal party and liberal capitalism from their enemies, Liberals understood that reforms were needed to dull the sharp edges of the capitalist system. However, individual and local government action could hardly be expected to meet the needs of the poor adequately. At the same time any reform on the massive scale was bound to be extraordinarily expensive.

Given the need for both low cost and the effective relief of poverty, it is not surprising that the Liberal government looked to the principle of insurance as a means for the alleviation of destitution. Since the mid-nineteenth century friendly societies had been providing both social activities and insurance against unemployment, sickness and death to their working class members. Insurance was also widely available from many private insurance companies whose agents were a common figure in working class life. The Liberals saw that the government could create its own system of compulsory insurance against the worst aspects of poverty -- unemployment, sickness and destitution in old age. Most importantly, however, state sponsored insurance would be cheap. The poor themselves would provide the bulk of the money and the central government had only to organize the collection of contributions and the payment of benefits without the taint of either charity or the Poor Law.

Insurance was never seen as a remedy for poverty, but it did hold out the promise of eliminating the most obvious and damaging results of distress. Moreover, it was a concept that appealed to both the rate payer and the working man and one that engendered very little partisan opposition. Therefore in 1908 the insurance principle was employed to create a national scheme of state sponsored old age pensions for the laboring poor. This was followed by an even larger measure of reform in 1911, when Lloyd George presented to Parliament a plan for national unemployment, sickness and health insurance. In this 1911 scheme the cash unemployment and sickness benefits were seen as being the most important and the health benefit (general practitioner care) was added almost as an afterthought. Nonetheless, the decision to include medical care in the national insurance plan was of tremendous importance. The government was no longer simply offering cash insurance benefits to eligible contributors in order to relieve poverty. For the first time in Britain's history the state had made a commitment to provide a minimum level of health care to the poor.

The importance of this decision, while not recognized in 1911, had a direct impact upon the lives of millions of Britons, who for the first time were offered the services of the medical profession without restriction. However, excluding the insured population, no group in Britain was more affected by the passage of the insurance act than the nation's doctors. For them the insurance act was more than a necessary social reform, a defense against socialist propaganda or a way to win votes. General practitioners became the part-time employees of the state and were placed at the center of a massive legislative scheme. Their heretofore personal services were organized for the public good and the medical profession becamse permanently linked to the state. Doctors became the linchpin in the daily operation of a health insurance system that provided benefits to nearly twenty million people by 1939.

The medical profession's new relationship with the state and the insured population was complex and far-reaching. On 15 January 1913, when the insurance scheme first delivered its medical benefits, the services of thirteen thousand practitioners were incorporated into the largest measure of domestic social reform before the second world war. Practitioners were thrust into a system of carefully balanced and competitive economic, bureaucratic and political interests. This shook the medical profession to its very foundation as practitioners found themselves the vehicles for social reform rather than simply the advocates of particular reform measures.[8] Doctors discovered that they had to deal with their new situation on three distinct levels. The conditions of medical practice, including the problems of securing adequate remuneration, the doctor-patient relationship, clerical work and professional discipline were of major concern to all medical men. On another level the nation's practitioners had to help to create a smooth working relationship with both local and national bureaucracies. Finally, the act put Britain's doctors in the heart of national social and administrative politics.

The story of the medical profession's interaction with the insurance act from 1913-1939 and the effect this had upon individual doctors, medical traditions and institutions as well as upon the profession as a whole is at the center of this study. Nonetheless, this examination of insurance medical practice also has a larger concern. It seeks to add a new dimension to the study of modern British social history. In the past historians, searching for the origins of the welfare state, have generally concentrated their attention upon the development of social institutions, political conflict and the advancement of social theory.[9] As a result social history has at times been marked by ideological debate and dominated by the collection of bloodless statistics. This approach and the issues that it has dealt with are of course important; it has a prominent place in the story of the insurance act and the general development of social policy in Britain. Still, this style of historical investigation has often ignored the actual results of particular pieces of reforming legislation. Each reform measure has quickly become obscured by those that follow.

Because of the creation of the National Health Service and its massive bureaucracy after the second world war the health benefit of the national insurance act has been especially victimized by a lack of serious attention. Many historians have actually forgotten that the health provisions of the national insurance act ever existed and those who do remember the insurance medical service see it as a halfway house on the road to the welfare state. But the act did have a life of its own. It represented a particular response to poverty and sickness that, while limited in scope, deserves careful attention. With the insurance act Edwardian society sought to raise the level of health care among the laboring poor who had long been denied by poverty access to adequate medical attention. The act operated smoothly until the creation of the National Health Service and was often the only means of medical care for millions of Britons. Unlike the modern historian, the doctors who formed the insurance medical service were never allowed to forget this essential human fact. Its practical meaning looked them in the face every morning as they entered their surgeries. Therefore, through the eyes of the medical profession we can examine health insurance not as an abstract idea but as the product of social legislation at work, providing care and comfort to those in need.

Notes

1. This is a problem generally associated with the history of science. An example of the limits of the history of medicine in the past are made clear by the survey of medical history by Charles Singer and E. Ashworth Underwood, _A Short History of Medicine_ (Oxford: Oxford University Press, 1962). Within its limits it is a very good chronological study of the advancement of medical science but it completely fails to take into account the wider interaction between medical science and institutions with the societies of which they are an integral part.

2. The Society for the Social History of Medicine was formed in 1970 in order to accomplish this end. Dr. George Rosen, a long time medical historian, was elected its first president. In his 1973 Presidential Address Rosen defined the social history of medicine, health and diseases "more than the study of medical problems.... It requires as well an understanding of the factors - economic conditions, occupation, housing, nutrition, family structure and others - which create or influence health problems, and of the ways in which they operate."

3. See George Rosen, "Levels of Integration in Medical Historiography: A Review," _Journal of the History of Medicine and Allied Sciences_ vol. 4, 1949 p. 465. Henry E. Sigerist, "The History of Medicine and the History of Science," _Bulletin of the History of Medicine_ vol. 4, 1936 p. 5. Charles F. Mullett, "Medical History: Some Problems and Opportunities," _Journal of the History of Medicine and Allied Sciences_ vol. 1, 1946 p. 190. Richard Harrison Shyrock, _Medicine and Society in America: 1660-1860_ (Ithaca: Cornell University Press, 1975). Charles E. Rosenberg, _The Cholera Years_ (Chicago: The University of Chicago Press, 1962). Among the more recent American contributions to this expanding field is Richard W. Wertz and Dorothy C. Wertz, _Lying-In, A History of Childbirth in America_ (New York: Schocken Books, 1979).

4. John Woodward, _To Do the Sick No Harm, A Study of the British Voluntary Hospital System to 1875_ (London: Routledge & Kegan Paul, 1974). R. J. Morris, _Cholera 1832_ (London: Croom and Helm, 1976). John Woodward and David Richards ed., _Health Care and Popular Medicine in Nineteenth Century England_ (London: Croom and Helm, 1977).

M. Jeanne Peterson, The Medical Profession in Mid-Victorian London (Berkeley: University of California Press, 1978). F. B. Smith, The People's Health 1830-1910 (London: Croom and Helm, 1979). Other books of interest are Richard D. French, Antivivisection and Medical Science in Victorian Society (Princeton: Princeton University Press, 1975). Jeanne L. Brand, Doctors and the State (Baltimore: The Johns Hopkins Press, 1965). Brian Abel-Smith, The Hospitals in England and Wales 1800-1948 (Cambridge: Harvard University Press, 1964).

5. By far the best book dealing with the details of the National Insurance Act is Bentley B. Gilbert, The Evolution of National Insurance in Great Britain (London: Michael Joseph, 1966).

6. Besides Gilbert's study there is a sizable literature dealing with the background of the insurance act. For the act's public health connections see, Arthur Newsholme, The Last Thirty Years in Public Health (London: George Allen & Unwin Ltd., 1936). William M. Frazer, A History of English Public Health, 1839-1939 (London: Harrison and Sons Ltd., 1950). Also see Newsholme's The Story of Modern Preventive Medicine (Baltimore: The Williams & Wilkins Company, 1929). C.F.G. Masterman, The Heart of Empire, Bentley B. Gilbert ed., (New York: Harper Row, 1973) is a must for the Edwardian background of the act. Equally important is Charles Booth, Life and Labour of the People of London (London: Macmillan, 1903). A political scientist's analysis of the New Liberalism that produced the insurance act and its origins is supplied by Michael Freeden, The New Liberalism (Oxford: Clarendon Press, 1978). Another view of the background of the scheme has been supplied by G. R. Searle, The Quest for National Efficiency (Berkeley: University of California Press, 1971). Finally a recent synthesis of the intellectual and political trends that produced the insurance act is John Grigg, Lloyd George: The People's Champion (London: Eyre Methuen, 1978).

7. There has been very little analysis of the actual work of the insurance act. Some information is supplied by Bentley B. Gilbert, British Social Policy, 1914-1939 (Ithaca: Cornell University Press, 1970). Also see Barbara Armstrong, The Health Insurance Doctor, His Role in Great Britain, Denmark and France (Princeton: Princeton University Press, 1939). There are few valuable contemporary sources but among the most useful are Herman Levy, National

Health Insurance (London: Cambridge University Press, 1944). Arthur Newsholme, Medicine and the State (London: George Allen and Unwin Ltd., 1932). Also see Newsholme's International Studies vol. 3 (London: George Allen & Unwin, 1931). Finally of special interest is Douglass W. Orr and Jean Walker Orr, Health Insurance with Medical Care (New York: MacMillan Company, 1938).

8. Jeanne L. Brand, Doctors and the State (Baltimore: Johns Hopkins Press, 1965). Brand discusses the activities of the B.M.A. in the late nineteenth century and points out the strict limits of the profession's political concerns. Generally, they remained within the boundaries of sanitary reform and the establishment of professional standards.

9. See Maurice Bruce, The Coming of the Welfare State (London: Batsford, 1960). Also see Charles Loch Mowat, Britain Between the Wars, 1918-1940 (Boston: Beacon Press, 1971).

CHAPTER I

On the Panel

Lloyd George's national health insurance scheme was introduced into the House of Commons in May 1911. On 16 December it received the royal assent, in time for the Chancellor to present it as the government's Christmas gift to Britain's workers. As the most comprehensive social reform before the First World War, the act represented the growing Liberal commitment to the ideal of state sponsored contributory insurance as a bulwark against both confiscatory socialism and unregulated capitalism. The act provided sickness and medical benefits to fourteen million workers, employed 13,000 general practitioners on a part-time basis and created a complex network of private and public administration. At the same time the insurance act had at its disposal a massive amount of money that for its first year of operation totaled £18 million -- an amount roughly equal to the annual income of the Post Office.[1]

For Britain's medical profession the passage of the insurance bill into law meant far more than the application of political theory, humanitarian concern or the creation of a tremendous pool of money and an administrative network to govern its allocation. Medical practitioners were asked to provide their professional services to millions of patients under the direct supervision of the government. Not surprisingly, many doctors balked at the prospect of non-medical control and government regulation of their professional lives and from 1911 until 1914 the medical community existed in a state of perpetual crisis. The profession's political arm, the British Medical Association, was shattered by its inept leadership of the opposition to the act. Left confused and bitter, 13,000 general practitioners entered the insurance medical service still believing that it was contrary to their personal and professional interests. This sense of crisis persisted only to fade as individual doctors began to discover during the act's first year that most of their fears about the scheme had been unfounded. Practitioners had not become prisoners of abusive non-medical administrators and the value of medical practice had not fallen. There would of course be administrative difficulties after 1914 but as the routine of solving these became apparent, medical men could begin to look forward to a still uncertain but far less unknown future.

The Profession and its Past

Of all the traditional professions, the church, law and the army and naval officer corps, medicine was the last to be recognized by British society as as honorable endeavor.[2] Doctors in the 1820s and 1830s were accused of being charlatans and ignorant men, who took advantage of personal tragedy to charge high fees for their ineffectual services.[3] Bleeding and mercury based potions were still widely accepted as the best remedies for illness. As in Thackeray's novel, _Pendennis_, doctors were thought of as tradesmen who "exercised the profession of Apothocary and Surgeon and not only attended gentlemen in their sick-rooms and ladies at their most interesting period of their lives, [but] would condescend to sell a brown-paper plaster to a farmer's wife across the counter or to vend toothbrushes, hair-powder and ladies perfumery."[4] Such activities were hardly the mark of complete respectability. As a whole, doctors during the first half of the nineteenth century seemed to be tied far more to the artisan world of profit and competition than to any higher code of professional honor. Gentlemen may have entered medicine but clearly not all practitioners of the healing arts were members of the gentle class.

Public confidence in the skills of medical practitioners in Britain was not enhanced by the arrival of cholera in 1832. Doctors, despite their scientific claims, could do little in the face of the mysterious epidemic. In order to meet this crisis medical men formed themselves into professional associations, one of which would emerge in 1836 as the British Medical Association.[5] With professionalism as its goal, the B.M.A. during the second half of the nineteenth century sought through national legislative reform to eliminate the "mischief and inconvenience arising from unqualified practice."[6] The Association promoted uniform standards of medical education, ethics and science. At the same time the B.M.A. closely guarded the right of the profession alone to establish those standards and the right of independence of individual doctors from outside interference. The ideal was a prosperous private practice with both fees and the privileged doctor-patient relationship unhindered by non-medical concerns. Unfortunately, as the twentieth century approached not all medical practitioners in Britain were afforded such absolute freedom. Most practitioners lacked the family connections or private capital to set up shop on Harley Street or become consulting specialists in large hospitals.[7]

For many men, medical work in the late nineteenth century held little of the glitter of a learned profession. Often living in desperate poverty, general practitioners in rural areas, coal districts and urban slums found that their patients were at times more the objects of charity than the sources of lucrative fees.[8] Thus the medical man and his patient both turned to the friendly societies. These societies had long been part of English laboring life.[9] As a result of the decline of guilds in the seventeenth century, they developed as voluntary associations that offered contributors annual fetes and burial benefits. During the last forty years of the eighteenth century the number of these societies expanded rapidly and by 1800 there were several thousand in existence throughout the British Isles, with a membership of perhaps 8 1/2% of the total population.[10]

As they grew, societies such as The Loyal Ancient Independent Order of Odd Fellows, the Ancient Order of Foresters and the Ancient Fraternity of Gardeners became more than social clubs. Contributions were collected for an increasingly wide range of insurance benefits including medical care and cash sickness benefits. In the smaller societies medical men were customarily paid an annual capitation fee per subscriber even if all the members had no need of medical care. In return for his fee the doctor had to agree to provide all necessary services to those contributors who did fall ill. In contrast the larger societies often hired practitioners on a full time contract basis, thereby reserving the doctors' services for their members alone. It was also ot uncommon for several societies to amalgamate and form medical institutes, in which their members could receive a broad range of health services from a resident medical staff.[11]

The existence of the clubs served the interests of both poor doctors and their patients. Medical men were guaranteed a minimum fee and the working poor were assured of at least a basic level of medical care. But as the club medical system grew, complaints about its abuses began to be heard within the medical community which saw the expansion of contract practice as an affront to the professional honor and social status sought by the B.M.A. Medical men claimed the clubs didn't care about the quality of the men they hired or the level of care delivered to patients. Their only concern was the highly unprofessional desire "to get as much as possible out of the medical profession at the smallest possible cost to their own pockets."[13] They bullied doctors in their employ to refuse illness certificates to patients, thus denying them their cash sickness benefits.[14] Societies also engaged in the open advertising and many did not impose income limits upon their members. Therefore medical men believed that the clubs were a direct threat to private medical practice among the middle and prosperous artisan classes.[15]

In spite of the abuses of club practice, there was never any shortage of practitioners willing to accept the average capitation fee of 4s. per patient per year. Indeed the competition for contract appointments was usually quite keen.[16] Despite this, the subject of contract practice kept the medical profession in a constant state of agitation from the 1880s onward. Led by the B.M.A. the profession carried on an organized struggle to end the evils of club practice. Warnings of especially bad situations were published in the British Medical Journal. Local organizations were formed in order to end specific abuses and boycotts of societies and the establishment of alternative medical services became the profession's favorite weapons.

In Coventry, for example, local practitioners formed the Coventry Public Medical Service in 1893 in an attempt to destroy a provident dispensary and several friendly societies.[17] In order to secure "a more satisfactory state of affairs," all but two of Coventry's private practitioners joined together in the new service. Each man subscribed two guineas as a guarantee fund. The service forbade canvassing and imposed a £2 weekly income limit for members. Once it was established, its founders asked all contract doctors to resign from club service. None of the contract practitioners quit their posts, but in three years of struggle against local societies, one club, a branch of the Star Benefit Society, was forced to close because it could not fill its open medical positions. Unfortunately for the Coventry medical men, the closed society's members were almost completely absorbed into the provident dispensary, which with public chartible support was able to offer cheap care and medicine. Still, by 1896, doctors reported that they felt that their resistance to club domination had been a success for both themselves and the laboring poor of Coventry. "If other towns," Dr. Edward Phillips, the Secretary of the Coventry Medical Service wrote, "were to adopt such a course as Coventry, we should hear less of the 'battle of the clubs' and there would be no need for medical aid associations and cheap dispensaries."[18]

Many areas, though, had already adopted the measures advocated by Dr. Phillips. In Lincoln a medical protection fund was established in order to publicize medical complaints and to provide aid to men who resigned from club service. Lincoln medical men also formed their own doctors' club to care for the poor. Malvern practitioners refused to treat women at a cheaper rate than men and nearly every other local medical association passed resolutions decrying the conditions of contract medical work.

Nowhere, however, was the struggle more intense than in Cork, where the local medical society managed to get all the club doctors to resign in 1894. In response to this boycott the societies imported scab medical men to break local professional solidarity. But rather than beating the Cork practitioners into submission, the clubs alienated many of their own members, who often refused to be treated by the new doctors.[19] Nonetheless, even though the medical profession was successful in fighting the clubs to a stand-off in Cork, the struggle continued into the new century.

In order to document the difficulties of contract practice, the 1903 annual meeting of the B.M.A. asked the Association's Medico-Political Committee to investigate club abuses fully. During the next year the Committee issued 12,000 questionaires to doctors and 1,548 replies had been returned by June. Only 856 of the respondents stated that they were actually engaged in contract practice. Nonetheless the final report of the Committee, authored by Dr. J. Smith-Whitaker, the B.M.A.'s Medical Secretary, provided ample evidence of the dismal conditions under which many doctors worked.[20]

The fight against club medical practice was an important milestone in the history of the British Medical Association. From the earliest days as an organization the Association had always been recognized as an elite body, dominated by London's consulting and specialist class. Throughout its history the B.M.A.'s political activities were centered on the legislative reform of medicine. The Association's efforts to secure various educational and institutional reforms, while they may have raised the general status of the medical profession, had little effect upon the economic lives of the ordinary general practitioner. But in its struggle against club domination the B.M.A. attempted to extend its ideals of professionalism downward through the lower ranks of Britain's doctors.

A secure medical income not only promised clinical freedom but it guaranteed the right of patients to their doctor's unhindered clinical opinion. This argument earned the B.M.A. not only the respect of the mass of medical men but the trappings of a political and economic fighting force. No longer did the Association appear to be simply a pressure group whose only objects were medical reform and scientific advancement. In the early Edwardian period the B.M.A. seemed to be acquiring the strength and authority of a medical trade union whose goal was to raise all medical men to the middle class -- for the sake of doctors as well as their patients. This new political awareness was directly linked to the fight against club abuses and in turn the experience of the struggle against the societies would shape the profession's attitude toward national health insurance. The old antagonism between the friendly societies and the nation's medical practitioners was never laid to rest and this bitter rivalry remained at the core of medical politics throughout the life of the health insurance act.

The Coming of National Health Insurance

Despite the apparent new found strength of the B.M.A. the battle of the clubs continued without resolution. At the same time, though, there were other forces at work within Edwardian society that would provide a greater test of Britain's medical profession than their fight against friendly society control. Britain's public health pioneers, Edwin Chadwick, Sir James P. Kay-Shuttleworth, and Sir John Simon, had, in the last fifty years of the nineteenth century, publicized the inadequacies of sanitation measures.[21] But it was not until the Boer War that the terrible physical condition of the poor was crystalized in the public's consciousness. In the years that followed, school feeding programs were begun, medical inspection efforts were redoubled and contemporary writers found poverty, ill health and ignorance a never ending source of material for an increasingly receptive audience.[22] In this soil of rising social awareness, the idea of social insurance took root. Insurance became, in the words of one historian of the period, "a magic word, lighting a new future."[23]

The concept of social insurance provided a model for domestic reform while avoiding the stigma of the Poor Law. Contributory insurance also appealed to many as an effective means of diffusing the social discontent that threatened the glow of Edwardian society. Moreover, the idea of state sponsored contributory health insurance was well established in Europe. By 1911 many continental nations had created compulsory insurance for sickness as well as for accidents and old age. Germany under Bismarck had launched the first insurance scheme in Europe and this had been followed by similar plans in Austria, Hungary, Luxemburg, Norway and Switzerland.[24] But perhaps most important, insurance was cheap. The insured carried most of the financial burden. Rate payers were expected to add only enough money to cover the cost of administration, which was an attribute that was clearly appreciated by all British politicians.

On 4 May 1911 David Lloyd George, Exchequer in the Liberal government, introduced a national insurance bill into the House of Commons.[25] The plan had two separate sides. The first offered unemployment insurance and the second health insurance and cash sickness benefits to an estimated fourteen million wage earners. Contributions from the insured and their employers were compulsory. For health insurance each male worker was required to pay 4d. from his weekly pay packet while female workers contributed 3d. Employers were required to add another 3d. per insured employee and the government added another 2d. per week, per worker to cover the costs of administering the essentially self-financing scheme.[26] The funds collected were assembled into local insurance benefit pools and each insured person carried a card to which were affixed insurance stamps (usually by the employer who purchased the stamps through the Post Office). This system therefore made it possible to separate those persons who were insured from those who claimed benefits but who were either ineligible or who had failed to make a contribution.

In return for their contributions to the health insurance scheme, the bill promised workers general practitioner care, necessary drugs, sanatoria treatment for tuberculosis and a 30s. maternity benefit for insured women and the wives of contributing men. Insured women whose husbands were also insured were granted a double maternity benefit. In addition the plan established a scale of sickness benefits for workers who became physically unable to work. Commencing the fourth day of illness insured men were paid a weekly benefit of 10s. for the first thirteen weeks of sickness. During the same period women were given 7s.6d. and both male and female workers received a weekly benefit of 5s. during their second thirteen weeks of sickness. Disability beyond twenty-six weeks was also worth 5s. weekly until the age of 70 and general practitioner care continued for the rest of the insured's life.

The administrative structure of health insurance was worked out during the political debate that both preceded and followed the introduction of the insurance bill into Parliament. The negotiations, which have been thoroughly discussed by Professor Bentley B. Gilbert, were intense and represented a clash between the old friendly societies, the industrial insurance industry and various levels of government.[27] While the story of the conflict among these competing interests is beyond the scope of this present study, an understanding of its outcome is necessary to a full appreciation of the position of doctors under the insurance scheme.

The result of the political struggle over the administrative provisions of the health scheme was a complex balance between central and local government and private institutions. At the top level was the Joint Insurance Commission. This Commission was responsible for establishing the broad outline of national administrative policy. England, Scotland, Ireland and Wales also had national insurance commissions that oversaw the working of the scheme within the separate parts of the Kingdom. But it was at the local level that the tasks of day to day administration were conducted.

Following the traditional boundaries of local administration, a national network of 199 local insurance committees was established to regulate the work of the plan in each locality.[28] Each committee was composed of forty to eighty representatives from the local medical profession, the insured population, local authorities and approved societies, who acted as the dispensing agents of the cash sickness benefit. The size of the committees was reduced by half after 1921 but approximately three-fifths of their members continued to be drawn from the approved societies.

These societies were the actual administrators of the insurance act. In an attempt to follow the friendly society model, the act provided that each insured person could become a member of an approved society. In turn each society was to be democratically governed and society officers were charged with the responsibility of overseeing the insurance funds contributed in the name of their members. The insured therefore did not receive their cash sickness, maternity and disability payments from the government but directly through their society. The only exceptions to this general system were the insured who chose not to join a society. These 200,000 individuals, known as post office contributors, received their benefits directly through the post office.

Despite Lloyd George's vision of approved societies as democratic and cooperative organizations, not all societies entering the insurance scheme had roots in the friendly society or trade union movements. Industrial insurance companies and collecting friendly societies which were business rather than fraternal organizations were also allowed to form themselves into approved societies for the purpose of administering national insurance benefits. These companies had long been part of the working class landscape. The industry employed about 100,000 men. Of these, as many as 70,000 were full-time door to door sales agents and collectors for companies such as The Prudential, the Pearl, Royal London, and the largest collecting friendly society, the Liverpool Victoria. By the end of 1910 there were 28,541,525 existing industrial insurance policies in force with a total face value of £285,809,757. The vast majority of these policies were held by the poor in Britain's industrial slums, for whom the few pennies a week spent on the unemployment premium were often the only thing that stood between the worker and starvation in case of illness or disability. Moreover, the industrial policy was the only way many workers had of protecting their families from the personal and social degradation caused by having to accept charity or relief from the hated Poor Law.

The sheer economic size of the industrial insurance industry made it an important center of political strength in British politics. Liberals who, in 1910, had seen their huge majority of 1906 reduced to a razor thin margin over the Tories could not afford to anger an industry which wielded influence at the top of English society as well as with those at its bottom. Therefore when Lloyd George was piecing together his plans for the insurance act the industrial insurance companies had to be included.[29]

All approved societies, whatever their origins, had to agree not to operate national insurance at a profit and to allow their members absolute control over society activities. This provision was consistent with Lloyd George's notion that the act should be anchored firmly to the principles of cooperation and self help. But at the same time, so as not to raise the ire of the industrial insurance industry, the approved societies were not required to be limited by geographic boundaries. The forging of this careful balance between the friendly societies and the insurance industry was clearly a compromise that was accepted because for both sides, national insurance offered the newly certified approved societies an unparalleled opportunity. Not only could they attract new business by offering cheap additional benefits but societies could also sell millions of new policies for dependents not covered by national health insurance. The government realized, however, that by throwing open the doors of Britain's working class to the army of friendly society and industrial insurance salesmen, it might encourage the mismanagement of insurance benefit funds that were held by the societies.

To avoid a wild competition for new members, the government insisted that approved societies be forced to draw upon their private reserves should insurance benefit costs rise above available funds. In this way the government hoped that the benefit fund pool would be well cared for and that the Treasury would never have to save the societies from bankruptcy. The approved societies, blinded by the prospect of millions of new members and policy holders, agreed to this stipulation. Despite this, societies were not unaware of the two weaknesses in their position. The actuarial estimates and the rate of the contributions made by the insured and their employers were controlled by the government. Also, the societies did not have the authority to oversee the doctors of the panel medical service. This meant that when a doctor issued a sickness certificate to an insured person, the patient's society had no choice but to pay the insured his cash sickness benefit, even if the society suspected malingering, fraud or clinical carelessness. It was this lack of control over benefit costs that would, throughout the life of the act, fuel the approved societies' hostility towards the medical profession and the panel system.

Any administrative link between the society controlled sickness benefit and the medical benefit would have been intolerable for Britain's doctors who for thirty years had fought club domination.[30] Therefore, while the insurance medical service was administered by the approved societies and nominally regulated by the local insurance committees, doctors were independent of non-medical control. All practitioners listed on the Medical Register were entitled to enroll themselves as panel doctors and accept insured persons as patients. The insured were allowed to choose a doctor freely from the local panel medical service. The term panel therefore was used in order to identify a doctor who was part of the local insurance service. In turn practitioners referred to those patients who had registered themselves upon his panel list as panel patients to distinguish them from private patients. Medical men, however, were guaranteed the right to refuse to accept undesirable or otherwise unwanted patients upon their panel list. But once he was part of a list, a patient paid nothing directly to his or her doctor unless the practitioner rendered a service that was beyond the range of the established medical benefit.

In general, panel doctors' incomes from insurance work were

determined by a capitation fee for each registered patient. The only exceptions to this were in the case of special payments for mileage, difficult cases or in the special case of non-resident insured persons. In such instances a fee-for-service payment system was employed. In addition all doctors had the local option of adopting a fee-for-service payment scheme. But in all cases the amount available for medical fees was limited by the size of the local medical benefit fund attributed to the insurance committee area.[31] As long as these funds were not exceeded, payments to doctors were calculated according to a capitation fee and this was beyond the authority of either local insurance committees or the approved societies. As an independent contractor within the insurance system, the medical profession's rate of remuneration for panel service was determined solely by negotiations with the central government.[32]

The Battle of the Doctors

Lloyd George's plans for health insurance had been conceived and drawn with very little consultation with Britain's medical leaders. This is hardly surprising given the tremendous political and economic strength of the friendly societies and the industrial insurance industry whose cooperation and peaceful co-existence seemed far from certain. Doctors, however, viewed this lack of attention as a serious snub. After all, it was apparent that the insurance plan promised to alter significantly the relationship between the nation's medical profession and the state. Health insurance was far more than another public health measure in the mold of the Vaccination Act, the Notification Acts or medical inspection. Rather the Liberal government's scheme proposed the hiring of 15,000 part-time medical employees to care for fourteen million wage earners on a full-time basis. The prospects were staggering. Even beyond the difficulties of actually providing the needed care, medical men were being drawn into closer proximity to the state and the dangerous territory of high national politics.

Britain's doctors were not completely unprepared when Lloyd George first unveiled his national insurance proposal. The notion itself had long been a topic in the medical press.[33] The B.M.A. had proposed a modest extension of the poor law health service in its testimony before the 1909 Royal Commission on the Poor Law. Lloyd George himself had given warning of his intentions during the debate over old age pensions. Moreover, as the bill was being framed, the B.M.A. conducted a canvass of its members in order to discover the profession's sentiments.[34]

Very soon after the initial survey of medical opinion it became obvious that many doctors had important reservations about threats to medical independence posed by national insurance. The clubs were bad enough, but now their abuses might be sanctioned by legislative mandate. Reflecting this concern a *British Medical Journal* editorial commented in April 1910 that "This is undoubtedly a very serious outlook for the profession, but we cannot stand still and lament the fact, we must endeavour to discover how the intellectual and financial independence of the profession may be secured under the new order of things which seem to be at hand."[35]

Throughout the remainder of 1910 and early 1911 the B.M.A. sponsored national meetings to discuss the implications of the insurance bill. One speaker, Professor J.T.J. Morrison, told a Birmingham audience that, "the bill opened the first chapter of a new volume in the relations between medicine and the state." Its immediate prospects, though, were no less momentous. "General practitioners were confronted with an extension of contract practice and with an immediate drop in the saleable value of their practices." But Morrison noted the impact of the scheme would also extend to salaried medical officers who would have to deal with new health authorities and an expansion of state sponsored institutions designed to treat tuberculosis. In addition public funds might be drained away from charitable institutions and "teachers and directors in medical schools [have] good grounds to expect a decline in the entry of medical students from all quarters of the Kingdom."[36]

By the spring of 1911, the fears among the medical profession about the uncertain consequences of the insurance scheme had reached a fever pitch. The government's original proposal, made public in early 1911, was little more than an extension of the already existing club system. The entire health insurance scheme was to be placed in the hands of the approved societies. Even though the outline of the scheme had remained vague during the early part of 1911, the medical profession stood steadfastly against any kind of linkage between itself and the approved societies. On 1 June 1911 a special representative meeting of the B.M.A. was held and with Lloyd George in attendance the delegates issued their Six Cardinal Points which were designed to guarantee medical independence. Without government recognition of these, the medical men stated that they would refuse to man the insurance panels, just as they had carried out a boycott of club contract practice. The representative meeting demanded "(1) an income limit of £2 a week for those entitled to medical benefit; (2) free choice of doctor by patient, subject to consent by doctor to act; (3) medical and maternity benefits to be administered by local Health Committees, and not by Friendly Societies; (4) the method of remuneration of medical practitioners adopted by the local Health Committees to be according to the preference of the majority of the medical profession of the district of that committee; (5) medical remuneration to be what the profession considers adequate (later arrived at a capitation fee of 8s. 6d. excluding medicines) having due regard to the duties to be performed and other conditions of service; and (6) adequate medical representation among the Insurance Commissioners, in the Central Advisory Committee, (which was to advise the commissioners on health and administrative matters effecting the scheme) and statutory recognition of a Local Medical Committee representative of the profession in the district of each Health Committee."[37]

After listening to the profession's demands, Lloyd George indicated that the government could or already had supported all of the points except two. An income limit of £2 was too low, but the issue was still open to negotiation. In contrast, any more than a 6s. capitation fee including the cost of drugs was out of the question. For most doctors, however, the capitation fee was the primary question. Therefore, in spite of the Chancellor's seeming willingness to compromise, the meeting adjourned with the medical men suspicious and their fears about friendly society control and the impoverishment of the profession unresolved.[38]

Soon after the June representative meeting Dr. James Smith-Whitaker, the Medical Secretary of the B.M.A., began a campaign to organize medical opposition and solidarity. Doctors were asked to sign a pledge that bound them "not to enter into any agreement for giving medical attendance and treatment to insured under the Bill, excepting such as shall be satisfactory to the medical profession and in accordance with the declared policy of the B.M.A. ..."[39] This pledge of non-cooperation was signed by more than 27,000 medical men by the end of the year -- a total that amounted to nearly two-thirds of all doctors on the medical register.[40] Other medical leaders attempted to keep a high flame under medical opinion. In Edinburgh on 13 October, Sir James Barr, President-elect of the B.M.A. roused a medical audience by claiming that insurance "would impair independence, increase sickness and hasten the degeneracy of a spoon-fed race." Barr further asserted that the scheme before

Parliament "was a step in the downward path towards socialism. It would lower the standard of medical eduction and prevent intellectual young men from entering the medical profession."[41]

By November 1911, Lloyd George had formally agreed to accept all of the Six Cardinal Points except the 8s.6d. capitation fee and the £2 income limit. On this latter issue the Chancellor had insisted that all persons earning less than £160 yearly must be covered by insurance. As for the capitation fee, Lloyd George seemed immovable from his position that 6s. including drugs was more than generous to a profession that had many members working for clubs for far less.[42] Medical opinion was incensed. In Lambeth on 22 November the local B.M.A. division passed a resolution stating that the "concessions of the Chancellor of the Exchequer are unsatisfactory and do not meet the just claims of the profession as set out in the six points..." Echoing this anger the B.M.A.'s Derby division also rejected the bill as it stood. It did not, they claimed, "satisfactorily embody the demands of the profession... the bill in its present form is unworkable, and will create a condition of affairs not only detrimental to the medical profession, but dangerous to the public health." These sentiments were shared by medical men from around the country and similar resolutions were passed in Northumberland, Lancashire, Oxford, Shropshire and Dover.[43] This excitement, however, did not appreciably slow the legislative progress of the insurance bill in the autumn of 1911. As a result some doctors increasingly began to consider the consequences of their promised boycott of the medical panels. In the words of one medical man, "the danger of actual ruin to the bulk of the profession looms larger and larger and our anxiety becomes daily more acute."[44]

Medical anxiety, however, was only intensified when the government invited Smith-Whitaker, despite his announced opposition to the bill, to become Deputy Chairman of the Insurance Commission.[45] The Medical Secretary replied cautiously to the government's offer and chose to put the issue before the B.M.A.'s Council.[46] At a special meeting of the body on 9 December 1911, a lengthy discussion took place out of which arose two definite positions.[47] The leadership of the Council generally favored acceptance of the appointment by Dr. Smith-Whitaker. They argued that the insurance act "was merely a harbinger of future development in the direction of the establishment of a Ministry of Public Health."[48] Moreover the bill was already assured of passage and those favoring acceptance concluded that the position of the medical profession "would be better not only as regards the present, but as regards the future, and the interest of the profession would be served in the best sense of the term."[49] The opposing viewpoint was represented by Dr. Major Greenwood who pointed out that the personality of the Insurance Commissioners would have little effect on the impact of the scheme upon the medical profession. Greenwood also strongly reminded the Council that many of the nation's doctors, their constituents, had sworn not to accept service under the plan. Any movement to condone or accept the scheme's provisions without their approval would only arouse more anger and disunity among the profession's ranks.[50]

After the debate ended, the Council voted 38 to 3 in favor of Smith-Whitaker's acceptance of the post. Within days the storm broke and Dr. Greenwood's warning about the sentiments of the Association's membership proved to be accurate. Many medical men felt that their pledge of honor had been betrayed by medical politicians.[51] Those most firm in their opposition to the act now had a cause to rally around. As the insurance bill became law on 16 December, 1911 medical solidarity was shattered. The elected leaders of the B.M.A. appeared to have conceded the inevitability of health insurance. In contrast extremists in the profession, led by consultants and specialists, urged complete opposition and the ordinary general practitioner, bound by his pledge, stood and watched.

During the next several weeks, those medical men who demanded recognition of all six points before granting their cooperation held large rallys across the country.[52] These were followed on 5 January 1912 by simultaneous meetings of doctors in every B.M.A. branch. In South Staffordshire, an angry group of practitioners adopted a resolution stating that the B.M.A. would "stultify itself by assisting to establish the administrative machinery of the measure."[53] Similar resolutions were issued from nearly every other division and most called upon the Council of the

Association to cease negotiations with the government. Moreover, many divisions demanded that the Council "call upon all members of the profession to refuse to form any panel or to undertake any duties including administrative duties [clearly pointed at Smith-Whitaker] that the Act assigns to them."[54]

Despite this uproar, many medical men still supported the moderate leadership of the medical association. The pages of the British Medical Journal were filled with pleas for unity as many doctors began to wonder whether the profession was capable of winning a victory over the government.[55] Passive resistance had not brought the friendly societies to their knees and Lloyd George was a far more formidable adversary. Nonetheless, the opening shots had been fired and the battle had already begun in earnest. It was far too late for an orderly and honorable surrender.

Lloyd George launched his counterattack against his medical opponents on 12 February 1912, before a generally Liberal audience at the London Opera House. In contrast to the B.M.A.'s noisy specialist leadership, the Chancellor understood that the sole issue for the majority of general practitioners was money and not professional pride. In the end the struggle could be won by showing the abused club doctor or the man living among his working class patients that the act could mean significant financial advantages. Realizing that these divisions within the medical profession could be exploited, Lloyd George was conciliatory toward the moderates. He hinted that the government was willing to continue the negotiations over the terms of panel medical service even though the bill had already become law. However, in a sterner manner, Lloyd George reminded the profession that if it did boycott the panels after 15 January 1913, when benefits were due to begin, he would not hesitate to use the supervisory powers granted to him by the act. Although he had earlier ceded doctors certain privileges, he stressed that these could easily be placed under the control of the friendly societies.[56] The meaning of this threat was clear. Should they lose their struggle, the profession would be forced to bargain with the approved societies for payment.

By mid-June, after months of internal dissention and with the medical provisions of the act to go into effect in only six months, professional solidarity had yet to be repaired. The government had not indicated any willingness to budge from the letter of the act and, if the doctors were to fulfill their pledges by not giving service on the panels, medical men realized that plans for the future would be needed.[57] Making an effort to consolidate professional opinion, the medical association, having learned its lesson from the Smith-Whitaker affair, put the question of continued negotiations with the government to their membership. The overwhelming number of doctors in the Association chose to break off all contact and to work on alternate schemes. These, it was hoped, would be ready for the government's consideration after the failure of the act to deliver its promised medical benefit. By July, two similar plans, which had already been under consideration by the B.M.A.'s State Sickness Committee, were unveiled in the British Medical Journal.[58] These then became the center of medical debate and doctors assumed that professional solidarity was unshakable.

With all this scheming taking place, the men making the policy decisions in the medical association nearly overlooked, or rather chose to ignore, a report by Sir William Plender. On 7 June, the government and the B.M.A. had met and agreed to co-sponsor a study which would determine how much in fact doctors in the United Kingdom earned. The medical leaders hoped that such a study would reveal to the government that the 6s. capitation fee offer was unjust when compared to private practice. Sir William Plender, a respected accountant, was charged with making the study.[59] He examined six towns -- Darwin, Darlington, Dundee, Norwich, St. Albans and Cardiff -- in which there were 265 practitioners. Of these 265 doctors, 51 refused to turn over their records for study. Forty of these were in Cardiff, so that city was excluded from Plender's examination. On 11 July 1912 the findings of the study were announced. They revealed that in the five towns sampled, the average income of a general practitioner in private practice was only 4s. 5d. annually per patient.[60] The report clearly established that the 6s. offered by the government for serving on the panels was more than most doctors earned in private practice, which most practitioners assumed to be the most lucrative. The report should have been a warning to the leaders of the B.M.A. who were increasingly being pushed into a corner by the consultant-led anti-insurance faction. Instead they continued to construct their alternate plans and to speak of medical freedom and professional honor while the average general practitioner was primarily concerned with monetary security alone.[61]

Near the end of the summer, while still threatening the doctors with friendly society control and even a full-time salaried state service, Lloyd George privately prepared a compromise that would break the profession's resistance. On 22 October he received cabinet approval to increase the amount alloted to the panel medical benefit. Doctors were offered a basic capitation fee of 7s. with an additional 2s. reserved for the drug fund. Should an area's annual drug and appliance costs fall below an average of 2s. per panel patient, the Chancellor proposed that the savings, up to 6d., be divided among doctors. This new concession did not meet the straight 8s. 6d. that was demanded by the medical association's Six Cardinal points. Nevertheless, it was more than the previous government offer and 3s. 1d. higher than the average fee discovered in the Plender report. Moreover, this was far in excess of what doctors believed they could secure should they be placed in the hands of the societies.[62]

Almost immediately the British Medical Journal was flooded with letters demanding, if not outright acceptance, then at least further negotiation.[63] The resistance of the medical profession and its facade of solidarity were collapsing. As the B.M.A. leadership stood helplessly the drama's last act was played out. Moderates sued for peace and despite their pledges, many made plans to undertake panel work. At the same time hard-liners, who accused their less strident colleagues of treason, grew more adamant in their opposition.[64]

As medical tempers flared the B.M.A.'s Council attempted to reassert its authority. On 25 November it sent five representatives to see Lloyd George in the hope that he would agree to further negotiations.[65] But Lloyd George had no reason to budge from his already stated offer of 9s. With medical opposition disintegrating there was obviously nothing to discuss. Unable to reopen negotiations, the B.M.A. had little choice but to submit the question of cooperation with the act to the nation's doctors again. Each medical man was asked to answer yes or no on the question:

> Are you in favour of the Association calling upon the profession to enter into any agreement with local insurance committes to give service under the act upon the terms and conditions now finally offered by the government?

The result of the polling was announced in the British Medical Journal on 21 December 1912. It was:

For refusal to serve 11,219

Against refusal to serve .... 2,408.[66]

The significance of this vote was not that the overwhelming number of voters desired noncompliance with the new law; that was fully expected. The importance of the poll is that more than half of those who had earlier pledged resistance abstained from voting. The battle had ended and the nation's medical men were now in full retreat, rushing to join the panels.[67]

Lloyd George announced on 2 January 1913 that nearly 10,000 doctors had joined the local panel network. The die-hards organized one last protest on 7 January at Queen's Hall in London, but their defiant rhetoric could barely be heard above the sound of their colleagues running to add their names to panel lists.[68] By 10 January more than enough practitioners had agreed to panel work and on 15 January as the medical benefit came into effect Lloyd George told the nation that the lists were complete.[69] The end of this rather dismal performance by the medical profession came on 17 January when a special representative meeting belatedly released all practitioners from their pledges.[70]

The struggle between British doctors and the government over health insurance was fought in the public arena. Large amounts of propaganda were churned out by both sides in order to win public support. Mass meetings accompanied by bold pronouncements for the press were used as ammunition. But in the end, the victory was gained by David Lloyd George, who, after all, was fighting on his own ground. The Chancellor used every political tactic in his sizeable arsenal and bested his less experienced opponents at every turn. Doctors believed that all they had to do to achieve success was to refuse service under the act, while claiming their struggle was for the preservation of professional honor and privilege. But the real issue for many among the medical rank and file was no more than money. Lloyd George exploited this essential weakness through the judicious use of promises and threats. Unlike the Harley street leadership of the B.M.A., the Chancellor understood the economic and social condition of the average British general practitioner. Moreover, while preventing the profession from closing ranks, Lloyd George appealed to the public on constitutional grounds by insisting that the medical men were trying to defy the will of Parliament.[71] This tactic proved to be a success. Alfred Cox, the B.M.A.'s medical secretary at the time, claimed later that, in the public eye, medical men came to be seen as "irreconcilable and unconstitutional... for the sake of sixpence."[72]

On the Panel -- At Last

After more than a year of concerted political activism Britain's doctors found that as a class they had been made to look ridiculous and selfish. The B.M.A. had been crushed as a political organization. Its enemies, the approved societies, were if anything, more powerful and individual doctors felt betrayed by their colleagues. The crisis however had not passed with the profession's political collapse -- it had only entered a new stage. Even before the dust of battle had a chance to settle, medical men had to face new difficulties that touched the heart of their professional lives. Immediately practitioners had to deal with the massive problems of attending millions of newly insured patients and adjust to the administrative demands of panel service and an untested bureaucracy.

Even though nearly 13,000 general practitioners had agreed to serve as panel doctors by the time the medical benefit came into existence, most practitioners had waited until the last moment to agree to panel service. As a result, medical men found that during the month following 15 January, their surgeries were swamped by hundreds of insured but unregistered patients. Dr. Harry Roberts in Stepney, who would later claim the largest panel in Britain, was besieged by patients eager to join his panel. Insured persons clogged his stairway, bedrooms and bathrooms anxious to test the system that offered medical advice and a bottle of medicine "for nothing."[73] Another London medical man reported that he had been seeing patients "until past midnight; there has been a regular rush, and my private patients have been driven away."[74] In the confusion, doctors had not only to identify and treat the sick, but had to spend precious time with the healthy attending to the clerical duties of panel practice.[75] Practitioners had to personally sign the registration cards and enter each insured patient in a day book. In addition, a separate form had to be filled out and forwarded to the local insurance committee as a confirmation of a patient's presence on the doctor's panel list. If the insured person was ill, a sickness certificate issued by the patient's approved society had to be signed, a detailed account of the patient's illness reported and drug prescriptions filled out in triplicate.[76] "Most doctors" one Edinburgh practitioner soberly claimed, were "unaccustomed to working with carbons."[77]

Uncomfortable with the heavy clerical work and sometimes with two or three hundred patients crowding surgeries and standing outside in the damp January wind, doctors became convinced more than ever that their opposition to the act had been well founded. Under these harried conditions, misdiagnosis and loss of life were real possibilities.[78] In the winter of 1913, with coroner's juries investigating several suspicious deaths, stories about patients dying because of rushed diagnoses and doctors collapsing from overwork circulated freely in the medical community.[79]

Finally, on 4 February, a deputation of panel practitioners brought the doctors' complaints to the Insurance Commissioners, who, after considering the grievances, issued a memorandum on clerical work. Panel doctors were assured that no more registration cards would be issued (all insured persons had already received their cards), and that in the future medical men would only have to fill out a single form of acceptance. Once completed, the new form was to be sent to the local insurance committee, which (upon reception) would return an index card with the patient's name and address. These cards represented the doctor's official patient list as recognized by the insurance officials and eliminated the need for the keeping of the day book. Moreover, under the new system, practitioners were relieved from the responsibility of making copies of drug prescriptions for panel patients. Finally, in response to panel doctors' uncertainty about the date and method of payment, the Commissioners declared that all doctors were to be paid quarterly unless an alternate system was approved by individual local insurance and medical committees.[80]

The reduction in the amount of clerical work and the assurances from the Commissioners that they were indeed sensitive to reasonable medical suggestions eased the difficulties of the initial patient registration. Lloyd George's political ally, Dr. Christopher Addison, in surveying the situation after a month of panel work commented that "medical men were themselves finding that the service could be made more attractive and good, and were making suggestions for the greater efficiency of the service..." C.F.G. Masterman, Chairman of the Joint Insurance Commission, was willing to listen to all constructive advice from those actually engaged in panel service. This sincerity, Addison concluded, "would very soon take away the bitterness of the recent strife and attract to this service the hearty co-operation of medical men from one end of the country to the other."[81] Still, as the bare outline of a normal and systematized routine began to develop from the former administrative nightmare, many panel doctors were aware that time and the good graces of the Insurance Commission would still not satisfy all their complaints about practice under the act.

Early on, medical men began to report a much higher than expected sick rate among the insured population.[82] This was especially true in the industrial areas where a significant number of medical men had begun to practice.[83] At first, the excessive number of persons claiming illness was blamed on curiosity, a natural desire to test the system, or malingering ("insurenza"). Yet, doctors soon discovered that much of the reported illness was genuine and chronic.[84]

Prior to Lloyd George's insurance act the poor only infrequently saw doctors. Now, however, medical attention for prolonged illness was no longer reserved for the privileged. The industrial and rural laboring poor were suddenly able to enjoy a standard of medical care previously unknown to them. As a result, many practitioners found that, as compared to their private patient work load, their new panel work load was far heavier.[85] Dr. F. B. Hulke of Deal reported that in a single month he was called upon to give 340 home visits and attendance in his surgery for an average of 9 1/2d. per service.[86] Another doctor, with a practice consisting of 416 panel patients in New Cross Gate noted that one thing had become obvious. "Either medical men had to work harder for the same money or receive less money for the same work".[87]

There is no way of knowing exactly how many panel patients actually demanded medical attendance on a daily basis but a commonly used average was 2% of the doctor's list. Thus, a practitioner with average size lists may have visited or attended at surgery ten to fifteen insured persons daily for 1s. each, whatever the service given.[88] Because of this, panel doctors complained that the yearly capitation fee, -- based on the total number of patients on their lists, -- was unfair. They insisted that while this system kept the cost of medical attendance down, it worked to discourage time consuming and expensive procedures.[89] In order to remedy this, panel practitioners petitioned local insurance committees to make special allowances for the cost of anesthetics, bandages, trusses, and mileage but, despite constant lobbying, few committees granted the requests for supplementary payments. Thus, some irresponsible medical men, thinking that they were required to attend patients at an unprofitable rate, reduced the use of common medical appliances.

In addition to attempting to reduce outlays, some doctors sought to squeeze extra payments from insured persons by insisting that private patients receive preferred treatment. Critics alleged that a few medical men "refused to lance a boil or to prescribe a lotion for inflamed eyes without charge. Others... handed out bandages or dressings and told the patients to put them on for themselves."[90] Extra charges were also illegally made for night and Sunday house calls even though insured persons were entitled to these services as part of their medical benefit under the insurance act. One current joke even told of a panel doctor who, upon finding out that a patient was not insured, asked the man back to his examination table, this time for an inspection with his shirt off. But despite the well publicized abuses of some panel practitioners, most doctors with insured patients readily followed both the spirit and the letter of the insurance act. Even though it was true that at first some panel patients received a less than superb grade of medical care, all the insured at least had some kind of medical service available. Before 1912, poverty had often denied them the most rudimentary attention.[91]

Abuses of the insurance system by individual panel doctors were given a great deal of publicity in popular newspapers such as _The Star_ which campaigned against the act.[92] "The yellow press" Alfred Cox later wrote, "sedulously quoted every attack on the system, especially when it came from a doctor. Many such attacks were made ... mainly by men who have never done any industrial practice and do not understand it."[93] For most practitioners, however, complaints about poor medical care were largely unfounded. Whatever abuses did exist were isolated problems that could be dealt with by local panel committees responsible for medical discipline.

Of much more general concern to the medical men was the controversy over the circumstances by which the insured the right to contract out of the panel system and be attended by a practitioner as a private patient. In their desire to see that the principle of free choice was upheld, many doctors had understood the government's promise to protect this right as a license to encourage patients to contract out of the panel system.[94] Doctors anticipated that local insurance committees would freely pay non-panel practitioners the 7s. capitation fee for treating insured persons even if they were not registered as panel practitioners. Furthermore, these men looked forward to collecting the difference between bills for private treatment and the insurance allowance directly from the patient.[95]

As the medical benefit came into force, those doctors who had counted on building up sizeable insurance-subsidized private practices outside the panel system found that the local insurance committees interpreted the act more strictly than they had anticipated. Following a decision by the Joint Insurance Commission, some local committees allowed contracting out only when special medical care not available from panel doctors was needed. Others simply refused all requests and insisted that even specialists join the panel. In most localities, complex bureaucratic procedures were used to discourage the insured from contracting out.[96]

In Gillingham, the center of resistance to the act in Kent, the story was slightly different because the local insurance committee actively attempted to end all contracting out. Insured patients who chose to be attended as private patients were told that their approved societies did not have to honor sickness certificates signed by non-panel doctors. Approved societies quickly complied with the committee's plan, and private arrangements abruptly ended. This, however, was a clear violation of the act's guidelines, which did not completely rule out attendance by non-panel practitioners. Gillingham doctors complained about the ruling of the local insurance committee and in May, 1913 the Insurance Commissioners noted that such blanket policies illegally denied the insured their rights. All certificates signed by doctors on the medical register were equally valid. But the Commissioners did not open the door to non-panel medical attendance. Instead they insisted that a hearing by the local committee had to be held before insurance funds were granted to non-panel men. In these hearings the billing doctor had to prove that the patient was in need of his special services and that the cure provided was within the scope of the insurance benefit. This decision ended the debate over contracting out and marked the final defeat for the medical profession's interpretation of the principle of free choice of doctor by the patient.[97] Some extreme members of the profession did attempt to compromise the panel system by securing "patient rights" but these efforts met with little success.

Besides the contracting out controversy, practitioners were concerned about many other unresolved issues. Of these, none made medical men more wary of their future under the insurance act than the expansion of medical aid institutes.[98] Local insurance committees in Chesterfield, Derby, the South Wales coal districts, and Swansea, pressed by the resistance of medical men, had been forced to follow Lloyd George's advice to close the panels and import doctors from other areas.[99] At the same time, by active advertising, medical institutes which had been sanctioned by the Harmsworth Amendment to the insurance bill moved to incorporate many of the newly insured persons into their body of subscribers.[100] Employing doctors on a full time basis, these institutes not only offered medical care to the insured. For a small weekly contribution they also provided cheap extended medical coverage to dependents.[101] In the small socially compact industrial areas, the threat to the established medical men was frighteningly clear. Both insured persons and their dependents would be removed from the available patient pool. Therefore, denied patients, independent doctors could in some cases expect to receive no more than £5 to £15 yearly from private practice.[102]

Facing financial ruin, medical men in areas with medical institutes complained, with some justification, that they provided inferior medical care and that the imported practitioners were largely young and inexperienced. Moreover, they objected to the control over medical men by non-medical bureaucrats. In an attempt to break what they envisioned as the tightening grip of the clubs on the medical profession, non-club men, both panel and non-panel, threatened in some areas to boycott any man taking service on a contractual basis with a medical institute.[103] In Swansea, the local hospital medical staff decided not to treat any cases except emergencies that had been referred by contract practitioners.[104] Practitioners in Gillingham let it be known that they would refuse to consult or advise doctors accepting club contracts.[105] But without any firm basis of political support the medical men in the areas with strongly organized medical institutes could do little except disapprovingly watch those in the profession who openly cooperated with the clubs.[106]

The failure to mount an effective resistance to medical institutes illustrates the single most important aspect of medical opinion after January 1913. Opposition or support for the insurance act was largely a local matter stimulated by local issues. Some things were perceived as being of national importance, such as the threat presented by the medical aid institutes, but such rural concerns as the need for mileage allowances and the advisability of contracting out to herbalists, elicited little concern in metropolitan areas.[107] Similarly, the city doctor's complaint about the abusive manners of slum dwellers was unimportant in rural districts. Moreover with the B.M.A. discredited there was no mechanism that could focus national discontent. Panel doctors were on their own, left to judge the value of panel work and its effect upon their professional lives according to their own experience. The National Medical Union, a London based organization of anti-insurance doctors, continued its attempts to bind the localized complaints into a national opposition but the union never managed to extend its membership beyond London. Recognizing the hopelessness of welding the nation's medical men into an effective fighting force, the State Sickness Insurance Committee of the B.M.A. determined in April, 1913 that while "it appeared that many panel practitioners strongly disapproved of the conditions of practice, ... after a full consideration the Committee came to the conclusion that no good purpose would be served by the Association calling upon practitioners to leave the panel."[108] The interests of the profession, it concluded, were best served by working peacefully with the government to make the act operate as smoothly as possible. The wisdom of this was soon confirmed.

During the last half of April local insurance committees began to distribute money to medical men based on the number of insured on their panel lists. The size of the payments surprised even panel doctors who, despite their complaints of overwork and bureaucratic tangles, were indeed pleased to find that their incomes had dramatically increased by 40% to 60%. For medical men in industrial areas, such as the Bermondsey and Poplar districts of London, the increase was sometimes more than 100%.[109] A London doctor reported that 250 persons who had previously been treated as private patients would yield an insurance income of £110 yearly as opposed to only £19 the year before. A doctor in Liverpool expressed a similar relief at not having to worry about bad debts. The same opinion was expressed by a Leeds practitioner who reported that his poorer patients had in 1912 been worth only £300 but in 1913 he anticipated an income from these same patients of £700.[110] Even Dr. Alfred Cox felt bound to admit "that financially the Insurance Act has been a blessing to the medical profession, who belatedly needed the stimulus it gave. It practically doubled the amount they were getting from all the people who were formerly attended on a contract basis, which I believe more than compensated for the fact that a smaller number of people who formerly paid bills and paid them well and regularly are now insured."[111]

Rural practitioners did not realize the same increases in earnings as did their urban brethren simply because the opportunities to build a large list were absent. Most panel men, however, gained some monetary advantage from working the act. Moreover, not only did the financial return from treating the poorer classes improve but, after the medical benefit began, fees charged to private patients by doctors tended to escalate too. Armed with the argument that the insurance act established a national minimum for medical services, practitioners in Aberdenshire, Northhampton, Plymouth, Liverpool and many other areas created basic fee schedules.[112]

While it is impossible to determine how stringently doctors applied the established rate schedules, they clearly provided a new standard for medical fees. "Without a doubt," as a Fabian writer for The New Statesman noted, "doctors have gained an increase probably greater than that ever before received by a learned profession at one step."[113] Most medical men felt that the increase, despite its uneven distribution, was well earned and long overdue. At the same time, they had more to be pleased about than the increase in medical incomes.

Because of the heavier patient loads, panel men were able to persuade local insurance committees to impose standardized rules of attendance and patient conduct which allowed doctors to regulate their work hours. The old club practitioners especially appreciated the movement toward regularization of medical practice. Furthermore, local insurance committees and the national insurance commissions proved to be sensitive to the legitimate needs of the profession and lent attentive ears to the panel medical committees.[114] Dr. A. E. Larking, a practitioner in Buckingham, noted in the _British Medical Journal_ that while he went on the panel only because his neighbors did, "We are getting on very well with the Insurance Committee. It has acceded to our wishes as to certificates, model rules, allocation of those not selecting a doctor, etc., and has courteously replied to other requests." Larking concluded, "We believe we shall, by tactful and diplomatic dealing, obtain more than by adopting an antagonistic attitude. We intend to give the Act a fair trial."[115] Such local cooperation and lack of hostility was often matched at the national level. The profession especially appreciated the Joint Commission's invitation in March, to all doctors who had resigned from the Medical Advisory Committee the previous autumn to rejoin the Committee.[116] In response to the concern shown by the insurance bureaucracy and the chances for increased incomes, more practitioners agreed in April, 1913 either to begin or continue panel service.[117]

Still, the decision of many practitioners to continue under the insurance act derived more from a feeling of relief that anticipated fears did not materialize than from complete happiness with the scheme.[118] The majority of doctors recognized that the act needed to be adjusted and refined in order to accomodate the needs of medical men and their insured patients. Altering the act, however, was a matter for organized political pressure, and the only professional organization even remotely able to carry medical opinion to the government was the B.M.A. Through its State Sickness Insurance Committee, which was originally established in 1912 to devise alternate insurance schemes, the Association's Council kept a watchful eye on the working of the act.[119] Nonetheless, there was little the Association could do except catalog the profession's complaints. But when, in April, 1913, C.F.G. Masterman announced the government's intention to modify the insurance scheme, the B.M.A. was ready with a list of suggested amendments which reflected its members' experiences under the act.[120]

The medical association hoped that the government would simplify many of the clerical duties of panel doctors by clearly outlining the administrative responsibilities of medical men, insurance committees, and approved societies. The B.M.A. Council further asked the government to require a mileage grant in rural areas, and make available additional funds to doctors who treated venereal disease, miscarriages, and performed medically necessary abortions. In addition, the Association requested that a special temporary residents fund be established to pay the costs of treating the insured who had been given medical attention by a doctor not on their home panel.[121]

Turning to the administrative side of the act, the B.M.A. asked the government to increase the medical representation on the local insurance committees and to appoint non-medical insurance deputies to serve on the local medical committees. The Council hoped that practitioners would be guaranteed the right to limit the size of panel lists in order to maintain a private practice, or exclude troublesome patients. Because many medical men, especially in isolated areas, found it more convenient to dispense their own drugs, the Council also informed the government that it felt chemists should be allowed to provide bulk medicines to doctors with rural practices.

Finally, the medical association supported the appointment of independent medical referees by the Joint Insurance Commission in order to examine patients accused of malingering.[122] This proposal was one of the most important of the Association's suggestions for amending the scheme. As the proportions of the sickness rate under the insurance act began to take shape, approved societies, especially the smaller friendly societies which had accepted many new members without adequate medical examination, began to complain that doctors were too freely issuing sickness certificates.[123] Since the introduction of the act, one society charged that "experience has proved that the taking away from the approved societies of the provision of medical benefit had been a costly mistake in more ways than one... They could have continued to provide the benefit in a satisfactory manner as in the past and at a less cost than at present, and by co-operation ... reduce the claims for benefits."[124] Friendly society "co-operation", though, was the last thing the medical profession wanted. While it was conceded that some certificates might have been issued without enough care by practitioners attempting to establish kindly reputations, in order to increase the size of their panel practice, most men were conscientious. The vast majority of practitioners were simply carrying out their responsibilities to patients, many of whom could for the first time afford the luxury of minor illness.[125] Still, the accusations of the societies could not go unanswered. Therefore the profession suggested independent medical referees as a check upon malingering, lax certification and the societies.

By proposing what they believed to be moderate and constructive amendments, the B.M.A.'s Council hoped to put forward an image of responsibility and gain the ear of the government. Therefore their suggestions were portrayed as practical and based on working experience rather than political demands backed by threats. The B.M.A. Council soon discovered, however, that the debate over the amending bill would again put Britain's doctors on the political defensive. Lloyd George, Christopher Addison, and C.F.G. Masterman, had made it clear that the amending bill would be the first step in the eventual expansion of insurance benefits to a greater part of the population. Faced with this prospect, the approved societies attempted to use the amending bill as a vehicle to assert their control over the medical benefit and secure a dominant position in the administration of any expanded insurance scheme.[126] Unsure of the government's position, the B.M.A. knew it had little choice except to state its position clearly and hope that the government, which had shown themselves "not unmindful of medical interests," would come to the profession's aid.[127]

After weeks of promising to make public the provisions of the amending bill, the government finally presented its recommendations to Parliament on 24 June 1913. For those members of the medical profession who had anticipated a complete overhaul of the insurance scheme, the proposed amendments represented a disappointment. Short and uncluttered by specific changes, the government's bill was limited to tying up loose ends rather than addressing the grievances of particular interests.[128] Special supplementary grants were promised to local committees to cover any deficit in local insurance pools due to the rising costs of drugs, high sick rates, and administration. In addition, the benefits of the act were extended to persons up to the age of seventy and those who had been denied insurance because they had more than one place of employment.[129]

These modest extensions of the insurance act were accompanied by provisions that relieved unemployed insured persons and their employers from paying the full contribution to the insurance fund. The amending bill also provided for better treatment of casual laborers and clarified and expanded the powers of the Joint Insurance Commission to make regulations. Of the thirteen clauses of the government's amending bill, only reaffirmation of the £160 income limit had been on the B.M.A.'s list of recommendations. Aside from this single provision, the government ignored the suggestions made by the B.M.A., preferring to leave specific regulations within the discretionary domain of the Joint Insurance Commission. The medical profession, however, had little opportunity to make its disappointment known. It found itself wedged between the approved societies which sought to seize control of the insurance scheme and the government whose singular interest was to see that the act worked smoothly and efficiently.

The B.M.A. was helpless in the face of the political muscle flexed by the societies.[130] The profession had barely begun to repair its internal divisions between the specialist leadership and the general practitioner rank and file. Clearly the already crushed B.M.A. would not survive another political fight.[131] Fortunately for the medical men, the government was also opposed to complete private control over the insurance medical benefit. Government spokesmen insisted that the local insurance committees should owe their allegiance only to the national commissioners, and represent no single point of view aside from that of seeing that the insurance scheme operated for the benefit of the insured. Maintaining this position, the government used its majority first in committee and later in the full House to beat back amendments offered by the societies. Forced to stand on the sidelines during the bill's final reading on 5 and 6 August, the medical profession was made fully aware of its political impotence and its reliance on the government's good graces.[132] The current scheme, Dr. R. L. Langdon-Down told the B.M.A.'s Metropolitan Counties Branch, "represents the best alternative. Let us consider the position. Pure private practice failed to meet the wants of the people; the old form of club practice stands universally condemned; the reception accorded locally to our carefully considered schemes for a public medical service organized by the profession showed that they were felt to be impractable ... In any case before condemning the new system let us remember how bad things were before and be sure that there is not already a great improvement."[133] Some solace could be found in the fact that while the Liberal government did not hold the interests of doctors in high regard, at least it was not openly hostile to constructive medical opinion.

Once the amending bill was approved by Parliament, the insurance bureaucracy wasted little time in revising the provisions that regulated medical practice. At the urging of the Joint Insurance Commission, the National Insurance Commissioners for England issued a memorandum adopting standardized medical certificates for use by all approved societies.[134] This action, taken on October 1st, resolved the last major complaint of panel doctors about excessive and complex clerical work. The standardization of certificates in England was followed by a complete revision of the regulations guiding the administration of the medical and sickness benefits throughout the nation. Issued by the insurance commissions on 7 November, the new regulations marked the final movement of the British medical profession away from outright opposition to limited, if still unhappy, support for the insurance act.

Changes made in the regulations for 1914 clearly showed the benefits of peaceful participation with the insurance bureaucracy. The profession could not achieve its demands by actively entering the political arena, but paradoxically, doctors found that recommendations based on working experience inside the system were carefully considered. The new guidelines for the act's second year gave the medical profession nearly everything that had been recommended by the B.M.A. in March 1913. The Insurance Commissioners, the B.M.A. Council noted in its annual report, had on the whole been "very cordial ... and the Commissioners have treated the Association fairly."[135] It was a success earned by political failure, and by responsible action within the act's administrative structure; a lesson that was not to be forgotten for the next thirty-five years.

Predictably, not all medical men were entirely happy with

the revised regulations of 1914. Nonetheless, in light of what they gained from the new guidelines, complaints from anti-insurance doctors must have seemed superficial to the practitioners serving panel patients. For these, making up roughly half of the entire active profession, the regulations forged the final link in the chain that bound them to the insurance act and the government. Most doctors, panel and non-panel alike, had begun as the new year approached to look to the future instead of the past. Wholly private practice seemed to be a relic of the past except for specialists and general practitioners working in isolated rural districts. The new standard for medical practice had become panel service and most medical men had resolved to make the system work smoothly, efficiently and in the profession's benefit.[136]

It would be a mistake to conclude that the amending bill and the subsequent issuing of new regulations governing the administration of the insurance act were alone responsible for reversing medical opinion. The events of the late summer and fall of 1913 were part of a larger process of slow conversion and reassurance that took place within the medical profession. Doctors, with their highly developed sense of independence, were pushed and shoved by outside forces. Practitioners had existed since 1910 in a state of crisis and had been, as a profession, dragged kicking into the panel medical service. Along the way the B.M.A. had been shattered by internal dissention and discredited in public.

Furthermore the act that the medical men had fought against so vigorously was far more of an experiment than its sponsors would have liked to believe. Never before had Britain undertaken such a massive social program. Its administration was a process of trial and error because no one, least of all the nation's doctors, knew what to expect. Some practitioners had accepted the insurance act without question while others were not won over until the insurance bureaucracy demonstrated its willingness to reduce the amount of clerical work associated with panel practice. More members of the profession came to support the act only when the sizeable increase in medical incomes became apparent. Finally, there were many who did not acquiesce until it became clear that continued resistance to the government could lead to control of the profession by the approved societies. It must be recognized too, that a small number of practitioners maintained a noisy, but ineffective, opposition that continued to embarrass the majority of their colleagues. Aside from specific issues, however, the British medical community was plainly tired, and if anything bound the profession together it was a common desire to get on with the work of doctoring. After a year of service under the insurance act practitioners realized that the new conditions of medical practice were not nearly as troublesome as politics.[137]

1914: Administrative Routine and Detail

Exhausted from its three year adversary relationship with

the government, the B.M.A. quickly tried to move to a new position of partnership with the health insurance administration. Finally, the promise of a smooth, efficient and politically peaceful medical service seemed assured. There were of course many difficulties that still remained to be resolved by negotiations but clearly conflict was a thing of the past.

In April, 1914 the Commissioners agreed to establish a national mileage pool of £50,000 in order to increase the remuneration of doctors responsible for treating insured persons in rural areas. Local insurance committees were invited to apply for supplemental grants from this fund and by the end of 1914 some panel practitioners were receiving additional payment for insurance related travel.[138] Nonetheless, the B.M.A. was not entirely pleased with the system. Medical spokesmen argued that the system of mileage grants should be based upon national standards and administered by each national insurance commission. Under such a national scheme of mileage awards, the B.M.A. could be sure that no part of medical remuneration would be funneled through local insurance committees with their approved society majorities. Here again, as in nearly every other insurance related issue, the profession feared any influence by the societies within the administration of the medical benefit. The government, though, refused to administer supplementary payments centrally and the issue remained unsettled throughout 1914.[139]

Many of the problems faced by urban practitioners remained

unsolved too. Some eligible urban workers, had yet to register themselves upon a panel list, either because of ignorance or out of opposition to the act itself.[140] Despite this, contributions from the pay packets of the unregistered continued to flow into the central insurance fund. Doctors, as noted earlier, were actually paid according to two standards. Panel men received quarterly checks reflecting the total number of patients officially upon their panel lists. At the same time, the payments made from local medical benefit pools could not exceed available funds. Theoretically only a small reserve should have remained at the end of each year to cover any extra costs. But because some insured failed to become registered on a panel list, a large pool of unallotted money was built up in some areas. Nationally fully 96% of all eligible persons were on panel lists but in the large cities the figure was less.[141] In London, where only 90% of the insured were accounted for, £91,000 had accumulated in the surplus medical benefit fund by June 1914 and doctors insisted that the money be distributed as part of their capitation payments.[142] Legally the money belonged to London's panel practitioners but to critics of the scheme, it seemed that doctors were asking for money they did not deserve.

For the first half of 1914 London was in a constant state of excitement over the disbursement of the unallotted funds. The Insurance Committee in London, for reasons that are not altogether clear, could not decide the fate of the surplus fund even though the money had been ordered to be distributed by the English Insurance Commission.[143] At the root of this indecision was the unhappiness of panel doctors with small insurance lists and approved society hostility towards practitioners with lists over 2,000 insured persons.[144] In a rare alliance of doctors and societies, it was argued that it was not equitable to divide the surplus funds strictly according to panel size. Some medical men would simply receive too much money.

The debate paralyzed the London Insurance Committee for weeks and when the London Panel Committee suggested in May that the funds be distributed without regard to list size, the Insurance Committee, faced with medical and society opposition, asked the Panel Committee to reconsider the question. Finally, on 9 June, the entire issue was again brought before the London Insurance Committee. The Local Panel Committee held firm to its insistence that no limit be established. The society spokesman in turn demanded that no practitioner with more than 1,500 panel patients should receive payment from the surplus funds. In the end, however, a compromise was narrowly approved by the Insurance Committee by a vote of 17 to 16. Under this plan the available money was to be divided proportionately among all panel medical men except those with more than 2,000 insured patients. These doctors were excluded from the scheme.[145]

The problem of surplus medical benefit funds was a minor problem, yet, like many of administrative questions, it was the cause of great anxiety. It was in effect a non-issue that should not have been a question at all. The principles behind the insurance scheme dictated that panel doctors deserved all money paid into the medical benefit fund (less the cost of drugs) just as they would have been expected to accept a decrease in income should the fund fall short of its ability to pay the agreed upon capitation fee. The issue, however minor, does illustrate the tone and quality of the working of the insurance act at the local level. Tempers often did flare and misunderstandings spread easily among doctors, approved societies and the insured. Most local disputes, unlike the one in London, were settled by the quick and decisive action of the local insurance committee or their clerk. Where this leadership was not forthcoming and questions were allowed to linger unresolved, relations within the health insurance community often became strained.

There were local difficulties, though, that became so widespread that they acquired a national scope. One such issue was the rather technical problem of the accuracy of the central indexes of insured persons maintained by each local insurance committee. Before the act came into force doctors had been promised that insurance practitioners would be given accurate patient lists. When these were not issued practitioners assumed that their own records would be used to value panel practices. Many panel practitioners were thus upset when they found that their quarterly payments did not correspond to their own income estimates. As a result, while some medical men received more money than expected, most received less. Doctors therefore found that it was difficult to predict with any precision each quarter's income from their panel practices. More importantly, it meant that some medical men were treating patients who were not eligible for health insurance without charge.[146] In large part local administrators were at fault. Many lacked an efficient method of keeping doctors notified of the proper status of the patients. Approved societies were also to blame because they were often slow and even sometimes negligent in their administrative duties. By 1914 the problem was chronic, widespread and seemingly beyond resolution. This was a constant source of irritation to panel medical men for whom the inaccurate patient index seemed to be another example of the approved societies desire to have the medical practitioner on the cheap.

Another issue of national importance revolved around the size of panel lists. A few panel men had built huge insurance practices in urban areas with as many as 7,000 patients. With the average panel list at 750 patients, these large insurance practices were an embarrassment to the B.M.A.[147] Because of them, the entire panel service was laid open to attack by those who felt that doctors were reaping huge benefits from the act. The establishment of a national patient limit had difficulties of its own. Many urban slums had a chronic shortage of medical men. To enforce a national limitation in the larger cities would mean that many of the insured would be forced to go without medical attendance. Therefore, despite the possibilities for abuse, which were legion, the Commissioners left the issue of limiting list size to each local and panel committee. By the end of 1914, some local committees responded by placing a 2,500 person limitation on panel lists, with larger lists, normally up to 5,000 persons, allowed if sufficient evidence of need and the doctor's capabilities were presented.[148]

Other relatively minor problems of administration continued to irritate panel doctors in 1914 as they had in 1913. Complaints about the burdens of record keeping and about the definition of the range of medical service under the act persisted. At the same time doctors disliked the administrative inefficiency of some local insurance committees as well as the harassment of certified patients by their approved societies and the lack of manners of some patients. But these problems were inconsequential for most practitioners when they considered their pre-1913 fears. Most were forced to admit that "there might be something in the Insurance Act after all."[149]

Planning For the Future

The national health insurance act was indeed a massive social program but it was not comprehensive. It had been simply placed alongside the existing public health bodies without any real integration. There was no link with the local authorities who controlled sanitation, infectious disease hospitals, maternity and child welfare schemes and the health of school children. Also the Poor Law continued to provide its services independently. At the same time, the act excluded the dependents of the insured and did not provide specialist, maternal or hospital care to contributors. In early 1914 this situation seemed ripe for change. Doctors as well as many others in society began to speak seriously of an expanded state sponsored medical service under the authority of a central health department. However, in light of their recent history, medical men had perhaps a more immediate concern than most, and the profession debated the question throughout 1914.[150]

A small but vocal element within the medical profession's ranks argued that the insurance panel system was simply a halfway house on the road towards a full-time state medical service. Led by Sir John Collie, the State Medical Service Association sought in 1914 to convince the profession to support a full-time contract system as the logical extension of the panel scheme.[151] The debate was at times heated but the advocates of a whole time service made little headway. As noted by Dr. J. Charles to "change from an elastic and adaptable panel to a rigid state medical service conducted by whole time officers ... would break with a system of practice which has long and adequately served its purpose, and which in virtue of a competitive regime, has guaranteed it [the public] satisfactory medical attendance ..."

Finally expressing the sentiments of many of his colleagues, Dr. Charles concluded that the state would depart from the panel system "which has already found widespread favour with the public and a general acceptance by the medical profession."[152]

The debate over a full-time service was of course academic but that made it no less serious. Moreover, it provides another insight into the state of the profession's collective mind as the scheme settled into its administrative routine. Sir John's proposals for a whole-time medical service were for most medical men radical and potentially dangerous. Not surprisingly, a June meeting of practitioners in London overwhelmingly rejected them.[153] But what is interesting to note is that they, as did Dr. Charles, looked to the panel medical service as a refuge, whereas before many had seen it as a prison.

While medical men rejected the notion of a full-time state medical service, they did advocate an expansion of the scope of the existing insurance act. Most of Britain's practitioners were not opposed to including the dependents of those already insured within the scope of the act and expanding the range of medical service offered, so long as doctors received adequate payment for their services. It seemed only natural to include within the medical benefit technical and clinical services that had been excluded from the 1911 scheme. On this point the doctors were in broad agreement with the government and their old adversary David Lloyd George. In May 1914, the Chancellor delivered his budget message to the House of Commons. In it he asked that at least some of the money raised from the new land valuation system be devoted to expanding the services offered to the insured and uninsured poor.[154] Local authorities were to be given Ƀ4,000,000 in order to assist them in establishing supplemental health services and facilities. Another Ƀ750,000 was earmarked for institutions treating tuberculosis and to create a system of nursing homes, laboratory facilities and other diagnostic and clinical services. In addition, the budget also proposed grants for continuing medical education and the establishment of special schools for handicapped children. Finally, the government asked that a national system of medical referees be created to serve as a consultation corps for panel doctors and as a bulwark against malingering and fraud within the insurance scheme.[155]

It was generally assumed that the health provisions of the 1914 budget were designed to lay the institutional foundation for a far-reaching expansion of both the insured population and the benefits available to them. Despite this, the proposed expenditures on health were overshadowed by Lloyd George's radical land rating scheme. Like the reform of land taxation, the funding of the additional health services was dropped by Parliament from the 1914 budget on 22 June.[156] Nonetheless, a fully integrated system of state sponsored health care, built upon the national insurance panel medical service, was given a public if short hearing. Health reformers such as Christopher Addison were indeed pleased because a full scale reform seemed to be in sight.[157] But as with many things in British society, the coming of the first world war in August, 1914, made what had seemed inevitable to contemporaries, improbable, as the war suddenly shifted resources, manpower and energy towards a new enterprise.

The discussion about the future of the insurance act that took place in 1914 shows how far the medical profession had traveled since 1910. In slightly less than four years the nation's doctors had witnessed the collapse of the B.M.A. Following this defeat half the profession was thrust immediately into a new and closer relationship with the state. The adjustment was not always easy. Each panel practitioner was left to judge the act according to his own experience. What most doctors found was that service on the national insurance panels was not "derogatory" to the interests of the profession. Clinical freedom was not challenged and medical men found that the act's administration in no way disturbed the traditional patterns of medical practice. The local and national administrators of the scheme, moreover, usually welcomed constructive suggestions from the medical profession. This and the distribution of £4.5 million to panel men in 1913 alone had gone a long way toward easing the profession's anxiety.[158] Difficulties however did remain.

Although the friendly societies and industrial insurance industry had long been competitors, they now shared a common interest as approved societies. Together they represented a tremendous reservoir of political power inside Parliament. Even though the government had kept them beyond arms length of the insurance medical benefit, doctors could not be sure how long they would be protected. There were also a variety of administrative questions, mileage, range of service and medical records, that could only be dealt with at the national level. At the same time, no one could predict how the war would effect the panel medical service. One thing was known, however. Without a rebuilt political arm the nation's doctors could do little to improve their lot under the act or defend medical honor against the encroachments of the approved societies.

Notes

1. Great Britain, Parliament. Sessional Papers (Lords), 1912-1913, (Reports, vol. 69), Cd. 6907, "Report of the National Health Insurance Commissioner, 1912-1913."

2. M. Jeanne Peterson, The Medical Profession in Mid-Victorian London (Berkeley: University of California Press, 1978), pp. 194-243.

3. R. J. Morris, Cholera 1832 (London: Croom Helm, 1976), pp. 159-192. The impact of the Cholera epidemics upon the medical profession in America was much the same as in Britain. As a class doctors were left discredited and their professional claims tarnished. See Charles E. Rosenberg, The Cholera Years (Chicago: University of Chicago Press, 1962), pp. 65-81, 151-172.

4. William Thackeray, The History of Pendennis (New York: Clarke, Given Hooper, n.d.), p. 5.

5. Ernest Little, History of the British Medical Association, 1832-1932 (London: British Medical Association, 1932).

6. The British Medical Journal (18 March 1876), p. 353. Hereafter cited as BMJ.

7. Peterson, pp. 90-135.

8. F. B. Smith, The People's Health 1830-1910 (London: Croom Helm, 1979). Medical fees were adjusted to account realistically for the income of the patient. A confinement for a wealthy patient could cost as much as 100 guineas in the 1860s while a poor patient might not be charged at all. Naturally the quality and kindness of attendance varied with the fee.

9. P.H.J.H. Gosden, Voluntary Associations in Nineteenth-Century Britain (London: B.T. Batsford, 1973), pp. 3-4.

10. Ibid., p. 12.

11. Jeanne L. Brand, Doctors and the State (Baltimore: Johns Hopkins Press, 1965), pp. 194-199. The laboring classes could also receive medical care through Provident Dispensaries. These lacked the friendly society model of member control but for a small weekly contribution these dispensaries offered drugs and medical care from the early years of the nineteenth century. Unlike the friendly societies, the provident dispensaries were usually semi-public institutions that allowed even the wealthy to join.

12. *Ibid.*, pp. 195-196. The quality of care in the club system is hard to evaluate. There were certainly clubs that provided a good standard of medical care within the limits of the age. But it seems clear that most did not provide care equal to that received by patients who paid their practitioners privately. This of course was a product of class division. The rich always had received better attention because they paid more for medical services. At the same time the club system attracted practitioners who were often inexperienced or who had failed to make their way in private practice.

13. *BMJ* (15 December 1894), p. 1392.

14. *BMJ* (22 July 1905), *Supplement*, p. 57.

15. Brand, p. 196.

16. F. M. Mackenzie, "The Battle of the Clubs and How to Win It," *BMJ* (4 July 1896), pp. 8-10.

17. *BMJ* (11 July 1896), pp. 96-97. Provident dispensaries were a widespread phenomenon by the Edwardian period. They were sometimes established by borough councils or through private charitable subscription. They supplied cheap medicines and medical care to the working class for nominal contributions. In contrast to friendly societies, they were not fraternal organizations.

18. *Ibid.*

19. *The Lancet* (18 March 1905), p. 738. Cited in Brand.

20. Medico-Political Committee of the British Medical Association, "An Investigation into the Economic Conditions of Contract Medical Practice in the United Kingdom," *BMJ* (22 July 1905) *Supplement*, pp. 1-96. For a more general comment see *BMJ* (22 July 1905), p. 195.

21. Sir Arthur Newsholme, *The Last Thirty Years in Public Health* (London: George Allen & Unwin, 1936). Also see Newsholme's *The Story of Modern Preventive Medicine* (Baltimore: The Williams & Wilkins Company, 1929). Other works dealing with the nineteenth century public health movement are: W. M. Frazer, *The History of English Public Health 1834-1939* (London: Balliere, Tindall and Cox, 1950) and R. A. Lewis, *Edwin Chadwick and the Public Health Movement* (London: Longmans, 1952). In addition see Samuel Finer, *Life and Times of Edwin Chadwick* (London: Methuen, 1952).

22. Bentley B. Gilbert, _The Evolution of National Insurance in Great Britain_ (London: Michael Joseph, 1966), pp. 21-158. There is a growing literature dealing with this period and social reform. Among the most interesting are: Michael Freeden, _The New Liberalism_ (Oxford: Clarendon Press, 1978) and G. R. Searle, _The Quest for National Efficiency_ (Berkeley: University of California Press, 1971). Also see John Grigg, _Lloyd George: The People's Champion_ (London: Eyre Methuen, 1978) for a composite picture of the period with Lloyd George at its center. There are of course many contemporary sources--far too many to name here. Among the most indispensible for sampling the flavor of the reform sentiment of the Edwardian period are: C.F.G. Masterman, _The Heart of Empire_ Bentley B. Gilbert ed. (New York: Harper Row, 1973) and Charles Booth, _Life and Labour of the People of London_ (London: Macmillan, 1903).

23. Brand, p. 210.

24. _Ibid._, p. 211.

25. Gilbert, pp. 289-399. To a large extent the story of the passage of the insurance bill is an account of negotiation between the government and the various interest groups that were to be made partners in its working. Gilbert presents the negotiations between the industrial insurance industry and the friendly societies in exacting detail.

26. _Ibid._, pp. 348-351.

27. _Ibid._, pp. 368-383. Essentially the panel medical service escaped the control of the newly formed approved societies because the industrial insurance industry did not want to become involved in the local management of the act. The friendly societies however demanded the right to oversee the work of the panel service in order to control sickness certification. Fortunately for the nation's doctors the industrial lobby won and they emerged as an independent group within insurance administration.

28. R. W. Harris, "National Health Insurance Medical Service in Great Britain," _Canadian Public Health Journal_ 22 (February 1931), pp. 63-64.

29. Gilbert, pp. 316-335. The societies were to be self-governing voluntary associations on the model of the old friendly society. This ideal never was a reality and as the act operated the old friendly societies died out giving way to the industrial insurance concerns, which were both better organized and better at attracting members.

30. The Lancet, "Battle of the Clubs," (25 April 1908), pp. 1240-1242.

31. These funds were simply the total amount of money collected within a local insurance committee's area of authority.

32. Mackenzie, pp. 9-10.

33. Brand, pp. 207, 216.

34. _Ibid_.

35. _BMJ_ (23 April 1910), p. 1008.

36. _The Birmingham Post_, 16 June 1911.

37. _BMJ_ (29 July 1911), _Supplement_, pp. 236-239.

38. Gilbert, p. 402.

39. Paul Vaughan, _Doctor's Commons, A Short History of the British Medical Association_ (London: Heinemann, 1959), pp. 200-203. Cited in Gilbert.

40. _Ibid_.

41. _The Times_, 14 October 1911.

42. _BMJ_ (22 July 1905), _Supplement_, pp. 12-16.

43. _BMJ_ (2 December 1911), _Supplement_, p. 565.

44. _BMJ_ (25 November 1911), _Supplement_, pp. 537-538.

45. Sir John Conybeare, "The Crisis of 1911-1913: Lloyd George and the Doctors," _The Lancet_ (18 May 1957), p. 1033.

46. _BMJ_ (9 December 1911), _Supplement_, p. 586.

47. _Ibid_., pp. 585-586.

48. _Ibid_., p. 587.

49. _Ibid_.

50. _Ibid_.

51. Conybeare, p. 1033.

52. _Ibid_.

53. _The Times_, 6 January 1912.

54. _Ibid_.

55. Conybeare, p. 1034.

56. _Nation_ (3 August 1912), _Medical Supplement_, pp. i-ii. Cited in Gilbert.

57. Conybeare, p. 1034.

58. _BMJ_ (6 July 1912), _Supplement_, pp. 23.

59. Gilbert, p. 402.

60. Great Britain, Parliament. _Sessional Papers_ (Lords), _1912-1913_ (_Reports_, vol. 91), "Existing Conditions in Respect of Medical Attendance and Remuneration in Certain Towns."

61. Gilbert, p. 408.

62. _Ibid_., p. 411. The charge upon the Exchequer was estimated to be £1.5 million over the previously anticipated contribution from the Treasury.

63. _BMJ_ (16 November 1912), _Supplement_, pp. 528-548.

64. _Ibid_.

65. Conybeare, p. 1034.

66. _BMJ_ (21 December 1912), _Supplement_, pp. 682-684.

67. Conybeare, p. 1035.

68. _The Times_, 8 January 1913.

69. _BMJ_ (25 January 1913), _Supplement_, p. 97. See Gilbert, pp. 415-416. The major exception to Lloyd George's announcement was in London where medical organization was at its strongest.

70. _Ibid_.

71. Alfred Cox, _Among the Doctors_ (London: Christopher Johnson, 1950).

72. Alfred Cox, "Seven Years of National Health Insurance in England," _Journal of the American Medical Association_ (7 May 1921), pp. 1308-1312. The article was continued in the next two issues.

73. Winifred Stamp, _The Doctor Himself: An Unorthodox Biography of Harry Roberts, 1871-1946_ (London: Hamish Hamilton, 1949), p. 75. Roberts was a prolific writer on reform and medical subjects. He claimed to have the largest panel practice in England.

74. BMJ (25 January 1913), Supplement, p. 104.

75. The Lancet (22 March 1913), p. 855.

76. The National Insurance Yearbook 1913 (London: The Insurance Publishing Co., 1913). Also see Cd. 6907, pp. 147-151.

77. BMJ (25 January 1913), Supplement, p. 104.

78. The Times, 21 January 1913. According to a coroner's inquest one patient even died because his doctor was overburdened with clerical duties.

79. The Times, 30 January 1913. The wife of Dr. Charles Duckett testified before a coroner that the East Ham doctor had died because of worry about the onerous duties of panel work.

80. BMJ (22 February 1913), Supplement, p. 197.

81. Great Britain, Parliament, Parliamentary Debates (Commons), 5th series, vol. 48 (1913), col. 281.

82. The fabian Research Department, "Interim Report of the Committee of Enquiry," The New Statesman (14 March 1914), pp. 3-5. The Webbs had opposed the act from the start. They objected to it being financed from worker contributions and during its early months they carried on their anti-stamp licking campaign. This of course refers to the stamps that contributors placed in their insurance benefit books to attest to their contributions.

83. The Times, 14 July 1913.

84. Great Britain, Parliament, Sessional Papers (Commons), 1914-1916, 30. (Reports, vol. 1), Cd. 7687, "Report of the Departmental Committee on Sickness Benefit Claims Under the National Insurance Act."

85. BMJ (1 March 1913), Supplement, pp. 218-220.

86. BMJ (15 March 1913), Supplement, p. 257.

87. BMJ (1 March 1913), Supplement, p. 218.

88. BMJ (15 March 1913), Supplement, p. 257.

89. The Times, 7 June 1913.

90. The Manchester Guardian, 28 March 1913.

91. Great Britain, Parliament, Parliamentary Debates (Commons), 5th series, vol. 48 (1913), cols. 302-303.

92. John H. Marks, <u>The History and Development of Local Medical Committees, Their Conference and its Executive</u> (unpublished dissertation, Edinburgh, 1974).

93. Cox, <u>Seven Years of Health Insurance</u>, p. 1398.

94. <u>The Lancet</u> (1 March 1913), pp. 653-656. In reality the regulations allowed contracting out not to individual doctors but to approved institutions that could offer specialty care to insured patients within the scope of the medical benefit. The origin of this is the Harmsworth Amendment which allowed existing medical institutes to continue under the act. See Gilbert, pp. 374-376, 402-403.

95. <u>BMJ</u> (15 February 1913), <u>Supplement</u>, pp. 151-152.

96. <u>BMJ</u> (7 February 1914), <u>Supplement</u>, pp. 67-68.

97. <u>BMJ</u> (10 May 1913), pp. 1014-1015.

98. <u>The New Statesman</u>, "Position of the Medical Institutes," (11 April 1914), pp. 5-7.

99. <u>BMJ</u> (11 January 1913), <u>Supplement</u>, p. 83.

100. <u>BMJ</u> (11 October 1913), p. 954. The <u>BMJ</u> warned any practitioner undertaking an appointment in an institute to first make sure that its benefits were not being unprofessionally promoted by canvassing.

101. <u>The Lancet</u> (8 November 1913), pp. 1347-1348.

102. <u>The Lancet</u> (20 December 1913), pp. 1796-1798.

103. <u>The Lancet</u> (15 March 1913), pp. 787-788.

104. <u>The Times</u>, 28 April 1913.

105. <u>BMJ</u> (8 March 1913), <u>Supplement</u>, p. 238.

106. <u>BMJ</u> (5 April 1913), <u>Supplement</u>, pp. 304-306. The State Sickness Committee of the BMA was given the authority to make monetary grants to doctors who had suffered financial losses as a result of cooperating with the association's boycott of the panel system. Through 31 March 1914 the fund had made compensation payments totalling £687.19.2. <u>BMJ</u> (2 May 1914), <u>Supplement</u>, p. 284.

107. <u>BMJ</u> (12 July 1913), <u>Supplement</u>, p. 88.

108. BMJ (3 May 1913), Supplement, pp. 379-386. This conclusion was based partly on a survey taken in February among the medical community. Asking its membership whether renewed action should be taken against the insurance act, the BMA received replies from only a third of its members. On the basis of this response the association's leaders concluded that the desire for continued political action was very weak.

109. The Manchester Guardian, 28 March 1913.

110. The Lancet (19 July, 9 August, 20 September 1913), pp. 176, 422-424, 892-893. The Lancet sent a special correspondent on tour to report about the working of the act in the various parts of the country. His reports were made weekly and are indispensible for an understanding of the act's first year of operation.

111. Cox, Seven Years of Health Insurance, p. 1098.

112. BMJ (1 March 1913), Supplement, pp. 209-210. In Aberdeenshire, for example, local medical men established a base rate of 2s. 6d. for each attendance, excluding anaesthetics, appliances, mileage fees and minor operations, or the setting of bones. In contrast it was estimated that an average visit to an insured patient was worth only 1s. 5d. Such attempts at fee setting were not new. Medical men had long tried to avoid the unprofessional aspects of medical competition through the establishment of uniform fees.

113. The New Statesman, "Medical Remuneration" (21 February 1914), pp. 615-617.

114. BMJ (29 March 1913), Supplement, pp. 281-285.

115. BMJ (12 April 1913), Supplement, p. 325.

116. BMJ (5 April 1913), Supplement, p. 304.

117. Cd. 6907, p. 158. The Times, 28 March 1913. A meeting of the newly formed National Insurance Practitioners Association in London issued a statement that its members were satisfied with the working of the act and the response of the Commissioners to the problems of clerical work. Also see C.F.G. Masterman's speech before the House of Commons of 30 April 1913. He estimated that 80-90% of all medical men who had been in industrial practice before the act were now members of their local panels. Great Britain, Parliament, Parliamentary Debates (Commons), 5th series, vol. 52 (1913), cols. 1314-1317.

118. Alfred Cox, Among the Doctors, pp. 84-100.

119. BMJ (25 January 1913), Supplement, p. 90.

120. BMJ (5 April 1913), Supplement, pp. 304-306.

121. The original insurance regulations established a complicated system for paying doctors who attended insured non-residents. Medical men had to submit bills to their local insurance committees. In turn the patients local committee was billed. Unfortunately payment was not always forthcoming. The BMA encouraged the government to change this process in favor of one that simply established a national temporary residents' fund. Doctors, especially those in resort areas, could then simply submit their bills to this fund and be paid on a fee-for-service basis.

122. BMJ (13 September 1913), Supplement, p. 241.

123. The Times, 24 October 1913). Also see, J. Staveley Dick, "The Working of the National Insurance Act," BMJ (25 October 1913), Supplement, pp. 330-332. BMJ (12 April 1913), Supplement, p. 319. A meeting of the Faculty of Insurance, a group representing the insurance industry, warned about the dangers presented by the increasing sickness rate among women. The Faculty accused many women of actually being malingerers.

124. The Times, 5 August 1913.

125. The New Statesman (6 December 1913), pp. 261-263. Also see BMJ (2 May 1914), p. 983.

126. The Lancet (19 July 1913), pp. 156-157.

127. The Lancet (14 June 1913), p. 1676.

128. BMJ (5 July 1913), Supplement, pp. 40-43.

129. BMJ (12 July 1913), Supplement, p. 70. An actuarial report estimated that this proposal would add an additional 240,000 persons to the insurance rolls at a first year cost of £260,900.

130. BMJ (2 August 1913), Supplement, p. 153. In an open letter to the medical professions Alfred Cox complained that the friends of the societies in Parliament were trying to weaken the independence of the panel doctor within the insurance scheme by pushing to bring the administration of the medical benefit under the control of the approved societies. In addition Cox warned that two of the amendments would allow an expansion of medical aid institutes.

131. BMJ (19 July 1913), p. 138.

132. BMJ (9 August 1913), Supplement, pp. 181-187.

133. BMJ (19 July 1913), Supplement, pp. 111-115.

134. BMJ (4 October 1913), Supplement, pp. 287-288.

135. BMJ (2 May 1914), Supplement, p. 285.

136. J. E. Moorehouse, "The Insurance Act of 1913 and the New Regulations," BMJ (22 November 1913), Supplement, pp. 453-455.

137. The Times, 13 November 1913. On 13 November Bonar Law commented upon the insurance act in a Norwich speech. He said that if the Tories regained power they would undertake a study and revision of the insurance scheme. In its commentary the BMJ stated that, "there is no doubt that these proceedings caused forebodings to many members of the medical profession, who feared that they were again to become the plaything of political parties, for, whatever may be said in favour of a remodeling of the insurance system on voluntary lines it is certain that such a course of action would mean a complete upset of the present arrangements with a renewal of the anxieties of the past two years." BMJ (24 January 1914), p. 211.

138. Cd. 6907., p. 155.

139. BMJ (26 December 1914), Supplement, pp. 295-296.

140. Great Britain, Parliament, Parliamentary Debates (Commons), 5th series, vol. 58 (1914), cols. 1859-1904. In Parliament the main thrust of the opposition to the insurance act came from the friends of the approved societies. They lost no opportunity to discuss the inadequacies of the panel system, its cost and its administration. Outside Parliament the act was continually the target of the Fabians. The Webbs carried on their anti-stamp campaign throughout 1913 and attempted to raise the level of working class discontent as late as 1914. The Nation, "Insurance Discontent" (24 May 1913), pp. 297-298. For a discussion of the Webb's early opposition see Brand, pp. 212-213.

141. Great Britain, Parliament, Sessional Papers (Commons), 1913-1914, 72 (Reports, vol. 3), Cd. 7496, "Report of the National Insurance Commissioners, 1913-1914."

142. BMJ (6 June 1914), Supplement, pp. 31-35.

143. The Lancet (2 May 1914), p. 1289.

144. *BMJ* (24 January 1914), *Supplement*, pp. 33-34.

145. *BMJ* (6 June 1914), *Supplement*, pp. 31-35.

146. *BMJ* (8 May 1915), *Supplement*, pp. 234-237.

147. *BMJ* (14 February 1914), pp. 379-382.

148. *The Lancet* (14 March 1914), p. 789. Typical of the distribution of panel patients was the situation in Bradford where there were 117 medical men on the panel. Seven men earned between £ 1000. and £ 1500. and 47 practitioners had panel incomes between £ 250 and £ 1000. The remaining doctors all earned less. In the London Metropolitan area there were 909 panel men. Of these 172 had lists over 2,000 and 500 doctors had fewer than 500 insured patients.

149. *BMJ* (21 March 1914), pp. 645-648.

150. *The Lancet* (17 January 1914), pp. 187-188.

151. Sir John Collie, "A State Medical Service: Does it Mean the Nationalization of Medicine?" 82nd Annual Meeting of the *British Medical Association*, 24 July-31 July 1914, BMA Archives.

152. *BMJ* (14 February 1914), *Supplement*, p. 82.

153. *BMJ* (13 June 1914), *Supplement*, pp. 432-436.

154. Great Britain, Parliament, *Parliamentary Debates* (Commons), 5th series, vol. 62 (1914), cols. 75-83.

155. *BMJ* (13 June 1914), *Supplement*, p. 436.

156. Bentley B. Gilbert, "David Lloyd George: The Reform of British Land Holding and the Budget of 1914," *The Historical Journal*, 21, 1 (1978), pp. 117-141.

157. Christopher Addison, *Politics From Within, 1911-1918* (London: Herbert Jenkins Ltd., 1924), I, pp. 28-29.

158. *BMJ* (14 February 1914), pp. 379-382.

CHAPTER II

The War and After

It is often pointed out that the declaration of war in August 1914 rescued British society from domestic chaos. Women, the Irish and the trade unions were all forced to put off their grievances in the name of national unity. Unlike other groups, doctors had made their peace with the government before the war began. The panel medical service was operating smoothly and practitioners were beginning to understand the administrative implications of their new relationship with the state.

The coming of the war did nothing to alter this trend. Still, the war years and those immediately following did provide the medical profession with an opportunity to rebuild its national political integrity. From 1914 until 1922 the B.M.A. re-established its political base among both panel and non-panel doctors. During this period the medical association also was accepted by the government as the profession's official mouthpiece. Once its position was secure the B.M.A. moved to play a role in two broad areas of national insurance policy. Within what the Association saw as the administrative question, the B.M.A. worked to improve the conditions of practice for panel doctors. Furthermore the B.M.A. prepared and argued the profession's case for an increased capitation fee after the war. But both levels of B.M.A. activity shared a common theme. Under no condition would the B.M.A.'s political leaders allow the Association to push the profession's relationship with the government and the insurance bureaucracy to the breaking point. This policy continued until 1922, when the medical profession learned the limits of cooperation.

After August, 1914 civilian medical practice was left in the hands of older medical men and those who were physically unable to serve in the armed forces. For these doctors, the war years were marked not by glory but by crowded surgeries and overwork. At the beginning of the war it was expected that any shortage of medical manpower within the civilian population would be offset by the demands of the armed forces for new recruits.[1] The anticipated drop in the insured population was soon realized. Throughout the country the number of insured fell by 12 1/2%.[2] It was clear, moreover, that there was a hesitancy among the civilian population in general to report illness out of deference to the national emergency. Still, nearly all medical men in general practice found that they were far busier during the war.[3]

The war brought into the job market, and therefore into the insurance scheme, several million women who had never before been eligible for health insurance benefits. As a result, the decrease in the number of insured persons was counterbalanced by an increase in the overall risk of illness within the scheme. In addition, casualties caused by military action aggravated the situation as the government expected medical men to care for discharged wounded and disabled soldiers as panel patients if they were eligible under the insurance scheme.[4] Finally, as the military's manpower demands increased after 1916, the proportion of persons who were poor insurance risks in the insured population rose, and the net value of insurance medical practice fell. But with the nation engaged in a life and death struggle, the medical profession hesitated to express its economic disappointment.[5]

Even had the profession wanted to, it could do little about its declining economic position during the war. Nonetheless, the conflict did provide it with an opportunity to organize for future action. In late 1914, the Council of the B.M.A. concluded that the Association needed a central committee to ensure that practitioners were prepared to deal with all issues affecting practice under the insurance act. The scheme had already mandated some medical organization. For example, on the local level there existed panel committees which through their annual conference provided a sounding board for panel medical opinion.[6] But these were unwieldly mechanisms ill suited to negotiation at the national level.

In order to assert its leadership of the profession, the B.M.A. proposed to make its Insurance Acts Committee (essentially the old State Sickness Insurance Committee) the link between itself and the Conference of Local Medical and Panel Committees. In doing so, the Committee would become the executive of the Conference and the B.M.A. could assume the role of permanent guardian of the insurance medical service.[7] During its October, 1914 meeting the Panel Conference agreed to allow the B.M.A. committee a place in insurance matters. Nonetheless, the powers of this newly founded Insurance Acts Committee were left undefined and the precise relationship between the B.M.A. and the statutorily established local panel committees remained equally unclear. It was apparent that it would be up to the Insurance Acts Committee itself to define the scope of its role within the insurance system. Despite this inauspicious start, however, the Committee was to prove a useful tool for panel doctors, the B.M.A. and the government alike.

Even before the Insurance Acts Committee was accepted by the Panel Conference it had begun to investigate the discrepancies between the payments received by panel doctors and the amount expected by them, based upon their own calculations.[8] On 9 October 1914, the Insurance Acts Committee met to review this problem. The Committee discussed the possibility of securing the cooperation of a single insurance practitioner with a small panel list who could prove beyond a doubt that he had been underpaid by the government. Such a case might then be used to challenge the Insurance Commissioners in court. However, the Committee realized that a court case was surrounded with numerous difficulties. Even if a carefully kept insurance list were used to test legally the veracity of the government's payment system, resolution of the issue could take years. Moreover, such a challenge in wartime would be a public relations nightmare and would only damage the stable but still fragile relationships between the doctors and the government. Therefore, the Insurance Acts Committee decided to ask the National Commissioners to meet with them.[9]

Sir Robert Morant, Chairman of the English Insurance Commission, met with the Insurance Acts Committee on 22 December in order to hear the doctors' complaints about the payment of the insurance capitation fee. The deputation of medical men told Morant that there had been a great deal of confusion among panel practitioners on the subject of how the system of payments actually operated. They complained that the regulations stated that each panel man was to be paid quarterly based upon the size of his insurance practice. But quarterly checks did not accurately reflect the doctors' own patient records. Hence, the medical representatives charged that the creditability of the entire insurance scheme was called into question. If the profession was giving free medical care to uninsured persons the government had the responsibility of correcting the situation.[10]

Morant, while admitting that the panel lists were not infallible, had a ready excuse. He explained that at the end of 1913, the number of insured persons in England alone approximated ten million. This figure reflected the first issue of medical cards through the post office. However, of those ten million benefit cards 8 1/2% had been returned to the dead letter office, representing some 850,000 workers who could not be traced by the

Post Office. These figures, Morant stated, proved that the panel lists were inflated at the end of 1913 and the panel practitioners were themselves indirectly responsible for the confusion. Furthermore, Morant told the Insurance Acts Committee that panel doctors misunderstood the details of their contracts. The agreement did not always entitle them to receive a particular rate per insured person. Indeed, their income was limited by the size of local medical benefit funds. In short, it was not open to a doctor to claim a rate reflecting the multiplication of a specific capitation fee by the number of insured patients on his personal list. Rather practitioners were awarded a capitation fee that was based upon the size of the local insurance fund. Thus the amount per patient could exceed or fall short of the announced fee, which Morant stressed had always been only an actuarial estimate. While errors were bound to occur in a huge bureaucratic system, the central indexes of panel patients had to be the final authority, but Morant did promise that the system would be rationalized as much as possible.[11]

Morant's reply to the medical men was thus a not too subtle lecture on the principles of an insurance scheme with which they ought to have been familiar. The Insurance Acts Committee, however did leave his office promising to make the details of the capitation system clearer to panel doctors. This promise illustrates the shape of the emerging pattern of relations between the medical profession and the government. The Insurance Acts Committee realized that legal challenges to the rulings of the Insurance Commissioners would lead to counterproductive confrontations between the government and the nation's doctors. In such an atmosphere, the efficiency of the insurance medical service would suffer and the still evolving organizational and political revival of the B.M.A. might be destroyed. Thus, this first formal meeting between the insurance bureaucracy and the new Insurance Acts Committee marks the beginning of a working relationship between the two that was based on far more than wartime patriotism.

Once matured, the Insurance Acts Committee would assume a dual role. It came to act as the representative of panel medical opinion and at the same time its members were responsible for keeping doctors informed about governmental activities. It is also important to note that the national insurance bureaucracy did nothing to discourage the link between the B.M.A. and the Panel Conference. Just as it was in the profession's interest to have a single negotiating body, the government too stood to gain from the existence of a single medical voice. Not only could the positions and directives of the insurance administration be made clearer but the government would also have a permanent finger on the profession's pulse.

A more immediate result of the Committee's meeting with Sir Robert Morant was a statement issued in January, 1915 by the Insurance Commissioners assuring all panel doctors that the matter of accurate payments was being resolved. New medical cards were in the process of being distributed and these, it was hoped, would end much of the duplication and greatly simplify the entire record keeping system.[12] The re-issue of medical cards gave panel doctors more confidence in the accuracy of local insurance committee patient registers. Other administrative problems remained unsolved, however, and these were aggravated by wartime conditions.

From the first year of the medical benefit's operation, temporary residents had been the cause of much confusion and misunderstanding between panel practitioners and their local committees. Before the war the problem was largely confined to resort areas, where insured holiday makers or other travelers sometimes needed medical care. They, however, did not pay anything into the local insurance pool.[13] Doctors objected that they were in effect treating other men's patients without collecting a fee. In 1913, the Insurance Commissioners decided that to expect local committees to reimburse other committees for the treatment of their out-of-district insured persons was far too cumbersome a system. Instead a separate temporary residents' fund was established and doctors were paid directly on a fee-for-service basis, according to a pre-arranged tariff.[14]

The war vastly increased the population's mobility. As a result local insurance committees had a difficult time maintaining accurate indexes in the munitions areas where there were large numbers of new and possibly temporary residents claiming insurance medical benefits. By 1915, much to the consternation of Britain's civilian medical men, late payments to panel practitioners had become a routine matter. Especially hard hit by this situation were the families of doctors who had joined the military services because locums had to be hired and the practice maintained. In 1915 the wife of a man serving in France drew attention to her plight in the British Medical Journal.

> "For the quarter ending December 30th, 1914, they kept back 50 per cent of the money due us, for the quarter ending March 30th lost 20 per cent., for the quarter ending June 30th, 35 per cent .... Their excuse is that, "it takes time to find out what men have joined the forces from each doctor's panel." I dare say it does, but a system or method which cannot "find out" by now is no method or system, but a chaotic muddle ... Patriotism is a very fine thing, but it will not pay our bills."[15]

The above doctor's wife, however, found little solace in the response of the Joint Commissioners to the inability of local committees to keep patient registers up to date.

In order to guarantee that the medical benefit pool would not be overdrawn the Commissioners ordered all committees to limit their quarterly payments to panel practitioners to £72 per 1,000 patients. Nationally, this meant that doctors would receive only 64% of what was actually due them until a final accounting for 1915 could be completed in 1916.[16] But because many medical men had yet to receive their 1914 settlement, the action of the Commissioners was hardly comforting.[17]

Some inside the profession insisted that practitioners demand interest on all delayed or partial payments from the government.[18] The leaders of the profession, however, refused to press this or any other complaint too hard because of the war. Therefore, up to 1917, conditions within the insurance medical service changed very little. This general stability, however, allowed the B.M.A. to consolidate its political leadership of the panel medical service.

Even after the establishment of the loose connection between the Insurance Acts Committee and the Conference of Panel Committees in 1914, the B.M.A. had no real structural tie with the insurance medical service. But the Association, which had been so badly defeated in 1912, hoped to use the Insurance Acts Committee to bind itself to the panel service and achieve recognition as the political mouthpiece of the whole profession. There were those in the profession, though, who opposed all B.M.A. influence and sought to use the Conference of Local Medical and Panel committees as the sole vehicle for panel medical opinion. This sentiment was particularly strong in London, where, led by Dr. H. G. Cardale, the London Panel Committee had at first refused to join the national conference and then had objected to ties between the Conference and the B.M.A.[19]

Dr. Cardale, a leading member of the Medical Practitioners Union and Chairman of the London Panel Committee, insisted that the B.M.A. had shown itself far too weak to defend the profession's interest in 1912 during the fight against the panel system. Moreover, since then the B.M.A. had been too conciliatory towards the government. What angered Cardale the most, however, had been the Association's refusal to insist that late payments for panel work be eliminated. From early 1915 he had led the campaign to force the B.M.A. into stronger action but he had consistently failed to renew the profession's will to fight and dislodge the medical association.[20] According to Cardale and his supporters (mostly London men), the B.M.A. was like a wet blanket smothering the true level of discontent among doctors. The Association, he thought, should be left to deal with clinical matters and the local panel committees should form the basis of a new medical trade union.

Until 1915 the London Panel Committee had boycotted the annual panel conferences, but in May 1915, Dr. Cardale and his London colleagues attended their first meeting. Immediately the London doctors pushed to eliminate the B.M.A. from panel politics. In an amendment dealing with future panel agreements they proposed that, "no action of the British Medical Association shall be deemed to interfere with the right of the Panel Committees to make representations to the Commissioners on their own initiative."[21] Cardale's amendment was lost by a large majority and the supporters of the B.M.A. followed its defeat with a motion of their own which asked the Conference to accept the B.M.A. as the "single voice of the opinion" of panel doctors. This was quickly accepted, without dissent, when the London spokesmen either abstained or left the hall.

In order to confirm this formal link with the B.M.A., the Conference selected six members to serve on the Insurance Acts Committee along with those appointed by the Council of the B.M.A. From this point on the Insurance Acts Committee became the permanent executive and negotiating body of the Panel Conference. This was an important victory for the B.M.A. and its policy of cooperation with the administration of the health insurance act. With this final step, it recovered its traditional position as spokesman for the nation's doctors. Never again would its standing as the political mouthpiece on insurance matters for the whole profession be effectively challenged.[22]

With the maturation of the relationship between the B.M.A. and the Panel Conference, the Insurance Acts Committee acquired an increasingly important position between panel doctors and their employer, the government. The Committee's chairman was Dr. Henry Britten Brackenbury who, unlike others among the leadership of the B.M.A., was representative of those doctors who had entered panel service. As a general practitioner in Hornsey he had long been known for his liberal politics and sympathy for social medicine. Under Brackenbury the Insurance Acts Committee strove to develop a smooth working association with the government as well as the Panel Conference. Following the pattern established in 1914, the Committee refused to play the government's adversary and Brackenbury led it into easy cooperation with the national Commissioners.[23]

The Insurance Acts Committee's prime duty was to represent the profession at the panel medical services' annual contract negotiations. Yet, it was expected to be far more than simply the spokesman for medical opinion. The Insurance Acts Committee was also given the responsibility of planning for the profession's future situation under the insurance act. In June 1916, the Faculty of Insurance, a lobbying group representing the commercial insurance industry and collecting friendly societies, issued a report on the future of national insurance. In it, the Faculty proposed a large scale expansion of the medical benefit with the implication that it should be placed in the hands of the approved societies. Partly in response to this report, which the B.M.A. was of course not invited to help frame, the Association requested that the Insurance Acts Committee issue its own proposal for future developments.[24]

On 17 January 1917 the Insurance Acts Committee sent a notice to each local branch of the B.M.A. and all local panel committees asking that they consider the future of health insurance. All doctors were expected to evaluate the clinical, social and political aspects of the scheme's effect upon the profession. These evaluations were then collated and incorporated into a report that was later considered and adopted by the Panel Conference. The results are a good barometer of the medical profession's temperament as many Britons began to look towards post-war reconstruction.[25]

The degree of widespread agreement within the profession was in the words of the Insurance Acts Committee "remarkable."[26] Many of the issues that had created the most excitement in 1912-1913 had disappeared. Criticism of the scheme tended to concentrate on a comparatively few points that, though of great local or regional concern, were really matters of administrative detail. Of more importance for understanding the mood of the profession in 1917 are the larger national issues revealed by the Insurance Acts Committee's survey. On one level, the report dealt with the profession's desire to see a sweeping extension of insurance benefits to the dependents of those already insured within the £160 income limit. As before the war, doctors favored adding new benefits, such as consultant and specialist services, institutional facilities, x-ray, pathological, clinical and laboratory services, to the range of insurance medical care. In addition, dental treatment, nursing and maternal services as well as massage and electricity treatment were put forward as other possible services that could be made available to insured persons.[27]

Expanded benefits and the extension of the insurance act to dependents were issues for the future. The interests of most panel men were far more mundane. Within the framework of the act as it stood in 1917, practitioners expressed concern about the range of service under the capitation scheme. The 1911 act dictated that doctors undertaking panel service were responsible for providing all usual and necessary general practitioner care to insured patients. Since the inception of the medical benefit in January, 1913, the meaning of this directive had been disputed, as many medical men tried to exclude certain procedures and diseases from the scope of panel service.[28]

The administration of anaesthetics, for example, was seen by many doctors as requiring the skills of a specialist. Therefore a better defined system of special payments, in addition to the capitation fee, was desired by the profession. Some appliances too, such as splints, trusses and braces were also considered by doctors to be beyond the range of the normal medical benefit. Just as Hugh Gaitskell did thirty years later, the profession argued that to give patients medical appliances led to waste because most recipients did not fully appreciate the value of freely given supplies.[29] Finally, the Insurance Acts Committee's report revealed that a majority of panel men desired to see treatment of venereal disease removed from the medical benefit. During the war, venereal disease rates had gone up sharply and doctors argued that it was a self-inflicted disease and that infected individuals and not the panel medical service should be made financially responsible.[30]

Another large area of concern by the profession was the administrative duties associated with the insurance scheme. Medical records still caused a great deal of worry because of the clerical work involved. The card system that had been in existence since 1913 was certainly more agreeable than the original day book method. The cards, however, had to be sent to the local insurance committee at the end of each year. This was required in order to evaluate statistically the work of the panel medical service and, more importantly, to coordinate each doctor's patient list with the central index. Medical men complained that the procedure often led to difficulties when the cards were not returned promptly to panel doctors because very often the cards represented the only clinical records many practitioners maintained. Thus the clinical usefulness of panel medical records was impaired.[31] Insurance practitioners also asserted that the annual surrender of records was a violation of the confidentiality of the doctor-patient relationship.

A similar complaint was also made about the insistence of some approved societies that explicit clinical information be noted on the insurance sickness certificates. Doctors claimed that approved societies had no right to demand full clinical details before awarding the sickness benefit to their members. The societies, the profession argued, should be forced to honor all certificates signed by a panel doctor.[32] Moreover, societies should not be allowed to exercise any other control over the issuance of certificates, such as accepting them only on certain days of the week. Administrative convenience should never be allowed to dominate the patient's right to benefits and the private counsel of his chosen panel practitioner. The profession also reiterated its desire to see the establishment of an independent national medical referee service in order to adjudicate medical questions within the insurance scheme. Finally the report of the Insurance Acts Committee revealed that the vast majority of the profession favored the creation of a Ministry of Health to oversee the working of the insurance act and to coordinate the entire range of state-sponsored health services in Britain including sanitation, the school medical service, child and maternal care and health inspection services.[33]

Fully half the report of the Committee was dominated by the eternal question of remuneration for panel service. The issues of the general method of payment, the amount of the capitation fee and the calculation of doctors' annual panel income have all been discussed previously and there is little need here to outline again the profession's complaints. But the Committee's findings do confirm that there was overwhelming support for the continuation of the capitation scheme as the basis of payment for panel service. Only in Manchester, where, as will be discussed in chapter six, a fee-for-service scheme was used, did doctors express an interest in any other system of remuneration. Secondly, rural practitioners held that they were unfairly paid as compared to their urban colleagues despite the system of supplementary travel grants in operation since before the war.[34]

To illustrate the plight of rural panel men, the Insurance Acts Committee noted that before the war it had been generally believed that the greater distances traveled by rural doctors were largely offset by the better health of their patients. It was thought that city dwellers were subject to more illness and their greater proximity to practitioners encouraged them to consult doctors more frequently. But examination of data collected by the B.M.A. showed that nationally there was little difference in the number of attendances per patient between rural and urban medical men. Yet, the great majority of rural attendances involved a visit by the doctor to the home of the insured, whereas urban practitioners saw most of their patients at their surgeries. Therefore the Insurance Acts Committee urged in its report that a new scheme of mileage grants be established to compensate country doctors for their extra costs. Mileage grants, the Committee suggested, should be not only larger but based upon a national payment formula that reflected miles traveled, the difficulty of terrain and the weather.[35]

The 1917 Insurance Acts Committee report is a good reflection of the state of the mind of the profession during the late war years. It was apparent that the profession had come to accept fully the act and its role within the panel medical service. Still, most medical men realized that so long as the nation's attention was focused on the war, their problems would receive scant attention. The Insurance Commissioners, however, did make an attempt to ease some of the pressure upon the profession. As with other groups, panel doctors were granted war bonuses in order to compensate them for the rising cost of living during the war and for the increased work load. Special supplementary payments were also made to men practicing in munition mushroom areas and to those attending discharged wounded soldiers who had returned to work.[36] In addition, the responsibility for keeping medical records was suspended in 1917 and the government promised that before resumption the whole bookkeeping system would be reviewed.[37]

For the vast majority of panel practitioners the concessions by the government in 1917, while important, were only secondary to their primary concern: the size of the capitation fee. War time inflation had eaten into medical incomes and practitioners did not doubt that the money issue would dominate the immediate postwar years. In order to prepare for negotiating a higher capitation fee, the Insurance Acts Committee began to collect statistics pertaining to the costs of medical practice that it hoped would bear out the profession's monetary complaints. The information gathered by the Committee in 1917-18 confirmed the general impression that while doctors had done exceedingly well in the prewar period of the insurance act, the war years were different.

In urban areas of Surrey, for example, incomes increased 23% but expenses rose 38%. Shropshire towns showed a 7.3% decrease in medical incomes while the rise in expenses equaled 47.5% and the number of miles traveled by practiioners went up by 46%. Semi-rural regions of Northumberland reported a 19.5% increase in income but an extraordinary cost rise of 105% and a miles traveled increase of 81%. West country Wiltshire doctors reported to the Insurance Acts Committee that they had witnessed only a 7.5% war-time rise in revenue while outlays rose by 40% and miles travelled by 70%. Rural areas in Devon and South Hampshire reported that they had a 13.6% and 14.3% rise in income respectively. Nonetheless in Devon outlays rose by 31% and Hants doctors complained of a 112% increase in costs. Moreover, in Devon, travel by 1917 was 32% above 1914 totals and in Hants the increase was reported as being 100% above prewar levels.[38]

The figures collected by the Insurance Acts Committee are certainly dramatic evidence of a decline in medical incomes. In spite of this it is impossible to determine their accuracy. The statistics were collected by asking a selected group of medical men to supply information about the overall value of their private and panel practices in 1917 as opposed to 1914. However, the basis for the costs of medical practice was left to the individual doctor. Without guidelines, participating doctors used expenditures such as schooling for their children and holidays in totaling their overall cost of carrying out medical work. Thus, most of the material collected by the B.M.A. was useless, if not completely misleading. To assume that the average man in general practice sent his children to expensive public schools or took holidays abroad was both absurd and naive. To be sure, doctors did suffer increased costs, but the evidence gathered in 1917 was hardly, as the government would suggest later, an accurate measure of their loss. Still the statistics are significant because the leaders of the profession believed them to be accurate and their later political actions were predicated upon their perception of the financial position of doctors after 1914.

As soon as the fighting came to an end in Europe in 1918, the Insurance Acts Committee was ready with its request for an increase in the panel capitation fee for 1920. The profession's arguments were familiar. A rising cost of living coupled with a greater insurance risk (more broken health due to the war and an increase in the number of women in the insured population) necessitated an increase in panel income. In addition, with the expected extension of the medical benefit to the dependents of those already insured, the duties of the panel practitioner were sure to expand.[39] An advance was necessary but in late 1918, it was left to a canvass of the profession to specify an adequate level of panel remuneration in time for the beginning of the 1920 contract negotiations.[40] In the meantime, the Insurance Acts Committee and the Insurance Commissioners sparred with each other through the early months of 1919 as each attempted to gain an advantage in the upcoming panel medical service negotiations.

The Insurance Acts Committee met on 8 May 1919 with Dr. Christopher Addison, then the President of the Local Government Board and soon to be Minister of Health. At the conference Addison announced that the government had decided to raise the insurance income limit to £250 beginning January 1920, due to the war time inflation.[41] The Insurance Acts Committee expected Addison's announcement. It voiced no objection, as long as the extension did not materially alter the range of services under the act before the larger question of the panel capitation fee was discussed. Given the case the Committee was building for an increased rate of payment for the insurance medical service, it could hardly have opposed the government's measure.[42]

A more difficult question for the government in mid-1919, however, was the problem of the medical profession's war bonus. The Insurance Acts Committee asked for an increase over the bonus awarded in 1918. This issue was one of the first topics taken up by the newly created Insurance Department of the Ministry of Health.[43] The 1919 war bonus had to be examined in a tactical light. There was no question but that the medical profession intended to push for a large advance in the capitation fee for 1920, although the amount was not yet known. A small bonus might only increase the panel doctors' mistrust of the government and heighten their anxiety over the 1920 settlement. In contrast, a large bonus could spoil the practitioners and encourage them to ask for more money from an increasingly tightfisted Treasury.[44]

Since some concession would obviously have to be made, the key to the situation was the Ministry's evaluation of how cheaply it could get off without jeopardizing either the 1920 negotiations or the future relationship between the medical profession and the government.[45]

In the end the Ministry judiciously awarded the panel medical service a slight increase over its war bonus for 1918. Every insurance practitioner was given an increase of 15% of his total panel income. Moreover, if a doctor signed a statement attesting that his net professional income was not more than £500 a year the Ministry awarded him an additional 15%. Those medical men claiming net incomes between £500 and £1,200 annually were given an extra bonus of 5% above the 15% awarded to all panel practitioners. Finally, men with rural practices were granted an additional supplemental sum to cover the costs of travel.[46] The settlement met with a mixed reception. Some doctors, led by the Medical Practitioners Union, argued that the profession should have been included in the much larger bonus given to the civil service. The Ministry, though, pointed out that panel doctors were not full-time government employees. Unlike civil servants, they were part-time contractors with adequate opportunities to earn outside income from private practice.[47]

The political posturing by the profession and the government over the war bonus issue was in obvious preparation for the more important capitation negotiations expected in the autumn. This, however, took place against the backdrop of the postwar influenza epidemic.[48]

Doctors, who had hoped that the end of the war and the return of military medical men to civilian practice would ease the burdens of panel work, discovered that they had more work than ever. Beyond their increased insurance risk during the pandemic, those engaged in panel practice found that the floating sixpence system of financing the drug fund was proving totally inadequate. During the war an average of 3d. per patient from the floating sixpence was awarded to panel doctors. But the influenza epidemic increased the pressure on the floating drug fund to such a degree that in July 1919 the Insurance Acts Committee petitioned the government to suspend the fund and replace it with an emergency bonus to dispensing practitioners and chemists.[49] The government refused this appeal because it had, unknown to the medical profession, plans for the complete abolition of the floating sixpence scheme as part of a comprehensive capitation settlement for 1920. In light of this upcoming change, the government was unwilling to establish a precedent for future appeals for supplementary grants.[50]

For the medical profession, the refusal of the government to provide extra money for drugs was another disappointment. But with the pace of the influenza epidemic slackening, the medical leadership turned its attention to planning for the negotiations for the 1920 panel contract. There was still a small but very vocal group of medical men who believed that the only way to deal with the government was as a trade union. One man, Dr. E.H.M. Stancomb of Southampton, wrote that "There was no reason why the profession should not adopt a constitutional method of action which the Government recognized." "Trade unionism," he concluded, "was indeed the only thing which could bring influence to bear upon a recalcitrant Government."[51] Similar suggestions were a constant thorn in the B.M.A.'s side and it was feared by the moderate political leadership of the Association that extremists might push the profession to disaster. The B.M.A. had not been carefully rebuilding its credibility only to see it again crushed by irresponsible action.

In July, 1919, the Insurance Acts Committee issued a circular to all panel doctors decrying the intransigence of medical trade unionists who, the Committee charged, were examples of the worst kind of professional self-interest.[52] To follow the trade union path would only degrade the professional standing of the nation's doctors and reduce medical men to the level of tradesmen -- an image the B.M.A. had historically worked hard to surmount. The Committee's target was most notably the journal Medical World which had carried on an often nasty propaganda campaign against the B.M.A. The journal sought to inflame professional opinion against what its editors saw as the too placid and conciliatory B.M.A. The moderate leaders of the profession realized, though, that the views of Medical World would not succeed so long as they continued to be guided by the sentiment of the whole profession and led rather than pushed panel doctors.[53]

Following this general policy principle, the Insurance Acts Committee began to gauge the profession's temperament by soliciting suggestions from local panel committees for their opinions about the proper capitation fee. On 11 September 1919, the Committee reported that it had received replies from 81 panel committees with recommended capitation fees as low as 10s. and as high as Ƚ1.3s.6d.[54] The Insurance Acts Committee was careful not to commit itself to any capitation figure until the entire profession could respond to the Committee's canvass. To do otherwise might have prematurely placed in the public's mind an erroneous view of the doctors' demands and begun the political debate before the medical men were ready to argue their case effectively. For its part, the Ministry of Health watched the slow and cumbersome democratic procedures of the B.M.A. and the Conference of Local Panel Committees take their course. Still, the Ministry was not blind to the profession's "wildmen" and it maintained close touch with the Insurance Acts Committee in order to ensure that medical radicals did not push the government or the B.M.A. down a road neither wanted to travel.[55]

There were, of course, other changes embodied in the 1920 regulations. A Ƚ300,000 mileage grant for rural practitioners was promised and the Ministry proposed a national unit system for determining the amount due to each doctor. Moreover, special allowances were offered to men who could show especially difficult conditions. In 1920 payment for treating invalid soldiers was placed on a fee-for-service basis. The Ministry promised to re-calculate the central insurance pool in order to provide more precise payments for panel doctors as well as to enforce a 3,000 patient limit per panel list.[56] Finally, the regulations for 1920 established medical referees through the creation of a Regional Medical Officer Corps.[57]

It was the capitation fee question, of course, that dominated center stage. Here the Ministry of Health found that it had significantly less flexibility than it had on administrative issues. The Ministry had notified the Treasury of its desire to raise the capitation fee and proposed that the government increase its contribution to the insurance fund to cover the cost of both increased payments to doctors and extended medical and sickness benefits. The Treasury, however, refused to provide the additional funds, thus assuring a stormy future for the ongoing negotiations with the medical profession.[58]

In November, 1919, the Panel Conference accepted the non-financial provisions of the proposed 1920 regulations but made their continued cooperation with the government contingent on the rate of panel remuneration.[59] On 4 December the Ministry sponsored a meeting to hear the profession's capitation demands formally. Speaking for the panel representatives, Dr. Henry Brackenbury officially put forward a request for a 13s.6d. capitation fee based upon the effect of war time inflation, the rising standards and expense of medical science and the anticipated expansion of insurance medical benefits.[60]

Addison had heard such arguments before but by late 1919 he was in no position to be swayed by them. In 1920 the employee contribution to the insurance fund was to be raised from 7s. to 10s. for men and 6s. to 9s. for women. The bulk of the new money was already earmarked for the cash sickness benefit fund and for administrative costs. Little or nothing was to be used for paying the doctors of the insurance medical service. Therefore Christopher Addison already knew that his freedom of action concerning the capitation fee was severely limited. He and some of his advisors inside the Ministry had before the meeting tentatively decided to offer 11s. rather than meet the profession's demands for 13s.6d. The Treasury, however, had yet to approve even the lesser rate and Addison stalled the doctors' delegation by reminding them that under the Ministry of Health widespread changes in the organization of health care were likely. An advisory committee was in fact already considering some proposals for preventive care legislation for the coming year. Therefore, he warned, all parties should take care not to allow the capitation issue to prejudice the future development of health care policies. This semi-conciliatory tone, however, was dropped when the Minister stated the core of the problem; quite plainly, the government would never agree to a capitation fee of 13s.6d. involving an additional £3.5 million Treasury grant to the benefit fund. Still the Minister promised to study the profession's case.[61]

Addison's delaying tactics had little to do with his desire to study the profession's capitation argument. Sir Eric Geddes, of the later budget cutting Geddes Committee, had begun to pressure him about the rapidly rising cost of houses being built under the control of his Ministry of Health. Given the Treasury's increasing fiscal intransigence on the problems of postwar reconstruction, Addison realized that a large and apparently generous capitation settlement would raise eyebrows among hostile Conservatives in Lloyd George's coalition government. It could also help to stiffen opposition to the increasingly expensive housing project that was at the very center of Addison's post war plans.[62] Moreover, his own political position might be further eroded. Finally, Addison's principal civil servant was of little help.

Sir Robert Morant was in fact pro-doctor. He argued that the government should meet the profession's request for a 13s.6d. capitation fee. On 13 December, 1919, Morant wrote a lengthy memorandum against the bullying of his own Ministry by the Exchequer. "The moderates in the medical profession," Morant correctly asserted, "had succeeded in keeping the extremists at bay and 13s.6d. was not an unreasonable figure." To deny it would court disaster for the entire panel system.[63]

Morant's point of view, while perhaps logical in terms of securing improved relations between the government and the panel medical service, certainly ran counter to the emerging tone of postwar government policies. Whatever Christopher Addison's personal opinion, his vision was obviously clouded by his concern for his housing scheme and his own fading political influence with Lloyd George. The capitation issue was not the place to stand firm against the Treasury.

Therefore, Addison on 14 January 1920, met with the Insurance Acts Committee in order to inform it that the government had decided that 11s. was a fair and proper capitation fee based upon the evidence of the nature of panel work. Dr. Henry Brackenbury, speaking for the Insurance Acts Committee, replied to Addison's announcement by charging that the Ministry had ignored the medical evidence in favor of political convenience. Furthermore Brackenbury doubted that the Committee had the power to accept anything less than 13s.6d. for panel doctors and suggested arbitration.[64] Addison, personally not unresponsive to Brackenbury's notion, demurred from making a formal agreement until he could first consult his colleagues.[65] However, he fairly warned the delegation that an arbitrated settlement might result in less, rather than more, than the already offered 11s. as any discussion of the capitation fee would necessarily involve a general investigation of the efficiency of the panel medical service.[66]

Immediately after the meeting adjourned, Addison carried the profession's suggestion to the Treasury. The response was not long in coming. Later the same day Addison summoned the Insurance Acts Committee in order to inform them of the Treasury's answer.

The Minister told the doctors that the government would agree to an arbitrated settlement and that the arbitration board would limit its inquiry to only the costs and not the effectiveness of panel medical practice.[67] In the interim, though, the Minister informed the medical representatives that doctors would have to accept a short-term capitation fee of 11s. Moreover, the benefit regulations as outlined in late 1919 had to be put into place for all of 1920 without revision. Sensing at least a partial victory and confident in their ability to win over an impartial board of inquiry, the Insurance Acts Committee readily agreed to the government's terms.[68]

To the medical profession, the 13s.6d. capitation fee was a matter of simple justice. But the profession as a political organization was in a precarious position. Its political arm, the B.M.A., remembering the defeat at the hands of Lloyd George in 1912, was hesitant to push its demands to the point of political conflict with the government. The leaders of the profession realized that the nation's doctors could all too easily be made to look greedy, unpatriotic and little better than a trade union. Yet, as Alfred Cox observed in a letter to _The National Insurance Gazette_ on 17 January 1920, he could "see no reason why anybody should believe that money is worth any more to a doctor than it is, for example a railroad servant."[69] Professional pride was one thing but Cox could see no reason why vanity should stand in the way of a vigorous pursuit of what were seen as legitimate financial claims. Therefore, the B.M.A. threw itself into the arbitration hearings, vowing to prove its case calmly and systematically.

When the arbitration panel did meet to hear the evidence it became apparent to all that the profession had based its position more on personal impression than statistical evaluation. It was, it seemed, as if 13s. 6d. had simply been plucked from the air. The Insurance Acts Committee put forward statistics from only 24 insurance practices to support its case for a 13s.6d. capitation fee. No where did the medical representatives show satisfactory figures of actual expenses, average incomes or the number of attendances by doctors per panel patient.

The doctors' case was, to be sure, weak. So frail, in fact, that the government hardly bothered to refute the profession's meagre statistics. Instead its spokesmen pointed out that the medical men were asking for nearly twice as much as they earned per patient in 1914. Inflation had indeed taken its toll but even Professor Bowley, the doctors' economist, conceded that the cost of living had risen only 50% to 53%. At this figure, the government claimed its offer of 11s. was adequate with the additions already made to the Central Mileage Fund. The medical profession's flimsy case was completely demolished and the Arbitration Board was forced to agree with the government that "there was unfortunately a surprising absence of evidence from the doctor's side."[70] Because of this, the arbitration panel felt that it had little ground for supporting the profession's demands and on 5 March 1920, it rendered its decision. For 1920, the capitation fee was to be set at the 11s. originally offered by the government.[71] The profession was naturally disappointed but it had agreed to abide by the decision, even if the settlement was thought to be unsatisfactory.

Following the capitation arbitration many within the medical community argued that the government had again missed an opportunity to increase the quality of medical service for the insured population. Few doctors ever admitted the possibility that insurance patients might not receive the same quality of care as private patients. Still, practitioners stressed repeatedly that the only way to improve the care given to the insured population was to pay the panel doctor more. Medical technology after all had not been stagnant during the late world war. New techniques and drugs had been developed and it was assumed that the skill of the average medical man would improve rapidly in the postwar world. A low capitation fee, it was argued, would effectively bar insurance patients from the new knowledge that was then beginning to change the face of British medical practice. Moreover, high medical incomes would ensure that highly skilled practitioners remained in the panel service. This argument was an old one. It had been used both with regard to the Poor Law Medical Service and the School Medical Service. There was, the B.M.A. argued, a commonality of interest between patients and the advancement of all doctors into professional financial security: the better paid the latter, the better treated the former.[72]

Whatever the truth of the profession's insistence that the government would get only what it paid for, such simple assertions could not alone raise the capitation fee. In March, 1920, the profession had lost its case before the arbitration panel because it had failed to muster sophisticated evidence. As the government easily saw, the doctor's claims were based on scant evidence. Clearly, the medical men should have considered themselves fortunate to have gained an increase to 11s. in the capitation fee.

In appreciation of this weakness the profession began to prepare for the 1922 negotiations by resolving to collect sufficient, indeed overwhelming, detail concerning the necessity of their demands.[73] At the October 1920 meeting of the Conference of Local Panel Committees, such statistical gathering efforts on the part of the Insurance Acts Committee were formally approved. In addition, the Conference renewed its efforts to build up a medical defense fund so that the profession would have at its disposal enough money to finance its future capitation appeals.[74] Still, statistical information and a large defense fund could not save the medical profession from the postwar reductions in government expenditures.

In March, 1921, under pressure from the Conservatives, Lloyd George shunted out one of his oldest political allies, Christopher

Addison, from the Ministry of Health. Sir Alfred Mond, a man with a far more businesslike mind and without Addison's emotional attachment to the act, became the new Minister. This, however, did not change the profession's tactics. The Insurance Acts Committee continued zealously to collect evidence of the underpayment of panel doctors in order to prepare a case for a higher capitation fee. But unknown to the doctors, Mond and his Treasury colleagues were making plans to cut the government's contribution to the insurance act's medical benefit.[75]

Rumors of a reduced capitation fee were heard by the medical profession in September of 1920. Commenting on these, the British Medical Journal stressed that "It is to be hoped that the suggestions that such a reduction is to be proposed are irresponsible. If not, a situation will arise of great importance to the medical profession and to the public, and the organized bodies of the profession must be prepared to defend their own and the public interest."[76] The nature of the profession's defense should such an emergency occur, however, was not disclosed. The reason for this was clear when the government finally did make its announcement to cut the panel remuneration. The profession had no effective means of resistance.

Mond met with the Insurance Acts Committee on 11 October 1921 and told the practitioners that the government intended to reduce the rate of panel remuneration in 1922 from 11s. to 9s.6d.[77] The Minister based his judgment upon the fact that the cost of living had steadily fallen since the beginning of the postwar trade depression and hence the foundation for the arbitrated settlement of 11s. established in 1920 was no longer acceptable. Mond appealed to the Committee to urge its constituency to accept the proposed cut out of patriotism to the nation which was threatened with economic chaos if the government could not control expenditures. He also issued a threat. The Minister stated flatly that he had

> "no desire or intention to enter into long haggling negotiations with the medical profession. That would be very undignified on both sides ... The conclusion which has forced itself on my mind, having regard to the economy which is enjoined upon us, and is being carried right through the remuneration of Government servants and Government expenditure generally, is that the sum of 11s should be reduced to 9s.6d., and that the arrangements in force now regarding mileage and things of that kind should remain in force as in the past ... I am sure that there is no one here who is in the least degree anxious to see a revival of the old conditions with regard to the medical profession and the friendly societies. You will remember, as I do, that at the time when the Insurance Bill was before the House of Commons, considerable pressure was brought to bear by the approved societies that there should be no interference with their practice or raising their own medical benefit and negotiating directly with the medical profession on that subject. I do not think that at the time the medical profession was very enamoured of being put in the hands of friendly societies - for many excellent reasons. But the pressure from that force has always existed and still exists... I am sure that you do not wish to escape from the Scylla of the Ministry of Health to the Charybdis of the friendly societies."[78]

Even had it been willing to agree to the Minister's capitation reduction, the Insurance Acts Committee was not empowered to accept Mond's offer. Therefore, after assuring the Minister of the profession's patriotic loyalty, the Committee promised to present the government's views to the annual Panel Conference due to meet in London, only nine days later, on 20 October.

When the Conference did meet all medical men in attendance understood that Mond's offer was an ultimatum backed by the specter of approved society domination. Following the Insurance Acts Committee's report at the opening session of the Panel Conference, the representatives engaged in a stormy five hour debate to consider their options.[79] Three courses of action were discussed: (1) the profession could attempt to negotiate with the government in order to secure either a reduction in the duties of panel practice or a smaller cut in the capitation fee, (2) practitioners could threaten to refuse to accept less than the 1920 arbitrated settlement and take the issue into the courts for a decision, (3) a boycott of the panel scheme could be undertaken in order to force the government to surrender. As the debate took shape it became clear that the majority of representatives would not support the third option, despite the urging of the London delegation which had always supported the use of the strike to achieve the profession's ends. The second option was ruled out because of time and expense. The only other alternative (besides outright acceptance) was to try to convince the Ministry to open the question to negotiation.[80]

At the close of the debate the Insurance Acts Committee was given the responsibility of engaging Mond in further talks about the capitation issue. Mond agreed to receive the Committee at

7:00 on the evening of October 20. At the meeting the practitioners offered a counterproposal of 10s. and a reduction in the range of panel service. Mond listened but stood firm. "I cannot alter my basic figure of 9s.6d. -- I told you that last time," the Minister of Health stated flatly. "I was not bargaining," Mond continued, "but was laying down a final figure, and that I must maintain." Backing up this stern reply the Minister of Health played what had always been the government's trump cards -- popular opinion and the approved societies. He warned the Insurance Acts Committee that they "should not be well advised to scrap the whole thing. It is no use shutting one's eyes to two important facts. One is the great desire of the taxpayer to be relieved of expenditure at almost any cost and in almost any manner. The other is the outcry of a not uninfluential section, both lay and medical attacking the panel system."[81]

An hour later the Insurance Acts Committee was again before the panel representatives informing them of the Ministerial pronouncement.[82] The only concession that the medical negotiators had wrung from Mond was an agreement that the duration of the new capitation fee would be two years instead of the eighteen months originally proposed by the Minister. In addition, Mond promised that he would consider not enforcing the new capitation level until April 1922. These minor points, however, were small consolation to the representatives of the annual panel conference who had been waiting anxiously for the return of the Insurance

Acts Committee. When faced with the Minister's refusal to discuss the issue further, most doctors attending the panel conference understood that the profession had few options.[83] A few alternative courses of action were considered, such as a direct appeal to the Prime Minister. But in the end the Conference had little choice but to cave in. Without the backbone for a boycott, medical men had to agree to the government's offer for the coming year "on the grounds of citizenship."[84] Nonetheless, the doctor's sense of citizenship was hardly rooted in an undying regard for patriotism. It was apparent that the medical men had been battered into submission again by the government. "The public," warned the <u>British Medical Journal</u> shortly after the settlement, "must not ... suppose that the medical profession in accepting it is satisfied with this figure as a fair and proper rate of payment for the work and the responsibility. It is not."[85] Patriotism was indeed a bitter medicine.

Alone, the capitation fee reduction was difficult enough for the profession to accept. What the medical men really resented however, was the government's willingness to rub salt in their open wounds. In what the Insurance Acts Committee considered a breach of faith the government announced on 19 December 1921 that it intended to enforce the 9s.6d. capitation from 1 January -- thus violating a long-standing agreement that three months notice would be given before any changes in the insurance regulations were made.[86] Two other announcements made by the Ministry of

Health left the profession even angrier.

Throughout the negotiations during the autumn of 1921 the Insurance Acts Committee had understood that neither the panel dispensing fee nor the mileage fund would be affected by economy measures. During the first week of December the Insurance Acts Committee was asked to meet with the Insurance Department of the Ministry of Health. At this conference the Ministry's spokesman announced that the dispensing fee for doctors (mostly rural men) would be reduced from 2s. to 1.9d. per patient.[87] While this equalled the rate chemists were to receive, the Insurance Acts Committee argued later in a December memorandum that from 1916 through the first six months of 1921 doctors' dispensing losses had ranged from 2.4d. to 8.8d per head. But the primary reason medical men deserved a higher dispensing fee than chemists, claimed the Committee, was that "the making up of bottles of medicine, mixing of ointments, and weighing out ingredients, the ordering of drugs, comparing of price lists, checking and unpacking of hampers, etc., is not the practitioner's proper function; it is a waste of professional time, and should be paid for at a higher rate than is paid to the chemist, whose trade it is."[88] This appeal fell upon deaf ears and on 1 January the panel dispensing fee dropped to the previously announced level.

Equally important, but perhaps less clear-cut for practitioners, was the reduction of the mileage allowance for travel. The Ministry had appointed a committee to report upon the Central

Mileage Fund and to suggest alterations in November 1921.[89] The Committee's report had two sections. The first, using the same methods as in 1920 to determine actual travel costs, concluded that on the basis of 1921 returns, the Ƀ300,000 mileage fund was too large. Not only had the earlier estimates of miles traveled been too generous but costs throughout 1922 had fallen as the nation's economy deflated. As a result, the Committee recommended a 15% reduction in the mileage fund. Speaking for the B.M.A., Alfred Cox did not take issue with this part of the report, stating that "if the methods of the Committee are sound, and the data accurate as can be obtained, the result arrived at must be a fair assessment."[90] The second part of the report, however, did not meet with the same kind response.

Since the 1920 panel agreement, rural practitioners had been paid mileage allowances according to a dual standard. A basic national rate was established. At the same time special payments were allowed to medical men where terrain and weather made travel difficult. These payments were made from a reserve portion of the Central Mileage Fund. This pool of money was eliminated after the committee dealing with the mileage question submitted its report. For medical men this seemed to be in direct violation of Alfred Mond's promise not to "interfere" with the method of calculating supplemental payments. "The blindest and most apathetic panel doctor must see the recent agreements between the Insurance Acts Committee and the Ministry of Health," one angry Northumberland doctor wrote, "are no better than Teutonic scraps of paper. Had we realized the possibility of a breach of faith over the mileage grant, probably the acceptance of a reduction of the capitation fee for 'patriotic reason' would not have been borne so meekly."[91]

In 1922 the medical profession had reached a political crossroad. By 1914 the nation's doctors had made their peace with the insurance act and its administrators. Throughout the war years the B.M.A. reasserted itself as the natural leader of the whole profession. It not only strove to rebuild its base of medical support but the leaders of the B.M.A. worked hard to gain the government's respect. Through a conscious policy of peaceful persuasion Alfred Cox and Henry Brackenbury avoided direct conflict with the government while trying to improve the profession's administrative and financial position within the insurance act. Admittedly the doctors had little choice in light of their recent history. Nonetheless the government appreciated the Association's cooperation and its unwillingness to adopt trade union tactics.

As each year passed the B.M.A. gained more confidence in its ability to influence insurance policy with reasoned argument. But after the end of the war the nation's practitioners found that administrative questions were far easier to resolve than economic issues in the atmosphere of tight-fisted government. Medical men failed to win their financial claims in 1919 and their appeal to the arbitration board was at best inept. Repeatedly the profession's spokesmen had to admit to a lack of evidence to support their demands for a 13s.6d. capitation fee. This failure was overshadowed by the reduction of panel remuneration, mileage allowances and dispensing fees for 1922 which taught the profession the grim realities of postwar British politics. Persuasion did not always end in success. So long as medical men denied even the possibility of a national withdrawal from panel service it was clear that the B.M.A. had reached the limits of cooperation. If doctors wanted the government to listen seriously to its economic claims for more money the profession had to "decline to be perpetually bullied."[92]

A more belligerent policy could of course achieve its aim and earn financial concessions from the government. But any doctor who knew the story of the profession's relationship with national health insurance was fully aware of the dangers inherent in confrontation. No one was more conscious of these than Alfred Cox, who had overseen the rebuilding of the B.M.A. after its political collapse in 1912. Repeatedly he pointed out that the position of the panel doctor was far better than anyone would have expected. Better, he thought, than the profession could hope for from an insurance system managed by approved societies or private enterprise. By following a conciliatory path since 1914, Britain's practitioners had become active partners in the daily operation of the act and the local panel committees had a considerable voice in how the medical benefit was managed. After eight years of working the national health insurance panels, 'doctors,' Cox asserted, had done well in a "process which all reasonable people know must be one of give and take..."[93]

To be sure, Cox was right in his assessment. Practitioners certainly could be placed in a more disadvantageous position. Medical unity had, it seemed, been rebuilt and the ability of the B.M.A. to claim the loyalty of all doctors appeared much stronger than it had ever been. But both the solidarity of the profession and the B.M.A.'s ability to lead it to success in a crisis stood untested in 1922. Should an attempted boycott of the panels fail, in a repetition of 1912, doctors could be sure that the government would not so diligently defend the panel medical service from approved society control. Furtunately for the profession in early 1922, it did not have to decide its future course immediately. It had until the autumn of 1923, when the capitation issue would again be opened, to weigh the merits of the panel system against the risks of confrontation and to prepare itself for the consequences of its actions.

Notes

1. BMJ (27 October 1917), Supplement, p. 76.

2. Ibid.

3. Insurance Acts Committee, session 1819-1919. IAC 118, 16 July 1919.

4. BMJ (26 June 1915), Supplement, p. 327.

5. BMJ (6 May 1916), Supplement, pp. 97-101.

6. One of the concessions won by the BMA in 1912 was that non-panel doctors would be represented at the local level. The BMA felt that this would prevent a split in the profession. Therefore, while panel committees were composed only of doctors working the act, local medical committees were established to provide a forum for all medical opinion. In most areas, though, the distinction soon blurred as non-panel men lost interest in the operation of the act. By the early twenties few localities had active medical committees as most had either ceased to exist or had merged with the panel committee.

7. BMJ (6 May 1916), Supplement, p. 189.

8. BMJ (8 May 1915), Supplement, pp. 234-235.

9. Ibid.

10. Ibid.

11. Ibid., pp. 235-237. For example, a patient might be seeing two separate panel doctors, with both assuming that the insured was on his list. Practitioners could also have been seeing patients who were in fact not eligible for the medical benefit, or carrying patients on their personal lists who were dead, or who had moved. Thus, Morant, despite unavoidable inaccuracies, chose to use the local insurance committees panel list over those kept by the medical service doctors.

12. BMJ (30 January 1915), Supplement, p. 333.

13. BMJ (17 January 1914), Supplement, p. 24.

14. BMJ (5 July 1913), Supplement, pp. 45-46.

15. BMJ (23 October 1915), Supplement, p. 165.

16. BMJ (26 June 1915), Supplement, pp. 320-321.

17. BMJ (23 October 1915), Supplement, p. 165.

18. BMJ (26 June 1915), Supplement, pp. 321-322.

19. The Panel Committee of London, minutes, 28 April 1914. These records are now in the possession of the Secretariat for the London Local Medical Committees. Although the secretariat is independent of the BMA, it is located in BMA House, London.

20. BMJ (1 May 1915), Supplement, p. 157.

21. BMJ (26 May 1915), Supplement, p. 329.

22. Ibid.

23. BMJ (14 October 1916), Supplement, pp. 102-107.

24. BMJ (3 March 1917), Supplement, pp. 42-43.

25. BMJ (23 June 1917), Supplement, p. 143. See Paul Johnson, Land Fit for Heroes (Chicago: University of Chicago Press, 1968).

26. Ibid.

27. Ibid., p. 145.

28. Ibid., p. 147.

29. Ibid.

30. BMJ (27 October 1917), Supplement, pp. 76-77.

31. BMJ (23 June 1917), Supplement, p. 147.

32. Ibid., p. 148.

33. BMJ (30 June 1917), Supplement, p. 154.

34. Ibid., p. 153.

35. Ibid.

36. BMJ (2 November 1918), Supplement, pp. 62-69. The government decided that a complete actuarial audit of the medical benefit fund should be delayed until the war was over and then the entire scheme could be reconsidered. Therefore the bonus system was established. Each doctor had his bonus computed individually, based upon the number of panel patients on his list. This raised the average per patient income from panel work to 8s. 6d. by 1918 for medical men earning less than £ 1000. from panel practice. For those with

larger incomes a maximum bonus of £ 60. was established by the government. Supplementary grants were also allowed for men with a high number of disabled soldiers on their lists and for those practitioners working in munition mushroom areas. The bonus system, while welcome, was seen as only an extension of the capitation scheme already in effect. Many doctors felt that it was not flexible enough to allow for special cases. Medical men would have preferred a fee-for-service plan instead. Insurance Acts Committee, session 1919-1920. IAC 110, 4 July 1919. Also see *BMJ* (27 October 1917), *Supplement*, pp. 76-77.

37. *BMJ* (10 February 1917), *Supplement*, p. 23.

38. Insurance Acts Committee, session 1918-1919. IAC 16 (M.3.), 29 August 1918.

39. C.F.G. Masterman, "National Insurance and Its Future," *The National Insurance Gazette and Sickness Societies Review* (14 June 1919), p. 239. Hereafter cited as *The National Insurance Gazette*. Also see Dr. Charles A. Parker, "Some Aspects of the Case for a State Medical Service," *The National Insurance Gazette* (10 May 1919), pp. 186-187. For the profession such ideas were not idle speculation. The Insurance Acts Committee had been asked in December 1918 by the Insurance Commission to make a list of formal recommendations for the future. Insurance Acts Committee, session 1918-1919. IAC 50, 5 December 1918.

40. Insurance Acts Committee, session 1916-1917. IAC 19, 31 August 1916. In 1916 the Insurance Acts Committee promised the conference of local panel committees that it would never put forward any ideas or proposals to the government unless they had the full approval of the profession. This policy was designed to avoid the obvious pitfalls of the recent past. Most importantly, the Committee agreed that it would never call for a boycott of panel service unless 80 percent of all panel doctors agreed in advance to resign.

41. Insurance Acts Committee, session 1918-1919. IAC 95, 8 May 1919.

42. *BMJ* (31 May 1919), *Supplement*, p. 116. This fact did not prevent the Council of the BMA from voting to oppose the £ 250 income limit. Its members apparently believed that new people might be added to the insurance scheme at the expense of those practitioners still in private practice.

43. Bentley B. Gilbert, *British Social Policy 1914-1939* (Ithaca, New York: Cornell University Press, 1970), pp. 98-158.

44. PRO. MH 62/124., 14 April 1919.

45. *Ibid.*, 6 February 1919.

46. BMJ (26 July 1919), Supplement, p. 31.

47. Insurance Acts Committee, session 1918-1919. IAC 127, 26 July 1919.

48. Richard Collier, The Plague of the Spanish Lady: The Influenza Pandemic of 1918-1919 (New York: Atheneum, 1974).

49. Insurance Acts Committee, session 1918-1919. IAC 109, 4 July 1919.

50. PRO. MH 62/124., 2 June 1919.

51. BMJ (2 August 1919), Supplement, pp. 50-51. An amendment was offered by the delegates representing Bournemouth that proposed a medical trade union to replace the BMA in political matters. It was defeated 75-17.

52. Insurance Acts Committee, session 1918-1919. IAC 116, 4 July 1919.

53. Typical of Medical World's attacks upon the BMA and the position of the panel practitioner is the poem entitled "The Panel Doctors Plaint." The poem (loosely defined) accuses the government and the BMA of exploiting the poor panel practitioner. Medical World (11 April 1918), p. 85.

54. Insurance Acts Committee, session 1919-1920. IAC 4, 11 September 1919.

55. PRO. MH 62/119., 19 & 20 September 1919.

56. BMJ (30 October 1920), Supplement, pp. 116-117.

57. Insurance Acts Committee, session 1919-1920. IAC 24, 21 October 1919.

58. PRO. MH 62/119., 18 October 1919.

59. BMJ (6 December 1919), Supplement, pp. 137-147.

60. BMJ (13 December 1919), Supplement, pp. 55-156.

61. Ibid.

62. Geddes to Addison, 4 December 1919, Addison Papers, 36/89 Bodleian Library.

63. PRO. MH 78/96., 13 December 1919.

64. BMJ (24 January 1920), Supplement, pp. 17-20.

65. Ibid.

66. *Ibid*.

67. Marks, p. 93.

68. *BMJ* (24 January 1920), *Supplement*, p. 19.

69. *The National Insurance Gazette* (18 January 1920), p. 129.

70. *BMJ* (13 March 1920), *Supplement*, p. 74.

71. H. B. Brackenbury, "Some Thoughts on the Arbitration," *The Lancet* (13 March 1920), pp. 621-622.

72. *Ibid*.

73. Insurance Acts Committee, session 1919-1920. IAC 99, 29 April 1920.

74. *BMJ* (24 October 1920), *Supplement*, p. 119. The National Insurance Defence Trust had been established in 1915 from funds left over from the 1912 struggle against the act. All panel committees were asked to subscribe but many did not. By 1920 the fund had a balance of £6,508 and the panel conference voted to pay the expenses of the Insurance Acts Committee, relieving the BMA of the responsibility. This is only another indication of the success of the BMA in solidifying panel medical opinion and organization under its leadership. It should also be noted that the panel conference defeated a motion to end the collection of money for the fund.

75. Gilbert, *Social Policy*

76. *BMJ* (24 September 1921), p. 497.

77. *BMJ* (15 October 1921), *Supplement*, pp. 147-150.

78. *Ibid*., p. 148.

79. *BMJ* (29 October 1921), *Supplement*, pp. 163-166.

80. *Ibid*.

81. *Ibid*., p. 169. The medical representatives tried to convince the Minister that a rebate scheme should be tried instead of an across the board cut. Under their proposal the reduction of the capitation fee was to be made temporary and a rebate system was to be established to give panel doctors an official remuneration of 10s. Under the scheme doctors would agree to voluntarily rebate a portion of the panel income to the government. The advantage to the doctors was that the official fee would not fall quite so far and in the future they could withdraw all or part of their voluntary rebate. The Minister politely refused the suggestion.

82. *Ibid*.

83. *Ibid*., p. 170.

84. *Ibid*., p. 179.

85. *BMJ* (29 October 1921), pp. 712-713.

86. *BMJ* (17 December 1921), *Supplement*, p. 231. The medical profession charged that the government was taking advantage of a technicality. Officially the national insurance commissioners had the right to alter the regulations any time they pleased. But since 1913 they had always given the medical profession three months notice of any change. Although the panel fee reduction had been made in early October, official notice was not given until much later.

87. *BMJ* (31 December 1921), *Supplement*, pp. 258-260. The single reduction in the range of dispensing service granted by the Ministry of Health was that cod liver oil and malt were now charged to the local drug fund. This was not an insignificant concession, as the two were the largest single items prescribed by panel doctors to their insured patients.

88. *Ibid*., p. 259.

89. *BMJ* (4 February 1922), *Supplement*, p. 24. The government at first refused to release the report but when pressured by the BMA it finally relented.

90. *Ibid*, Alfred Cox to Sir Alfred Mond.

91. *Ibid*., p. 27.

92. *Ibid*.

93. Alfred Cox, "Does the Medical Profession Wish the National Health Insurance System to Continue?" *BMJ* (8 October 1921), *Supplement*, p. 138. With this article, which argued that the medical profession would be foolish to give up on the insurance act, Cox appears to have been preparing his fellow doctors for a possible cut in the capitation fee. Later he told the Insurance Acts Committee that Sir Arthur Robinson, the Permanent Secretary in the Ministry of Health, was keeping him posted on insurance issues. Insurance Acts Committee, session 1921-1922. IAC 54, 22 March 1922.

CHAPTER III

This Panel Business

By 1923 the national health insurance act had been in operation for ten years. As we have seen, in those first ten years, doctors had to deal with a variety of political and administrative issues that were at the very core of the profession's relationship to the act and its administrators. Up to this point, however, this discussion has had as its primary focus the political activities of the B.M.A. and its leaders. To be sure, an understanding of this view of the doctors and the act is important. The willingness of the insurance bureaucracy to consider medical views on administrative questions and the constant threat of approved society control were beyond a doubt central to the formulation of professional opinion and political activity after 1913. Still, the attitude towards the panel system was shaped far more by each doctor's personal experience than by the political activities described in the medical press.[1] By the early twenties, medical men had a large stake in the continuation of the insurance act. Not only had they done well monetarily but their professional interests had also been served by the scheme. The importance of these factors cannot be divorced from the political story of the profession's relationship with the government.[2] Therefore, just as Britain's doctors undertook an evaluation of panel work in 1922 before deciding their political future, it is appropriate that this study too step away from the capitation issue and explore the act from the perspective of the panel doctor -- not only as it existed in 1922 but as it evolved throughout the interwar period.

Money and Medical Incomes

In spite of the ongoing capitation dispute, there was little doubt that insurance income had become the economic bedrock of general practitioner medicine. A sample of many advertisements in the pages of The Lancet may suggest the importance attached to panel work and the fees it produced. A London medical practice offered for sale in 1922 was described as a "middle and working class practice with some very good patients. Receipts over £3000. Panel 1800 appointments £200." A more modest Northumberland practice also for sale in 1922 offered the prospect of a total income of £800. Of this, appointments and panel work produced £250 annually.[3] In 1938 a female doctor placed an advertisement seeking a position, asking for a "private and panel practice ... with a minimum income of £400" annually.[4] The Bovril Medical Agency of London in June 1939 placed with The Lancet a list of thirteen medical practices for sale located in all parts of England. Eleven of these prominently touted the value of their panel patients.[5]

Unpaid medical bills among a sizable class had been eliminated and while the panel fee was a matter of contention, it was at least steady. Contemporary wisdom dictated that a single doctor could effectively handle a maximum of 3,000 panel patients in addition to those who paid private fees.[6] Naturally, most medical men had far fewer insured patients, but it was thought that a sound practice should have a third to half of its patient load covered by the act. This provided a measure of stability previously unknown in middle and working class medical work.

Panel lists ranged in size from only several insured patients to those with 5,000 or more. In London, for example, in 1922, 33% of all doctors had fewer than 500 patients while 13.5% had more than 2,500.[7] Despite such wide disparities, however, the average list size nationally ranged from 750 in 1920 to nearly 1,000 patients in 1938.[8] Thus, subject to the precise capitation fee, the average panel practitioner could expect from £400 to £900 annually from insurance work alone.[9] However, from this gross income, doctors had to pay the costs of some appliances, including bandages, trusses and splints.[10] The net value of panel work was also subject to the frequency of attendance per patient. Fortunately for those men serving within the panel system, most insured persons were prudent in their demands, although patients did tend to call upon their doctors more often as they became accustomed to the scheme.[11] In 1924 the Ministry of Health calculated the rate of panel attendance at slightly less than 3.5 per person each year with 60% of all insured persons receiving some kind of annual medical care under the act. The B.M.A. did not dispute this latter figure. Nonetheless it did claim that its evidence showed that the average rate of panel attendance was 3.77 visits per person. In contrast the attendance rate for private patients stood at 3.95 per year.[12]

Doctors pointed out that while attendance rates were similar, panel practice yielded far less per service than the average annual private fee of 14s.9d. per head. Yet, despite this disparity, few practitioners ever realistically entertained the notion that private and panel fees should be equal. Charges for medical services had always been geared to the financial status of the patient.[13] A rich man was invariably billed more than those of more modest means, even if the services rendered were identical.[14] Moreover, doctors realized that no matter how unhappy they were with the capitation fee, the insurance scheme had broadened the economic opportunities of medical work.

Usually an insured wage earner brought members of his family to his panel doctor as private patients when they were in need of care or advice. Prior to the coming of national health insurance, medical care among the poor was limited by economic necessity. It was reserved either for the very young or for those whose health was vital to the family income.[15] Little money was available to pay a private doctor for attending non-wage earners and charity, to say nothing of the Poor Law Medical Service, was always a last resort. As a result women especially were victimized by such poverty. The insurance act changed this pattern of neglect. With insurance-financed care extended to wage earners, other family members were in a better position to receive at least limited medical attention as private patients. This meant that for panel doctors each insured patient was also worth additional money because of his dependants. An accepted rule of thumb stated that, including the capitation fee, every panel patient was worth in total gross income about £1 per year in an average mixed industrial practice.[16] For practitioners this meant extra income of around 10s. to 12s. annually per panel patient that, but for the insurance scheme, would have been lost.[17] Thus, while panel work may have produced less money per attendance than private practice, an average list could generate as much as £600 from a class that in the past had been the object of charity and the source of bad debts.[18]

The Changing Face of the Profession

How much the average practice gained in value as a result of the insurance act varied. Some doctors gained more than others but all practitioners witnessed changes in the nature of medical practice. Expanded opportunities for income from insurance practice meant that many doctors who had cared almost exclusively for the middle classes found it profitable to extend the boundaries of their practices.[19] Branch surgeries, while not unknown in pre-insurance days, became far more common after 1913. Usually located in commercial districts of working class neighborhoods, they were sparsely equipped and locked up except for specific hours and days of attendance.[20] Critics charged that they denied panel patients the advantages of having a family doctor because the practitioner was not constantly available at his surgery. Moreover, it was pointed out that branch surgeries were often staffed by young and inexperienced assistants who provided inferior medical care for the insured class.[21]

Panel patients were indeed sometimes victims of high volume insurance mills that made use of branch surgeries. Nonetheless, when seen as a whole, the increased number of branch surgeries was a positive advance. Their growth represents an expansion of the availability of medical care to the poor who because of housing patterns were already isolated from most doctors. Medical men who did not want to have a large industrial practice in the past avoided poorer districts because a small working class practice was a liability. After the passage of the act, doctors invaded impoverished areas in search of panel patients while maintaining their profitable private practices.[22] Branch surgeries, lock-up or otherwise, expedited this medical migration without upsetting the doctor's non-panel work and allowed the insured primary care in the familiar surroundings of their own neighborhoods. While patients legally had the right to be treated at a main office, most preferred the closer branch surgery. At the same time, it should be noted that the existence of a branch surgery did not free the panel doctor from his obligation to make home visitations when called upon. Moreover, all surgeries serving panel patients were subject to inspection in order to guarantee their cleanliness and medical adequacy.[23]

The expanding scope of medical practice and modern innovations (such as branch surgeries) made some older practitioners uncomfortable despite the obvious economic advantages. They often felt the disappearance of the personal aspects of the doctor-patient relationship. Younger doctors generally disagreed with this view, finding the panel system to their liking. The larger patient loads meant that it was easier for newly trained medical men to secure employment as assistants and to become accepted as partners in already established practices. The act also enabled young doctors without private means or family connections to begin their own practices earlier than in the past. In addition the relative financial stability created by the capitation payments protected many medical men with small private practices from professional ruin during the worst years of the depression.[24]

This increased economic stability of doctors had a wide impact upon the profession as a whole. Before the insurance act, the general practitioner was often perceived as little more than a tradesman. The financial stability spawned by national health insurance began to change this and the profession began increasingly to be drawn from, in the _British Medical Journal_'s view, "a better class of man".[25] The overwhelming majority of students entering medical schools were by the early thirties of middle class origin. In 1938, for example, almost 90% of the students attending St. Mary's Hospital Medical School were entirely self-financing. The vast majority of these students entered general medical practice and therefore panel work upon graduation.[26] This increased competition did not mean, however, that British training institutions produced more doctors. Limited facilities and the profession's natural inclination not to flood the market prevented this. But the competition to enter medical schools resulted in rising admission standards and thus a natural improvement in the quality of medical education.[27] Even though the evidence may be circumstantial, it does seem apparent that the economic motivation provided by the working of the insurance act as well as the growing acceptance of medicine as a science shared responsibility for these changes.

Whatever benefits there were from these rising standards, however, urban based practitioners gained the most. Large towns and resorts always attracted medical men because of their greater cultural amenities and economic possibilities. Rural districts remained as chronically short of doctors after the act's passage as they had been before. In part this was because medical men with exclusively country practices did not benefit from the act's financial advantages nearly as much as their urban colleagues. The distance between patients was far greater and the country practitioner could therefore attend fewer insured persons.[28] This was true not only because there were fewer people in rural districts but because the insurance act itself had increased competition among doctors. The act sought to encourage more men to work in rural areas. This goal was achieved but not in the manner that had been expected. Instead of more men moving to the country, the motor car made it possible for doctors living in towns to provide care for those in adjoining rural regions. Rather than providing security for the exclusively rural medical man, the result was often unwanted competition from his town brethren who with the telephone and motor car were now invading his territory.[29]

Doctors and Patients

Payment for the provision of medical care did little to ease class bias. There were indeed medical men who clung to the old practice of keeping the classes isolated from each other. Insured workers sometimes were required to enter the surgery by a side or back door while better class patients were allowed to use the front. Separate waiting rooms, as shown by a 1922 *Lancet* advertisement, were also maintained and these almost certainly differed in comfort.[30] However widespread these distinctions, they were not the making of the medical profession or of the insurance act. Even today, after thirty-one years of the national health service, class continues to plague British medicine and society as a whole despite the best efforts of social levelers. Thus, simply to write off the panel system as a class ridden experiment in working class medical care is a mistake. For both doctors and patients it was indeed far more.

Whether or not an individual doctor greatly increased his income from panel work or discriminated against insured patients, all agreed that the act had a tremendous psychological advantage. Before the coming of the act many practitioners, no matter how kindhearted, found it difficult to provide even a basic level of care for fear of trampling upon patient pride. The panel system alleviated this. Insured persons and their doctors no longer had to worry about anything but health and illness.[31] While not all practitioners were sensitive to such changes in the nature of medical practice among the laboring poor, there is little doubt that on the whole the comfort of easier relationships with poor patients was greatly appreciated.[32]

On another level, though, it is difficult to assess the daily routine of medical work under the act once money was removed from the doctor-patient relationship. Whether doctors gave less attention to panel patients or were swamped by patients with minor complaints are important questions. They are questions, however, that can only be answered in the most general terms. The records of individual practices, even if they could be assembled, would be of little use in reconstructing the most mundane daily routines. Moreover, after thirty years of the National Health Service, there are not many doctors still living who participated in the panel medical service.

The above limitations make any account of panel work especially interesting. They provide a human element that cannot be easily gleaned from official documents. Such evidence is given by an anonymous author who simply titled his 1926 discussion, On the Panel.[33] The work is essentially a manual outlining the nature of general practitioner care in a modest urban medical practice. Because of this, the author's description of an average morning's work bears retelling.

The practice described was shared by two men. Between them they had a list of 2,500 panel patients. Each morning's surgery session began at 9:00 a.m. and patients seeking attendance, both insured and private, usually arrived before 10:00. The doctors customarily arrived at the surgery at 9:00 and they remained there until the last of the morning patients had been seen. There was also an afternoon hour of attendance from 2:00 to 3:00 and an evening period from 7:00 to 7:30. In the summer each of the partners was present at the surgery only twice a day but in the winter both men attended patients at all three sessions. There were, of course, home visits to panel and private patients alike to be made in between surgery hours.[34]

According to the writer, roughly half of the patients who came into the surgery on any given day were insured. However, on the specific morning described, more insured patients than usual were seen but the private patient load was lighter. In all, the writer attended fifteen panel patients in an hour and a half. This number of patients normally required more time but the doctor noted that only four were new and of these, two were men suffering from boils. These two needed only a simple dressing, a prescription for a tonic and a few words of advice. Another new patient was a boy who had had an attack of appendicitis in London. He had been sent home by a panel doctor for treatment. The boy had not had an operation and had nearly recovered. The last new patient was a more serious case. A man, aged 50, suffered from chest and stomach pains. This case, the doctor reported, took the most time and eventually the man was told to return later for further attention. He was sent home and advised to rest and eat simply.

There were eleven remaining panel patients treated and all of these had been seen earlier in the week. One patient had a broken wrist and another man needed a dressing changed on a hand that had received eight stitches. In both cases, the doctor signed certificates attesting to each man's continued incapacity to work. Next the physician attended a man to whom he had given an anaesthetic earlier in the week while a dentist removed decayed teeth. The patient had been off work for three weeks with "indigestion" but now, with the teeth gone, he was improving rapidly. Another patient came to the surgery to sign off the sick list. Even with the promise of an extended sickness certificate the doctor failed to convince her that her bad teeth should be removed. The practitioner next saw a young girl who had had an abdominal operation the previous year and had been off work since. She was a temporary resident and the doctor was supplying her with sickness certificates and prescriptions for drugs. Then came an elderly farm laborer who had been convalescing after a severe attack of shingles on the face. He came to acquire a final sickness certificate, in order to return to work. The laborer's wife, who was also present, asked the doctor to refuse. Agreeing with the man's wife, the doctor advised several more days rest. Two other women came to ask the doctor's advice about ill relatives and finally the practitioner saw a widow who was suffering from "general weakness."[35]

If the above was typical of the daily routine of panel practice, and all the evidence suggests that it was then it should be apparent that the general practitioner care given the insured did not vary much from that given to the uninsured. Private and panel medical practice was too closely allied for the situation to be otherwise. Patients and their families could always select a new doctor should they feel abused or ill-treated. More importantly, though, it should be recognized that even as late as the 1930s the level of sophistication among general practitioners was not high. Doctors worked very hard and had far more patient contact than is now customary. The doctor visited frequently so as to monitor the patient's progress and his choice of drugs was severely limited -- most being harmless and some useless.[36]

Such technological advances as x-rays and other diagnostic facilities were for the most part reserved for use by specialists in hospitals.[37] Therefore, in a period when codliver oil was the most widely prescribed remedy and regular bowel movements the most common advice, the opportunities for setting insured persons apart from private patients were minimal at best. Of course gentler words may have been used when lancing uninsured as opposed to insured boils during the early years of health insurance. However, despite the occasional charges of critics, such ignoble medical attitudes faded as the act became a customary part of general medical practice.[38]

Although the act had succeeded in blending private and panel practice, there was a governmental attempt to separate the two sides of medical work. In 1920, the Ministry of Health insisted that panel doctors be barred from establishing a precuniary interest in their panels and that the sale of panel lists be stopped after January 1924.[39] Medical men, however, opposed the ministerial contention that the sale of panel lists was to the patient's disadvantage. Indeed, they insisted that the opposite was true. The traditional practice provided both continuity and safety for the insured whose interests were guarded by the selling doctor. They also pointed out that a practice, like other businesses, represented a lifelong investment of time and energy. As the only real property owned by many practitioners, it seemed natural that upon retirement some return should be secured. After all, patients, whether insured or private, could always refuse to be attended by the purchaser and select a new practitioner.[40]

Between 1920 and 1922 the Ministry refused to reconsider the issue. By the end of 1922, however, with the B.M.A. developing ways to circumvent the spirit of the regulation, the Ministry realized how difficult it would be to exclude the value of panel lists from private negotiations. Insurance and private practice were far too interwoven. As a result the Ministry withdrew the ruling before it went into effect. The only stipulation was that every time a practice changed hands all panel patients had to be personally informed of their rights of transfer. Those insured patients who took no action within six months were then credited to the purchasing doctor's panel list.[41]

In spite of the profession's demand that the sanctity of private practice be maintained some doctors began to worry about the long-term effects of this all but automatic transfer. In the early thirties the speculative buying and selling of medical practices began to occur at an increasing rate. Wealthy doctors and even some lay investors were purchasing panel practices and then placing recent medical graduates in them as hire purchasers. The young men were paid a small salary and asked to sign a contract which bound them to buy the practice gradually. The terms of these contracts, however, usually made the purchaser into little more than a "share cropper."[42] Interest rates were high and the annual payments sometimes exceeded the net worth of the practice. As a result many doctors failed to honor the terms of their contract and were turned out, leaving the speculator with money in his pocket and a panel practice for sale to any man with a down payment. Understandably the B.M.A. objected to such abuses and eventually the Association established a list of approved loan companies as well as its own loan fund for deserving medical graduates.[43]

Medical Records

Had the Ministry succeeded in stopping the sale of panel practices, the change would still have done little to alter the daily routine of general practitioner care. Equally, it was also beyond the Ministry's power to improve the technical sophistication of the average panel doctor. Such improvements had always been products of scientific advances and rising educational standards. The government had no desire to usurp the profession's primacy in such matters. Nonetheless, the act did contribute in one particular respect to the modernization of daily medical practice in Britain. For the first time in the history of British medicine general practitioners widely kept patient clinical records.

Before the passage of the insurance act, the keeping of medical records, while encouraged, was not widespread. To keep records for lower class patients who might never be seen again seemed to be a waste of time and for the better class of fee-paying patient, rough notes, except in cases of scientifically interesting afflictions, would often suffice. More often than not, the practitioner's memory served as a clinical record file.

The framers of the insurance act hoped to amend to such unscientific behavior by requiring panel doctors to keep medical records. In October, 1912, the excuse for the special Exchequer grant of 2s. per doctor that finally defeated medical resistence was that it would go to pay medical men for record keeping and other additional administrative duties.[44] As seen in chapter one, this extra money did little to quell the strong undercurrent of professional dislike for the clerical work demanded. The fundamental objection, though, was not for the keeping of clinical records. Rather, professional criticism stemmed from a dislike of the bureaucratic regulations that dictated the form the panel patient records were to take.

The war brought new pressures to panel doctors as older men were asked to take on the insured patients of practitioners serving in the Royal Army Medical Corps. The burdens of clerical work became all the heavier and in response to a request by the B.M.A. the Insurance Commissioners, in 1917, agreed to suspend the responsibility for keeping patient records.[45] In 1920, though, the newly created Ministry of Health, decided to require doctors again to keep clinical records and appointed an Inter-Departmental Committee chaired by an eminent surgeon, Sir Humphry Rolleston, to devise an improved system.[46]

Prior to 1917 the medical record cards (of even the most trivial attendances) kept by all panel men had to be surrendered at the end of each year. Because of this doctors were deprived of a continuous clinical account of their insurance patients unless separate duplicate records were maintained. Drs. Brackenbury and H. Guy Dain, who led the medical delegation appointed to the Inter-Departmental Committee, complained that this practice destroyed the value of the records. Over the long term, statistics derived from such disjointed clinical accounts would be of only limited use. Doctors, knowing that the cards would disappear after a year, were bound to be careless. Moreover, the necessity of beginning new record cards each year ironically increased the amount of clerical work during January and February, two of the busiest medical months of the year.[47]

The Committee took no public evidence. But all sides agreed that the responsibility for keeping clinical records should be reimposed. Without much hesitation the Committee also decided in favor of leaving the record cards permanently in the hands of practitioners so that the cards might be used as a continuous clinical account. The cards would only be handled by the local insurance committees when a patient changed doctors.[48]

Of a more controversial nature was the question of what panel doctors should be required to note on their panel record cards. This problem went beyond simply listing symptoms, diagnosis and treatment. Arriving at even tentative conclusions about the nature of illness was difficult enough but the Committee was forced to wrestle with deciding how much precision should be required of medical men. Sir James MacKenzie, the noted clinical researcher, warned that even by appearing to require or encourage practitioners to record absolute diagnoses on medical cards, the Committee might inadvertantly harm the patient. Doctors might conclude that they were required to make precise diagnoses even if the scientific evidence was inconclusive. MacKenzie reminded the other Committee members that the vast majority of medical work was based not on certainty but on probability. Some doctors might forget this and unnecessarily limit their field of vision. Moreover, should the records of an erring doctor be placed in the hands of another practitioner, the second man could easily be misled. Dr. MacKenzie's arguments were accepted and the Committee recommended that all mention of diagnostic precision be removed from the regulations even though this eliminated all hope of using panel clinical records for statistical purposes.[49]

Finally, the Rolleston Committee turned its attention to the actual physical form of the medical record card. This question had been the cause of much dissatisfaction in 1913 when an over-sized daybook was used. The daybook was eliminated in February, 1913 and was replaced by the card system. This second format had proved to be a success and the Committee suggested that it be readopted. Each doctor was to receive a window envelope colored according to the patient's sex in order to expedite filing. An enclosed card would contain the patient's name, address, approved society and number, name of doctor, local insurance committee cipher and date of issue. During the patient's first attendance, the doctor would fill in the age and birthdate, the insured person's occupation, and, for a woman, a note indicating whether married, single or widowed. The remainder of the card was reserved for clinical notes.[50]

The Inter-Departmental Committee's recommendations were accepted by the Ministry of Health without hesitation and on 1 October 1920 panel practitioners were again made responsible for the keeping of medical records. The new system was seen by most practitioners as an improvement over the one that was used until 1917. Its very vagueness was a blessing to a profession that was sent into fits of rage even at the hint of bureaucratic entanglements.[51] The reimposition of record keeping duties for insured persons also raised a broader question of medical ethics. This was not anticipated by the Rolleston Committee which had assumed that the confidentiality of patient records would be preserved.

Ownership of panel clinical records had not been discussed. Therefore, it was unclear whether panel records belonged to the state, doctor or patient. For the profession this legal question touched the very heart of the doctor- patient relationship -- confidentiality. If the records were public property and available even to limited inspection by approved societies or local insurance committees, then the doctors argued it would be ethically difficult for them to carry out their panel duties. Moreover, there was the issue of the immunity of clinical records from the power of subpoena. For the B.M.A., all medical records had to be completely confidential and protected from uninvited inspection. To give in here would have been to abandon a basic ethical position of the medical work. Making records available to the public could also, the B.M.A. must have suspected, make the doctors more vulnerable to charges of negligence and malpractice.[52]

The issue was, of course, hypothetical. During the first five years of record keeping it had not even been raised. Despite this, Christopher Addison was worried enough about the legal problems surrounding panel records that he asked Lord Chancellor Birkenhead for an opinion in February, 1921.[53] Before the Chancellor's decision, in May, 1921, a divorce case brought the question of the confidentiality of medical records before the public when a doctor was ordered to give evidence in court based upon his panel records. At first the practitioner refused but eventually he relented, without legally challenging the court's competence in the matter.[54]

In July, the B.M.A. Council formally objected to all court-room demands for medical records. The Times also, in a leader, supported absolute privacy.[55] Despite the seriousness of the issue, it was never really resolved. In 1930 the Ministry of Health declared that the records of panel patients were the property of the Ministry but at the same time they refused access to the records by non-Ministry officials including those working for approved societies.[56] Still, there were occasional court cases involving medical records and passing questions in Parliament. The issue faded quickly however.[57] Few doctors were ever asked to produce their records as public testimony. Moreover, it was apparent that no one really wanted an answer. The moral questions were simply too hard and were clearly best left untouched. Nowhere is this general attitude more apparent than in Lord Birkenhead's memorandum issued in October, 1922, after he had resigned from office. The confidentiality of the doctor-patient relationship, he stressed, had to be guaranteed. Nonetheless, in special cases such as abortion or attempted suicide doctors were to exercise an overriding social sense of moral responsibility and provide the court with evidence.[58] Doctors could readily concur with such an opinion. As a profession, they had always been more comfortable with ethical rather than legal boundaries anyway and the issue remained undecided.

Whatever the problems surrounding the reestablishment of medical records as a contractual duty of panel doctors, the overall effect was to make the keeping of records central to the general practitioners' daily routines. Such practices often spilled over into the private side of general medical work and must be counted as a modernizing effect of the insurance scheme.

The act was also responsible for another improvement in medical practice. A rigid professional class structure had always assured the complete intellectual isolation of the general practitioner from the specialist. The B.M.A. naturally encouraged postgraduate training but it was a luxury few doctors could afford. The Ministry of Health began to promote additional study by making money available for advanced training to doctors serving in the insurance medical service. The number of participating panel men was never large but such opportunities certainly proved to be of benefit to the participating practitioner and his patients.[59]

Local Administration

Panel medical service meant more than simply the keeping of clinical records, postgraduate training stipends and the additional income. Health insurance did bring the medical profession closer to the state than it had ever been before. For most panel medical men, the central bureaucrat in their lives was the clerk of the local insurance committee.

As the chief full-time administrative employee of the local committee, the clerk was the backbone of local administration. All paper work was channeled through his office, as well as most of the complaints and questions about the panel medical service. He had the authority to inspect surgery accomodations for panel patients in order to determine that the insured were not isolated from the mainstream of private medical practice. Clerks also regulated branch surgeries and were responsible for seeing that lock-up surgeries did not restrict the access of the insured persons to medical care. The insurance clerk also saw that panel practitioners maintained their agreed hours of work and that locums were hired when panel men were absent. The use of medical assistants for panel work also fell under the authority of the insurance clerk. Not only was it his job to see that all assistants were qualified but that the senior practitioner did not assign assistants to care for his insured patients while he attended only to the private patients.[60] In the vast majority of cases the clerks were sensitive to the needs and temperaments of medical practitioners. Rarely was there anything but a smooth working relationship with individual panel doctors. When the ease of this relationship broke down, however, disputes invariably developed.

The most notable illustration of such a breakdown occurred in 1927 in Dorset.[61] Dorset panel practitioners complained that the local clerk had always been hostile to the panel medical service. The tone of the clerk's communication with doctors was said to be abrupt, irritating and sometimes offensive. Mr. Henry Moore, the clerk, was also accused of traveling about the country with the expressed intention of soliciting complaints against panel men. At the same time the clerk also took it upon himself to act as sometime informer, full-time prosecutor and adjudicator of totally frivolous charges against doctors.[62] Speaking in support of local medical men, the Insurance Acts Committee wrote to the Ministry of Health that "owing to the long continued antagonistic attitude, insurance practitioners throughout the county are extremely discontented that their grievance in this matter is not in any way remedied."[63] In his own defense the insurance clerk denied that he had ever exceeded his authority. From his perspective, he was simply carrying out the precise letter of the law. Panel patients were often hesitant to complain about abuses due to their respect for doctors and Mr. Moore argued that it was his job to see that the insured received the full medical benefit.[64]

The Local Insurance Committee tried to defuse the dispute by compromise. It conceded that its clerk was sometimes dictatorial and perhaps too zealous.[65] Still, the Committee came to Mr. Moore's aid by stressing that "trivial" and "frivolous" were matters of definition. Dorset panel doctors were hardly prepared to accept such a reply. As a result, by the last week of December, 1927, the matter fell into the Ministry of Health's lap, when the county's doctors refused to cooperate with the act's local administration. Still the Ministry's officials refused to intervene in what was purely a local dispute. The Committee then hardened its line and demanded that the doctors provide indisputable proof in support of their charges. At this point the Insurance Acts Committee of the B.M.A. stepped in to aid the Dorset practitioners and escalated the dispute to the national level.

In the eyes of the Ministry of Health the entire Dorset affair was ridiculous. Both sides had placed themselves in the wrong by allowing a minor administrative problem to assume such emotional intensity. In order to untangle what had become a very messy situation, the Ministry agreed to establish a board of inquiry in February, 1928, but the wrangling between the doctors and local insurance committee continued unabated.[66] The Insurance Acts Committee, normally quite moderate in its approach, allowed the local doctors to take the lead. First the Dorset practitioners insisted that the inquiry be removed from the Ministry of Health in order to guarantee independence but the Ministry naturally refused.[67] Later, further delays were caused by the Dorset Insurance Committee's refusal to meet with a board of inquiry until a full list of charges was laid before it by the county's panel medical men. Not until June did both parties agree on a date for the beginning of the inquiry, by which time, the Ministry and the Insurance Acts Committee were both sorry that they had been dragged into the dispute.

When the board of inquiry finally issued a report in August, 1928, it found that the clerk's activities had been within the scope of his legal duties. Mr. Moore, the board noted, had meticulously followed procedures and regulations. But the Ministry's investigators concluded that Moore had done so without being conscious of their intended flexibility. The Local Insurance Committee also received a share of the blame. The inquiry concluded that it should have carefully watched the preliminary investigations against doctors so that frivolous cases might have been prevented. Finally, the report agreed with the complaining practitioners that on occasion the clerk had been too short and disrespectful in his dealings with the Dorset panel medical service.[68]

The Ministerial board of inquiry recommended that the dispute be settled by all-around apologies. While some were given, bitterness and mistrust continued to sour the relationship between Dorset's panel medical service and the local insurance bureaucracy.

The Dorset case highlights the most important aspect about the relationship between the panel medical service and the local insurance bureaucracy. The working of the insurance scheme was designed to be an informal affair among gentlemen. The Ministry demanded a flexible administration. If bending guidelines increased medical efficiency, improved care for patients, and greased the wheels of the bureaucracy, the Ministry was willing to accept local variations. In Dorset this underlying principle was ignored by the Committee and its clerk. Dorset, though, represents the extreme. Throughout the entire history of the insurance act the relations between the panel medical service and local bureaucracies were usually cordial.[69] For the late twentieth century mind, burdened with overly heavy bureaucracies and legal entanglements, the reason may seem improbable. However, it is clear that the success of insurance local administration depended more upon a shared sense of good will than upon the bureaucrat's whip.

The Range of Service

Manners and good sense reduced the friction between administrators and panel practitioners but this kind of administration had its problems too. Doctors found that once in insurance practice, they were often confused about the range of care for which they were responsible. The insurance act asked all panel medical men to provide accustomed general practitioner care. What was meant by this vague directive was naturally subject to varying interpretations. Moreover as technical or procedural innovations altered medical work, the scope of panel practice automatically expanded. This previously unforeseen growth in the range of panel service was a problem of vital economic importance for doctors. Even without a conscious policy the medical benefits of the insurance act would expand and a once limited medical scheme could approach a full-time general practitioner health service for the insured.[70]

The profession demanded that something be done to prevent the complete transformation of the panel medical work. The Insurance Acts Committee consistently asked that the Ministry of Health specify those procedures that lay within the scope of the doctor's responsibility.[71] Understandably, this was always rejected and the open-ended system was maintained. It was therefore left up to the local insurance committees to decide whether or not a doctor could collect extra fees for performing medical services beyond the range of the medical benefit.

The majority of panel practitioners took a broad view of their insurance duties. Nonetheless when a dispute did arise the burden of proof was squarely placed on the shoulders of the individual medical man. Not only did a doctor have to prove that the needed service was beyond the ability of most of his colleagues but he had to show evidence that, as a practitioner, he had been specially trained to carry out such work.

With the aid of medical advisory boards, local insurance committees routinely considered cases dealing with the provisions of anaesthetics, vaccination, venereal disease treatments, birth control advice and minor surgical operations performed in the doctor's surgery.[72] Because of the local emphasis and case by case investigation, it is hard to discern any particular pattern from the decisions made by local committees. Nonetheless, in general, items of service such as those below were most commonly declared to be within the boundaries of general practitioner care:

(1) Treatment of fracture of bones of legs and dislocation of ankle.

(2) Treatment of gonorrhea by irrigation and medicine.

(3) Opening and scraping abcess of thigh.

(4) Curetting of uterus.

(5) Suppurative mastitis: opening and breaking down all pockets and inserting rubber drainage tubes.

(6) Opening and draining an ischio-rectal abcess.

(7) Advanced cirrhosis of the liver with very severe

aseitos and general dropsy; local anesthetic injected. Incision made; cannula and trocar inserted; drainage tube fitted to cannula.

(8) Operation for fissure *in ano*.

(9) Removal of facial sabaceous cyst.

(10) Deep abcess of neck due to byuelficcition of gland. Incision made; sinus forcep inserted and creamy material evacuated. Syringed out with iodine.

(11) Dislocation of left elbow; reduction under chloroform.

(12) Opthalmoscopic examination for occipital headache.

(13) Removal of epithelioma of lower lip.

Some of the operations and services that were usually judged to be beyond the skill of the majority of general practitioners and hence outside the range of insurance care were:

(1) Removal by dissection of Bartholin's gland.

(2) Passage of Eustachian catheter.

(3) Operation for hemorroids.

(4) Examination of eyes by retinoscope.

(5) Colpo-permeorrhaphy and stitching of cervix.

(6) Gastro-jejunostomy.

(7) Removal of varicose veins.

(8) Intravenous administration of novarsenobillon.

(9) Enucleation of eyeball.

(10) Radical cure of left inguinal hernia.

(11) Operation for suppurating fibroid.

(12) Removal of tuberculosis glands in neck.

(13) Extreme genu valgum in both legs.

(14) Application of radiant heat and ionization.

(15) Amputation of toes.[73]

In most cases local insurance committees followed the medical advice of the practitioners who studied each case. As laymen they were normally intimidated by the clinical jargon of medical practice. This effectively eliminated non-medical interference but the system for determining the range of service was always a source of embarrassment for the profession. Having to be supported by evidence showing a particular expertise, appealing practitioners often appeared to be bragging about their skills. The results were sometimes petty personal disputes between members of a profession that was sensitive to every nuance of class distinction.[74]

The system for defining the scope of insurance benefits on a case by case basis worked to the advantage of panel patients. For doctors the appeal process was slow, cumbersome and sometimes costly. Practitioners, as businessmen, knew that once a patient left the surgery it might be impossible to assess further charges -- even if the local insurance committee decided extra fees could be collected. In order to protect themselves some practitioners asked insured persons for fees without consulting the local insurance committee. Although this practice was quite illegal, an experienced panel practitioner usually knew where the line was being drawn in his local panel area.

More difficult to decide was whether or not a particular

patient who claimed to be insured was in fact eligible. Various parliamentary extensions of the insurance medical benefit, due to chronic unemployment, meant that many persons moved in and out of the panel scheme. Since the patient list kept by the doctor was not officially recognized as the basis for payment, insurance practitioners could never be absolutely sure who was insured and who wasn't.[75] When in doubt, practitioners would often ask that private fees be paid. If the panel doctor was correct in his judgment, all went smoothly. However, inappropriate fee charging could result in having to return money to the patient, a reduction being made from the next capitation check or, in extreme cases, expulsion from the panel medical service. At the same time failure to treat a panel patient because of suspicion about eligibility or the status of a needed treatment was also a violation of the medical benefit regulations.

Panel Discipline and Oversight

The vast majority of cases involving a breach of the panel rules were dealt with informally by a visit from a friendly colleague or a member of the local insurance committee.[76] Therefore, it is difficult to know for sure how widespread violations were among doctors serving on the insurance panels. But for those doctors who did not comply with the regulations after repeated warnings, a formal disciplinary procedure was established. Consistent with the general design of the insurance scheme, medical discipline was kept beyond the control of the approved societies. While it was overseen by the local insurance committees, discipline, in practice, was in the hands of a medical service subcommittee. These committees usually consisted of three doctors selected by the panel committee and three persons chosen by the insurance committee to represent patients. Despite this, the subcommittees were dominated by the medical representatives, who usually dictated the guilt or innocence of doctors accused of violating panel regulations.

Normally a guilty verdict by the subcommittee resulted in a deduction being made by the local insurance committee from the capitation check of the violator. In serious cases, doctors might even be removed from panel service. Still, the disciplinary procedures were entirely administrative rather than legal. Throughout the period the B.M.A. asked that panel doctors be given the right of legal appeal. But as no fines were levied, the Ministry of Health refused to surrender its position as final arbitrator of all discipline cases and the Association never tested the issue in court.[77]

The scope of problems dealt with by the local medical service subcommittees ranged from violations of insurance regulations to breaches of professional ethics among panel practitioners. Strict confidentiality was maintained at all times and the remaining accounts of disciplinary hearings are not very informative about the work of these committees. Fortunately, the records for

London, while discrete, do reveal at least some of the details surrounding individual cases of panel misconduct. At the same time the minutes of the London Medical Service Subcommittee show how few disciplinary cases reached the formal hearing stage.

In all of London there were a total of only 78 cases heard in 1916. Of these, 28 were substantiated; thirteen for neglect of treatment, two for fee charging, seven for careless certification, two for refusal to order drugs, three for special reference, and one for refusing to issue a sickness certificate. In 1926 the same committee examined only 58 complaints and found 29 medical men to be in violation of the medical benefit regulations.[78] The cases heard were far from simple to judge. They often involved conflicts between moral and legal responsibility. For example, in a 1921 case the London Committee was asked to examine a panel doctor who was accused of refusing to provide care to a chronically ill patient. The practitioner had been informed that the patient in question had been removed from his list because the medical man had already agreed to attend 3,000 insured persons. The patient, though, had not been informed of the change and when he asked for attendance the doctor refused to see him. Immediately the insured man complained to the clerk of the London Insurance Committee. The doctor was eventually absolved of guilt but the Medical Service Subcommittee did reprimand him for his handling of the problem.[79]

The relative flexibility of the act's administration usually made it possible to avoid the type of difficulty noted above. More common were problems arising from procedural indiscretions: investigations of doctors who had failed to make arrangements for a locum while on holiday; the violation of stated surgery hours; the employment of unapproved medical assistants. On occasion, however, more serious charges were brought to the attention of the London disciplinary body. These included accusations of drunkenness, taking liberties with female patients, the over-prescription of dangerous drugs and incapacity due to illness or old age.

These were always professionally embarrassing questions but none was more delicate than an accusation of incompetence. As a general rule, panel practitioners were rarely charged with clinical incompetence. Much more likely was an assertion of professional negligence, but even this charge was uncommon. An example of such a case occurred in Worcestershire, where in 1929 the local Medical Service Subcommittee ruled that a panel doctor was incompetent. The conclusion was based upon the doctor's misdiagnosis of a serious illness which ended in death.[80] The accused practitioner appealed the case and was later vindicated by the Ministry of Health which disallowed the Committee's ruling not because the Worcestershire doctor was free from blame but because it would have established the dangerous practice of administrative diagnostic hindsight.[81]

Unlike administrative discipline, the enforcement of ethical standards was left entirely under the control of the profession. Traditionally the ethical code of the profession had been enforced by the B.M.A.'s Council. The formation of the local panel committees, however, created a mechanism for local peer review. The cases heard by local committees were often complex and usually involved disputes between panel medical men.[82] Open canvassing and theft of particular patients were the most common complaints and resulted in financial penalties. For more serious ethical violations, such as moral laxity or fraud, panel doctors could be removed from the insurance medical service.[83]

The number of doctors completely banned from panel work was small and these men were often reinstated after an appropriate waiting period. Reinstatement cases were usually not given to the local panel committees to decide. Instead, if readmittance was desired, a practitioner had to apply directly to the Ministry of Health. Nonetheless local practitioners and the local insurance committee were normally consulted. One case in London involved a doctor who had previously practiced in Bristol. In September, 1927, he resigned from panel work after an investigation had shown that he had failed to give medical service when requested by several of his panel patients. The charges were never formally heard because of the man's resignation from the Bristol panel. In July, 1928, the same practitioner, after moving to London and beginning a private practice, applied to join the panel medical service. Despite a good recommendation from the London Panel Committee, the Ministry of Health ruled that the medical man would have to wait until 1930 to undertake the care of insured persons again and then only as an assistant. It was not until 1932 that the doctor received permission to join the panel with independent status.[84]

For most panel practitioners the disciplinary side of local administration was more a concern of gossip than daily contact. In general doctors had very little direct contact with the local insurance bureaucracy. Quarterly checks, occasional information circulars and the filling up of sickness and prescription forms were usually the only reminders of panel service.[85] The same lack of weighty bureaucratic regulation was also the hallmark of relations between panel doctors and the Ministry of Health. Here familiarity was provided by the Regional Medical Officer Corps. R.M.O.s were not originally part of the insurance scheme. Nonetheless, as early as 1913 the B.M.A. and approved societies had both advocated the hiring of medical referees to provide advice to panel doctors, coordinate local medical services and root out malingering.[86] In October 1913 the London Insurance Committee hired a small number of medical referees to deal primarily with malingering among the insured population.[87] In 1914 Parliament appropriated funds to create a national network of R.M.O.s. This provision was suspended during the war but the idea was not lost. In 1920 the Ministry of Health hired thirty fulltime medical officers and during the next twenty years this number was to increase steadily to nearly a hundred.[88]

The work of the R.M.O.s fell largely into three areas. First, as doctors they were viewed as representing a pool of experienced medical knowledge that was freely available to panel practitioners. The Ministry of Health encouraged panel men to seek the R.M.O.s' advice on especially difficult cases. Secondly, the medical officers acted as sickness referees within the insurance scheme. Malingering by insured persons had always been the greatest fear of the approved societies. Without any control over certification procedures the societies had no way of safeguarding their funds from fraudulent sickness claims. The creation of R.M.O.s gave the societies a means to call claims into question by referring ill members to the local R.M.O. for examination. Doctors too, could refer suspected malingering cases, although they rarely did. Finally, the medical officers alone had the power to inspect the medical and prescription records of insurance practitioners in order to be sure that they were being properly maintained.[89] Instances of obvious neglect were rare but those cases that could not be resolved by a friendly word of advice were turned over to the local medical service subcommittee for discipline.[90]

Another part of the R.M.O.'s inspection duty was to see that statistical information was gathered about panel work within his area of responsibility. The R.M.O.s were to act as health statisticians, collecting information concerning disease among panel patients. By 1926 this duty, however, had fallen into disuse, except for the purposes of determining prescription and certification averages. Despite this the Ministry of Health's bureaucracy harbored hopes of making some use of the records and made an effort to study the medical records of 25% of all panel doctors kept between 1923 and 1926. The result was complete frustration. The several million record cards examined were far from standardized. Clinical entries were often made in the attending doctor's private shorthand or written in an illegible scrawl. Under such conditions interpretation was impossible and after 1926 the Ministry of Health lost all hope of making statistical use of panel medical records.[91]

The Quality of Care

Taken as a whole, the duty of the R.M.O.s was to ensure that health insurance in Britain operated smoothly, efficiently and effectively. Smoothness and efficiency of operation could usually be assured by friendly talks over tea in a panel practitioner's surgery. In contrast, oversight of medical quality within the panel system presented a far more difficult task for the medical officers because the definition of what constituted quality medical care was then, as now, not very clear. Few doctors would have ever suggested that the medical attention received by panel patients was in any way inferior to that received by private patients. Yet, it was an article of faith among representatives of approved societies and their political supporters that practitioners did shave medical corners when treating the insured class. It was often heard that dual surgeries were maintained and that those visited by panel patients were dirty, small and drafty. Societies charged that too little time was spent with insured persons and that doctors were often impolite.[92] Such broad indictments could, however, never be substantiated because the charges generally were not true. Still, the societies, who wished to see themselves made part of the panel disciplinary procedure, rarely stopped complaining that such abuses lessened the quality of care received by their members.

The B.M.A. was never able to put the accusations of the approved societies to rest. In part this was because the profession's leadership, showing its class bias, often suspected the skill and efficiency of the general practitioner as much as did the approved societies. But more importantly, the reason for the confusion surrounding the quality of panel care was due to a general inability to define the aims of the insurance act. Prior to the creation of the panel system reformers argued that medicine should change its emphasis from curative to preventive care. Doctors for too long had given priority to severe illness and had ignored potential diseases that, if diagnosed early, might ease the destructive course of debilitating sickness.

The state was seen by health reformers, such as Arthur Newsholme, George Newman, Christopher Addison and Sidney and

Beatrice Webb, as being the only effective agent for the encouragement of preventive care on a massive scale. Through self-financing sickness insurance, the economic barriers that mitigated against effective primary care were to be removed with the result being improved health for laboring Britons.[93]

At least on the surface the dreams of the Edwardian health reformers were realized in the 1911 insurance act. They, of course, recognized its obvious limitations but their hopes were high for further enlargements of the insured population and a widening of the benefits beyond general practitioner care. Nonetheless, advocates of state sponsored preventive medicine rarely considered the difficulties of the implementation of their dreams. Like private medical care, health insurance was limited by ability and willingness to pay the medical bills. No politician was likely to open the floodgates of unrestricted medical attendance without placing some controls upon both doctors and patients. Thus textbook preventive medicine, in which their are no barriers between an ill patient and his practitioner, hardly had a chance once the framers of the act came up against the realities of administration and politics.

The act mandated a three day waiting period between the signing of the sickness certificate and the first cash benefit payment. This gave societies an opportunity to review each claim. Moreover, sickness certificates had to be renewed each week by the attending physician and many societies employed sick visitors to check up on disabled or ill members.[94] In addition most societies routinely submitted cases of lengthy sickness (6-8 weeks) to regional medical officers. Therefore it was unlikely that a person placed upon the sick list because a panel doctor perceived the threat of severe illness would have continued to receive benefits for very long.

Finally, approved societies were not consistent in their policies concerning ill members. Pregnancy was not a certifiable illness under the act and some societies referred all pregnant women with sickness certificates to the R.M.O. However, other societies, sensing the sale of a new insurance policy, paid benefits to women six weeks prior to the expected delivery date.[95] Therefore, even if a pregnant woman's doctor felt that cessation of work was necessary, he could never be sure that she would actually be allowed to stop working. Societies also tended to accept signed sickness certificates on particular days of the week.[96] An Insurance Acts Committee survey of several societies between January and March 1934 showed that 52% of all certificates were accepted on Mondays while Saturdays accounted for only 9% of the week's totals. At the same time the opposite pattern was revealed for final certificates, which gave the doctor's approval for a return to work. Of all these sampled, only 9% were accepted on Mondays with 50% taken on Saturdays.[97]

This pattern was no accident. Societies usually organized their finances according to benefit weeks beginning Monday and ending Saturday. Therefore it was clerically convenient to begin and end the benefit of patients on those days. At the same time employers preferred to have workers return to work on Mondays rather than on Thursdays or Fridays. As a result, the insured were often forced to conform to work or clerical convenience instead of illness patterns. Thus, while at times patients were given extra days on the sick list by their societies, many were turned away and told that their signed certificates would not be honored until a particular day.

Medical men too worked against the panel system becoming truly preventive in nature. Few doctors really wanted to be bothered by dozens of patients each week seeking routine medical checkups when payment was upon a yearly capitation basis. Such visits meant a higher overhead and were often discouraged. Profits, though, were not the usual reason doctors working the act did not usually engage in the kind of preventive care advocated by health reformers. Most practitioners simply had more ill patients than they could treat and naturally they preferred to expend their energies upon those in the most immediate need of attention. Those complaining of seemingly mild maladies could always be given a prescription for cod liver oil or malt or told to eat less fried food. In a sense this is what primary care is all about, but it was hardly the sort of medical attention desired by advocates of preventive care on a grand scale. Finally, the insured class itself was partly to blame for the act's failure to promote preventive medicine. Calling on the doctor is often an experience that is filled with anxiety, even if the visit costs nothing. Fearing what might be found or simply not wanting to bother an already busy man, insured patients preferred not to give up a morning's wages to be examined. Therefore, the tendency of most panel patients was to wait until illness made a visit to the doctor's surgery unavoidable.[98]

With these bureaucratic and natural limitations, it is not surprising that for the most part the panel medical system provided only essential primary rather than preventive care. Yet, even had preventive care become a fixture of the act, an evaluation of the effectiveness of the medical service given by panel doctors would remain difficult. Regional medical officers, given the responsibility of review, had no standard, except their own, with which to judge the work of panel practitioners. What was, or in fact is, the measure of a good doctor and effective medical care? Obviously little is known of what is meant by normal health or what constitutes a restoration of good health. Here medicine is not far advanced from Hippocrates, who defined good health as the ability to breathe freely, digest food, excrete regularly and move without pain. Moreover, the disappearance of disagreeable symptoms does not necessarily indicate cure or medical success. Therefore, in evaluating the effectiveness of the medical care provided by panel doctors to insured patients, opinion is far more a product of personal prejudice than reasoned observation.

Without a yardstick to place beside panel practice the dispute between those who felt that panel practitioners were making a significant contribution to the health of the insured and those who saw it as minimal could never really be settled. Individual examples illustrating either viewpoint could always be found but this approach does little more than aggravate the controversy. Still, the question is a nagging one because it cuts to the very heart of health insurance as a social policy.

If critics were correct in asserting that the panel system made no appreciable improvement in the health of the insured class then the entire scheme and the money devoted to it was for naught. If, as reformers believed, ready access to doctors improved medical care and thus health, then the nation's vital statistics should show improvements that might plausibly be due to the work of the insurance act. In looking at the _Yearly Statistical Review for England and Wales_ throughout the period, however, it is difficult to find a sound correlation between health insurance and the health of the nation, despite the fact that by 1939 half the population was insured. Britain's vital statistics had, since the mid-nineteenth century, been steadily improving, with the greatest gain coming between 1900 and 1912 when the crude male death rate fell from 19.5 to 14.2 per 1,000 persons.[99]

During the life of the insurance act, no similar improvement can be found. In fact, the steady decline comes to an end. In

1921, after the influenza pandemic, male death rates per 1000 stood at 12.9, precisely the same rate as in 1939. In the intervening years there was only slight fluctuation, with the rate reaching a high for the interwar period in 1922 of 13.5 and a low of 12.3 in 1930.[100]

Mortality rates for specific diseases reveal more telling evidence of improved health among the general population. The fatality rate of scarlet fever per 1,000 notified cases fell steadily from a 1911 level of 18.1 to 2.8 in 1939. The incidence of death in confirmed diptheria cases declined from 103 per 1,000 cases in 1911 to 46 in 1939.[101] Each of these diseases are infectious and certainly were especially prevalent among the laboring poor.

The most chronic illnesses among the poor, both before and after the coming of national insurance, were of course respiratory diseases. Here the evidence of the impact of the panel system may be clearer. From 1911 to 1920 the combined death rate for bronchitis stood at 2,069 per million.[102] By 1937 the rate had declined sharply to only 611 per million of population. Mortality from pneumonia fell by 35% between 1911 and 1920 and a further substantial improvement was made after 1920. From 1927 to 1929, for example, pneumonia deaths per year amounted to 214,489 for England and Wales but in 1937 only 55,896 deaths were recorded from this cause.[103] The incidence of death from tuberculosis also declined throughout the period, falling at an average rate of

2.5% per year for men from 1913 to 1933. For the same period rates for females were reduced 2% annually. An even sharper decline occurred from 1933 to 1937 when death from tuberculosis among males fell by 3.5% and women enjoyed an improvement of 4% annually.[104] At the same time though, it is interesting to note that the incidence of diseases of longevity -- most notably cancer -- had increased by 1937 to 111% for men and 57% for women over their respective rates between 1901 and 1910.[105]

The insurance act, with its maternity benefit, could also have been expected to bring a decline in child mortality. From 1871 to 1875 the yearly average death rate for infants stood at 153 per 1,000 live births. A significant improvement was made only after 1900 when the death rate among children was in excess of what it had been in 1871. From 1900 the rate of infantile death dropped from 156 to 117 per thousand births in 1911. From that time there is a steady decline until 1934 when the rate leveled off at 59 per 1,000 in England and Wales.[106] Britain's progress in this area was not unusual. It was mirrored by other European countries throughout the period -- with the English and Welsh statistics trailing those of New Zealand, Australia, Holland, Norway, Switzerland, Sweden and the United States. Denmark, Germany, Canada, Belgium, Italy and Greece all had higher rates.[107]

Early detection by panel medical practitioners no doubt played a role in the decline of mortality and illness among the population. Many cases of bronchitis and pneumonia, among other illnesses, were caught before they became chronic or deadly. Improvements in prenatal and postnatal care too, certainly played a role in reducing the incidence of infant death, as did the 30s. cash maternity payment to insured and dependent mothers. But whether or not, as the *Times* wrote in 1933, the act was responsible for the falling death and disease rates is far from clear.[108]

Despite its press, medicine rarely deals in cures or for that matter in the prevention of disease. The great killers of mankind; plague, malaria, small pox and others have not been stamped out or controlled by the endeavors of the general practitioner. Rather, they have been eliminated by scientific, technological and social innovations. Decent housing, wholesome food, sanitary reforms and cotton underwear have perhaps improved health far more than doctors have.[109] Thus it is hardly fair to hold the insurance act's panel medical service up to such high standards. The act provided only primary care to an insured population that by 1939 had reached twenty million. Each day panel practitioners stitched hands, set bones, pulled teeth, gave out dietary information and literally prescribed tons of cod liver oil. By the mid-thirties eight million patients a year sought the advice of their panel doctors and these medical men reported giving over fifty million attendances.[110]

Whatever can be said of this, however, one thing is clear. To look for the clinical effectiveness of the panel system is to misunderstand the importance of the act as an instrument of social policy that sought to raise the level of medical care among the laboring poor. Unlike the earlier Poor Law, the health insurance act did not isolate its patients from the larger sphere of general medical work. Instead the scheme successfully blended panel and private practice, thus preventing the establishment of a separate standard of medical care for the insured. Within the limits of the act's benefits, the scheme recognized the individual nature of illness and medical practice. Despite its national scope, health insurance, according to Sir Edward Hilton-Young, Minister of Health in 1933, had avoided the pitfalls of "mechanical uniformity" and had adapted to "local peculiarities and interests." This, the Minister concluded, "was no small asset."[111] The scheme's flexibility allowed doctors nearly absolute clinical freedom. Patients, within certain time limitations, could always change practitioners and the value of the personal doctor-patient relationship was, if anything, enhanced for the insured class.

In addition, the insurance act finally eliminated the widespread abuses of unqualified medical attendance that had long been the hallmark of medicine among the poor.[112] Members of the insured class, and to some degree their dependents, no longer had an economic incentive to seek the least expensive and usually worst level of medical service. Untrained and sometimes unskilled individuals were excluded from the panel system. Only those practitioners listed on the Medical Register could participate as panel doctors. This, in effect, firmly established a national minimum for medical care that had in the past been absent. As a result, the quality and effectiveness of primary medical service for the insured came to approximate closely the care that was given to private patients within the limits of personal and class bias. Thus, for the first time in the history of British medicine and public health, the poor, at least at the general practitioner level, became full partners in both the advantages and shortcomings of contemporary primary medical care.

For the general practitioner, the work of the scheme must be unquestionably judged a success. Individual doctors increased their incomes, relations with poor patients were eased and bureaucratic entanglements that limited professional independence were largely avoided. There was, however, a much broader if less tangible advantage produced by the insurance act. Since the mid-nineteenth century, the central theme of British medical organization had been the notion of professionalism. In the name of the professional ideal the B.M.A. had led the way in eliminating quackery, inadequate training and subserviance to non-medical interests.[113] Despite this activity, the British medical profession remained sharply divided along class lines. For the majority of general practitioners, professionalism, with its claims of middle class status, was an elusive ideal reserved for the specialist class and those men with large incomes.

It was the search for professional standing for all practitioners that guided the B.M.A. in its fight against the friendly societies. Similarly, it was in part, a fear that thousands of practitioners were being permanently condemned to economic and thus social inferiority that drove medical men in their struggle against the insurance act in 1912. Practitioners, it seemed, were only trading non-medical masters and they feared that what had once been private abuses would become institutionalized in Parliamentary law. But as we have observed, the act had quite the opposite result. Leaving monetary concerns aside, doctors found that the government honored their claims of professional privilege and status. In fact, these were guaranteed in statute by the establishment of local panel committees and in practice by the working relationship between the B.M.A. and the government.

Never before had the profession enjoyed so much authority, both on the local and national levels. Medical men worked with the knowledge that they and their brethren held nearly absolute control over professional ethics, discipline and scientific standards within the insurance act. Thus, the working of health insurance had propelled Britain's medical men past a barrier that they had long sought to surmount. Even though the link between work and pay had been broken for an insured population of twenty million by 1939, the standards of professionalism so long advocated by medical leaders were now enjoyed by all and not just some practitioners. Whatever the complaints about the level of panel remuneration, this was an advantage that the profession did not take lightly as the negotiations for the 1924 capitation fee approached.

Notes

1. Dr. E. Colin-Russ. Interviewed by author, Bournemouth, July 1, 1978. Dr. Colin-Russ was active in BMA politics from the late thirties and still serves occasionally as an advisor to the government on health matters. He had a medium sized panel practice in London from the mid-twenties.

2. Leonard Shoeten Sack, "Starting a Panel Practice," *The Lancet* (23 February 1924), p. 396.

3. *The Lancet*, "The General Advertiser" (15 July 1922), p. 60.

4. *The Lancet*, "The General Advertiser" (25 June 1938), p. 56.

5. The Lancet, "The General Advertiser" (24 June, 1939), p. 58.

6. Colin-Russ.

7. Insurance Acts Committee, session 1921-1922. IAC 83, 22 June 1922.

8. I. S. Falk, *Security Against Sickness* (New York: Da Capo Press reprint, 1972), p. 157.

9. Colin-Russ.

10. A.G.P., *This Panel Business* (London: Bale Sons and Danielson, 1933), p. 194.

11. Insurance Acts Committee, session 1931-1932. IA la, undated. Using the statistics gathered by the association, the Insurance Acts Committee determined that in 1925 the attendance rate per insured stood at 4.52. By 1929 this rate had increased to 5.07. The size of the sample, though, was not large and not reported. This trend, however, was noted by Colin-Russ.

12. Falk, p. 157.

13. Colin-Russ.

14. F. B. Smith, *The People's Health 1830-1910* (London: Croom Helm, 1979).

15. Dr. Frank Gray. Interviewed by author, London 10 July 1978. Dr. Gray was a prominent member of the London Panel Committee and was active in the BMA throughout the thirties. He is still active in the association and is a sometime contributor to *The Daily Telegraph* on medical issues. His panel practice was near Clapham Junction.

16. Colin-Russ.

17. *Ibid*.

18. *Ibid*.

19. Gray.

20. Harry Eckstien, *The English Health Service* (Cambridge: Harvard University Press, 1958), pp. 61-62.

21. *The Sunday Pictorial*, 4 March 1923.

22. Great Britain, Parliament, *Parliamentary Debates* (Commons), 5th series, vol. 48 (1913), cols. 302-303.

23. *The Lancet* (27 February 1932), p. 478.

24. Herman Levy, *National Health Insurance* (London: Cambridge University Press, 1944), pp. 122-137.

25. *BMJ* (4 September 1937), p. 445.

26. Rosemary Stevens, *Medical Practice in Modern England* (New Haven: Yale University Press, 1966), p. 56.

27. *Ibid*., p. 57.

28. Insurance Acts Committee, session 1931-1932. IAC 1A, undated.

29. *BMJ* (21 April 1923), *Supplement*, pp. 117-120.

30. *The Lancet*, "The General Advertiser" (15 July 1922), p. 59.

31. Dr. Solomon Wand. Interviewed by author, Birmingham, 15 July 1978. Dr. Wand served as a member of the Insurance Acts Committee in the mid-thirties and was intimately involved in many of the Committee's negotiations with the government. His panel practice was in Birmingham where he has now retired.

32. Colin-Russ, Gray, Wand.

33. A Panel Doctor, *On the Panel* (London: Faber and Gwyer, 1926).

34. *Ibid*., p. 9.

35. *Ibid*., pp. 9-12.

36. Colin-Russ.

37. *Ibid*.

38. *National Insurance Gazette* (6 October 1923), p. 475.

39. BMJ (22 November 1919), Supplement, pp. 678.

40. Insurance Acts Committee, session 1921-1922. IAC 58, 30 March 1922.

41. BMJ (11 February 1922), Supplement, p. 34.

42. Douglass W. Orr and Jean Walker Orr, Health Insurance with Medical Care (New York: Macmillan Company, 1938), p. 147.

43. Insurance Acts Committee, session 1934-1935. LAC 6, 15 November 1934. In Lancashire, where the problem was at its worst, there were 102 cases by 1934 of a third party being consigned a medical practice. The total value of these was estimated to be £45,000 and for hire-purchasers the down payments averaged £500.

44. Department of National Health and Welfare (Research Division), "Health Insurance in Great Britain, 1911-1948," Social Security Series, Memorandum No. 11 (Ottowa: 1952), p. 65.

45. BMJ (10 February 1917), Supplement, p. 23.

46. PRO. MH 62/130., 17 November 1919.

47. BMJ (31 July 1920), Supplement, pp. 53-54.

48. Ibid., p. 54.

49. PRO. MH 62/130., January 1920.

50. BMJ (31 July 1920), Supplement, p. 55.

51. Annual Report of the Chief Medical Officer of Health for the Year 1930, p. 40. Despite the widespread acceptance of record keeping the Chief Medical Officer reported that in 1930 only 70 percent of the panel doctors kept adequate records.

52. The Daily Mail, 16 July 1921.

53. PRO. MH 62/131., 4 February 1921.

54. The Daily Herald, 28 May 1921. It should be noted that once in court the doctor's records were of little value because the doctor himself could not decipher the handwriting. In the end the Justice was only able to direct the doctor to use more care when making clinical entries upon panel medical cards.

55. The Times, 16 July 1921.

56. PRO. MH 62/74., 30 July 1930.

57. The Daily Express, 20 January 1922.

58. The Evening Standard, 28 October 1922.

59. Annual Report of the Chief Medical Officer of Health for the Year 1928, p. 60. Although the funds were available for post graduate education beginning in 1928, only 86 practitioners took advantage of the opportunity in the first year that grants were awarded. For that year the total government expenditure was £2,557. Panel doctors could also petition the Ministry of Health for special modernization grants in order to install telephones, maintain automobiles or open branch surgeries. By 1934 these grants for education and modernization amounted to £8,900.

60. The Lancet (27 February 1923), p. 478.

61. PRO. MH 62/82., 29 November 1927.

62. Ibid.

63. Ibid., 27 November 1927.

64. Ibid., 13 December 1927.

65. Ibid.

66. Ibid., 21 February 1928.

67. Ibid., 24 February 1928.

68. Ibid., August 1928.

69. Colin-Russ.

70. Insurance Acts Committee, session 1929-1930. IAC 17, 9 January 1930.

71. Insurance Acts Committee, session 1923-1924. IAC 22, 25 March 1926.

72. Some local committee minute books are preserved in the Public Record Office, Kew, where those for Bedfordshire and Luton, Manchester and Salford are available. Most however are still in the unknowing hands of local authorities. Those for Yorkshire for example, were thought to be lost until the author encouraged a search in Wakefield where a complete set was found, dusty, but in good condition. These local records are of limited use because they are rarely more than the barest of accounts of local insurance committee meetings. Most of the time decisions concerning the panel service were referred to the local panel committees and these records, except in the case of London, have not been located.

73. <u>The Lancet</u> (18 September 1926), pp. 618-619.

74. Insurance Acts Committee, session 1925-1926. IAC 41, 11 March 1926. Beyond this more general level doctors also feared that a broad definition of the medical benefit would end public payment for other medical services. Special payments for vaccination had been ended during the first world war and the money for treating accident victims or for acting as police surgeons was being eliminated as many boroughs claimed that they did not have to pay for insured victims.

75. Insurance Acts Committee, session 1934-1935. IAC 14, 30 January 1935. As proof of status the insured carried insurance books in which they placed their stamps. Despite this, societies were not always as efficient as they should have been in seeing that the books were issued immediately. In addition books were reportedly used sometimes as collateral for loans made by loan sharks. Therefore not all insured persons could provide evidence of their standing. At the same time local insurance committees were often slow in crediting the accounts of panel practitioners for new patients. While there was a year end settlement of panel accounts, doctors complained that there was no excuse for the delay.

76. A Panel Doctor, pp. 129-140.

77. PRO. MH 62/139., undated memorandum.

78. The Panel Committee of London, Medical Service Sub-Committee, minutes, 1916-1926.

79. The Panel Committee of London, Medical Service Sub-Committee, minutes, Case No. M 21/3. 8 July 1921.

80. PRO. MH 62/2., 15 June 1928.

81. <u>Ibid</u>., 24 July 1928.

82. Colin-Russ.

83. The Panel Committee of London, Ethics Sub-Committee, minutes, 1914-1939.

84. The Panel Committee of London, Medical Service Sub-Committee, minutes, 30 April 1930.

85. Orr, pp. 150-151.

86. <u>BMJ</u> (19 April 1913), pp. 840-841.

87. <u>The Lancet</u> (3 January 1914), p. 22.

88. *Annual Report of the Chief Medical Officer of Health for the Year 1920*, p. 199.

89. PRO. MH 62/132., 11 September 1929.

90. Colin-Russ.

91. PRO. MH 62/102., undated.

92. *National Insurance Gazette*, "Doctor May be Rude" (11 April 1931), p. 175.

93. Jeane L. Brand, *Doctors and the State* (Baltimore: Johns Hopkins Press, 1965), p. 213. Also see George Newman, *The Rise of Preventive Medicine* (London: Oxford University Press, 1932) and Arthur Newsholme, *Evolution of Preventive Medicine* (Baltimore: Williams and Wilkins, 1927).

94. H. A. Parker, "National Health Insurance," *National Insurance Gazette* (4 February 1933), p. 56.

95. Insurance Acts Committee, session 1933-1934. IA 6, 3 November 1933. The societies with the most generous policies were as a rule the industrial insurance societies. By the interwar period the older friendly societies could not have financially borne such a burden, even had they wanted to. In turn this made them even less attractive to prospective members.

96. Insurance Acts Committee, session 1930-1931. IAC 5, 25 September 1930.

97. Insurance Acts Committee, session 1933-1934. IA 4A, 29 March 1934.

98. Colin-Russ.

99. *Statistical Review of England and Wales for the Year 1939,* New Annual Series, No. 19. Tables part 1, Medical (London: H.M.S.O., 1944), Table 4.

100. Ibid.

101. *Statistical Review of England and Wales for the Year 1938-1939*, New Annual Series, Nos. 18 & 19. *Medical Text* (London: HMSO 1947), Table 31.

102. *Statistical Review of England and Wales for the Year 1937*, New Annual Series, No. 17. Tables part 1, Medical (London: H.M.S.O., 1938), pp. 133-136.

103. *Ibid.*, Table 74.

104. Ibid., Table 52.

105. Ibid., p. 108.

106. Ibid., Table 11.

107. Ibid., p. 58. Diagram 5. Also see Table 26.

108. _The Times_, 15 July 1933.

109. Smith, pp. 414-415.

110. _Annual Report of the Chief Medical Officer of Health for the Year 1935_, p. 72. This was an official figure that was disputed by the medical profession. According to the Chief Medical Officer only 50.4% of all insured patients claimed some portion of their medical benefit in any given year. The medical profession pointed out that this figure was based upon returns from the approved societies. With some merit they claimed that this accounted for only certified illness. Many patients, it was argued, visited their panel practitioner without ever receiving a certificate. The BMA held that the attendance rate was therefore nearer 60% of panel patients.

111. _BMJ_ (22 July 1933), _Supplement_, p. 44.

112. M. Jeanne Peterson, _The Medical Profession in Mid-Victorian London_ (Berkeley: University of California Press, 1978), pp. 5-39.

113. Brand, pp. 150-164.

CHAPTER IV

The Doctors Common Health

The gains made by Britain's medical men under the national insurance scheme represented for most general practitioners a significant financial and professional achievement. This success did not escape the notice of those outside the medical community. On the twenty-first anniversary of the beginning of national health insurance, the medical correspondent for The Times noted that "The doctors themselves are so much better off under the new system that their contentment rather than their dissatisfaction offers a target of criticism."[1] Indeed, as discussed in the previous chapter, practitioners had become partners in the insurance scheme that many had so greatly feared and opposed in 1912. Since 1914 the nation's medical men, led by Alfred Cox and Henry Brackenbury, had pursued a conscious policy of peaceful cooperation with the act, its administrators and the government. In return, the insurance bureaucracy at both the local and national levels had allowed panel men independence and influence within the act's daily operation. Constant negotiation and adjustment was the dominant theme of insurance administration and, as Alfred Cox noted privately in early 1922, the national bureaucracy "is certainly playing the game with us."[2] Nonetheless the game had its limits.

As long as the medical profession confined its interests to the problems of insurance administration, doctors found the government responsive and eager to improve the act's efficiency. The monetary complaints of panel practitioners, though, had not met with such a cordial reception. Politically the medical profession had been bashed about for ten years by 1923 and had consistently failed to win its financial demands. Moreover in the wake of the capitation reduction for 1922 and the deepening economic depression, there was every prospect that when the remuneration question was again opened in the autumn of 1923, there would be a further cut in panel income. As a result, the members of the panel medical service and their leaders faced a profoundly difficult choice in 1922 and early 1923. Doctors could either accept the government's capitation offer, which in light of the fiscal conservatism of postwar politics, would likely be even lower than the 9s.6d. granted for 1922. Or, practitioners could, as they had in 1912, threaten to boycott the health insurance panels in the hope of forcing a higher settlement from the government's tightening purse.

Both avenues were clearly full of danger. But medical men knew that whatever the outcome, their activities in 1923 were likely to shape their relationship to the panel system, its bureaucracy, the government and the approved societies, for the foreseeable future. Fortunately for the medical profession, it was better served by both its leaders and by the restructured political organization throughout the capitation crisis of 1922-1924 than it had been in 1912 and 1913. As a result, significant emotional and political victory was achieved by the nation's practitioners -- a victory that not only left the professional gains made under panel service intact but created new political opportunities for the B.M.A.

The Capitation Crisis, 1922-1924

The political maneuvers and negotiations associated with the capitation crisis surrounding the 1924 panel fee are central to an understanding of medical politics up to the second world war. From the perspective of Britain's doctors, the crisis had three distinct phases. The first, in which the B.M.A. sought to neutralize the approved societies, lasted from the early spring of 1922 until January 1923. The crisis entered its second stage after the B.M.A. failed to eliminate the societies from the capitation negotiations set to begin in 1924. During this period, which did not end until October, 1923, the nation's medical leaders rallied medical opinion. In what was a remarkable show of professional solidarity, doctors stood firm against any further reduction of the capitation fee and forced the government to accept an arbitrated settlement in October, 1923. This success marked the beginning of the third phase of the crisis which ended in January, 1924, with the decision of the capitation board of inquiry.

Phase One, The Approved Society Menace

The months immediately following the reduction of the capitation fee for 1922 and what was seen as the government's bad faith in regard to mileage and dispensing fees were confusing for politically minded panel doctors. Once again the B.M.A. and its constituency had been swept aside in a political struggle despite what medical men believed to be the justice of their financial claims. The profession was certainly disenchanted -- more because it had been a victim of outside forces than because it had been failed by its political leaders. Despite this general malaise, which even silenced the correspondence pages of the *British Medical Journal*, Alfred Cox and Henry Brackenbury realized that if the profession was to have any hope of success in the autumn of 1923 Britain's doctors could not be allowed to sulk.

As the B.M.A.'s Medical Secretary since 1912 and Chairman of the Insurance Acts Committee since its founding, Cox and Brackenbury, respectively, had been the architects of the profession's policy of cooperation with health insurance. Since 1920, the two men had been actively engaged in the collection of statistical information concerning the net income and rates of attendance of panel doctors.[3] The information assembled revealed that despite the steady deflation of the national economy, the costs of medical practice had risen. Moreover, the range of service and the incidence of attendance within the panel scheme were growing.[4] Medical men, it seemed, could no longer afford to be intimidated by the government.

Cox and Brackenbury were both prudent men and increasingly adroit politicians.[5] Neither was willing to throw over ten years of significant professional and economic gains under the insurance scheme in a sudden declaration of open hostility to the government. The medical profession had far too many enemies, very few real friends and no tested political leverage. The B.M.A.'s leaders understood that any demand for an increase in panel remuneration for 1924 would be a direct challenge to the fiscal policies of the government. The great fear of the profession was that if it became too troublesome the government might allow the approved societies a freer hand in the administration of the insurance medical benefit. In 1919 Christopher Addison had made such a threat as did Alfred Mond in 1921. The leaders of the B.M.A. had no doubt that in the event of a dispute over the capitation fee, the society card would be played. Therefore, in the spring of 1922, Cox and Brackenbury kept the profession upon a moderate course. It was a course, however, that was not designed to maintain political options alone. Medical leaders also worked to neutralize the panel service's most persistent and dangerous critics, the approved societies.

On 30 March 1922, the Insurance Acts Committee met with representatives of the Ministry of Health in order to discuss issues affecting insurance practice. Both sides were fully aware that it was the approved society question that was foremost in the profession's mind. From the outset the medical representatives, led by Cox and Brackenbury, were placed on the defensive. Sir Arthur Robinson, Principal Secretary to the Minister of Health, opened the conference by reading a stern statement about the relationship of the societies to the medical benefit. Robinson reminded the doctors of the medical benefit's history. Since 1912 the Treasury had subsidized payments to panel practitioners through a series of Exchequer grants. These raised the capitation fee from the original offer of 4s.6d. to the 1913 level of 7s. plus the floating sixpence. In addition, during the war years bonuses were given to the doctors. But after the war, as the economic slump began, the government desired to end its supplemental payments and shift the burden for supporting the panel fee to the societies' surplus funds which stood at £17,273,887 in 1918.[6] In 1920 the societies loudly objected to this proposed policy and when the capitation fee reached 11s. after the arbitrated settlement they resented the government's lack of concern for what they saw as the act's financial integrity. The societies had felt the prewar panel fee was artificially high and wartime inflation had only reduced it to its proper level. Seven shillings was more than enough for insurance doctors, they argued, especially in light of their view of the quality of care provided by the panel medical service.[7]

The government gave into society pressure and continued its support for the panel system. In order to keep Treasury grants stable the level of contributions by the insured was raised and a general review of the financial standing of the act was promised before 1924. The Geddes Committee Report on National Expenditures, however, intervened. It called for the complete abolition of the government's supplemental payments of Ł1,700,000 annually.[8] Even though the capitation fee had already been reduced to 9s.6d., additional money still was needed to make good on the loss. The societies knew that the government could not be expected to raise the contribution level of workers for the second time in two years. Therefore either the doctors would have to suffer another reduction in pay or the societies would have to draw upon their insurance reserves, which by 1922 had increased to Ł42,000,000.[9] Because nothing could be done about the capitation fee until January 1924 the government informed the societies that they would, at least until then, make up for the government's withdrawal of support.[10]

Arthur Robinson told the medical leaders that the new financial arrangements would not alter the administrative machinery of the medical benefit. But the ministerial spokesman pointed out in his prepared statement that "in return for accepting these new charges the approved societies have made it clear that they intend to claim a voice in the negotiations with the medical profession both in regard to the capitation rates and the conditions of service after the expiry of the present agreement at the end of 1923." To this, Robinson added that because of "the extent of the societies' contribution to the cost of medical benefits under the new scheme, it is difficult to contest their right to be represented in any future negotiations with the profession."[11]

The doctors were, to say the least, taken aback by Robinson's formal statement. Throughout the ten years of insurance negotiations the societies had made their opinions about the capitation fee known. Still, never before had they been given an official hearing as part of the negotiation process. Not surprisingly, the medical representatives who had thought the meeting might be used to preempt the societies, objected to the government's new position. Henry Brackenbury argued that any direct involvement of the societies was unacceptable. "With regard to the improvement of the service we are perfectly ready to meet with anyone and everybody who can suggest a means of making the service better." "But," the Chairman of the Insurance Acts Committee insisted, "we cannot consent to negotiate with the approved societies on remuneration and terms of service."[12] Alfred Cox added to Brackenbury's comments, somewhat more diplomatically, that the profession did not intend to be "discourteous ... it is only necessary to make it plain that when negotiating on terms of service we prefer to carry on the negotiation directly with the Government."[13]

The conference went on to discuss some minor adjustments in panel service but the minds of the medical leaders were clearly fixed on the societies. On 18 May, the B.M.A. convened a special conference of representatives of panel committees at Central Hall, Westminster. The sole topic was the seemingly new position of the societies revealed by the meeting with the Ministry of Health in late March. The conference engaged in a lengthy discussion and finally a resolution opposed to approved society interference was carried unanimously.[14] The statement issued by the conference, however, was far from tactless. The vast majority of speakers recognized that the political power of the societies would grow in direct proportion to the government's reduction of its support of the insurance act. It was obvious that the government could no longer be relied upon to stand between the profession and the societies. Therefore, in a separate resolution the conference asked that the question of a meeting with the approved societies and all interested bodies be put before the annual panel conference in October.[15]

Many attending the conference hoped that a truce could be worked out with the societies without allowing them a direct role in the upcoming negotiations. Dr. S. P. Matthews, representing West Sussex doctors, pointed out that a "friendly conference was a far more expedient course than fighting the approved societies, and by such conference some curb might possibly be placed on the despotism of the Ministry of Health."[16] Others at the May meeting, however, were not so sure of the desirability of such a meeting with the societies. "On some Insurance Committees the medical representatives had to be continually on the defensive," Dr. A.

Foster of Worcester reminded his colleagues. "How could those who made such attacks be met in conference?"[17] Despite these differences, all those attending the meeting would have agreed with Dr. P. L. Benson of Buckinghamshire. Writing in the British Medical Journal, Dr. Benson stressed that "we doctors must stir ourselves or else at the end of 1923 we shall be in the the same state of unpreparedness as that which we were caught before, and our present inadequate remuneration will be still further reduced. We must be up and doing and let the Government and the friendly societies see that we will not be ground down. We must not lose the opportunity of stating our case; it will lose nothing in the telling."[18] The profession's leaders were to waste little time in following Dr. Benson's advice.

After receiving the blessing of the annual panel conference in October, the Insurance Acts Committee moved to bring doctors and society spokesmen together in a public forum.[19] The profession hoped to show its goodwill by exposing itself to the criticism of the societies. At the same time, medical men looked forward to showing the societies and the larger public "the good work that is done every day for the insured population."[20] The conference met formally on 30 January 1923. In attendance were representatives from the National Association of Local Insurance Committees and the approved societies. The spokesmen for the local insurance committees from the outset offered only minor criticism. But when the medical representatives came face to face with those of the approved societies the outcome proved to be cordial but far less friendly than the doctors had expected. The societies clearly intended to use the occasion to launch a frontal attack upon the panel medical service. Mr. Alban Gordon of the United Women's Approved Society, declared that "it was only right to emphasize the fact that there did exist the profoundest dissatisfaction with the panel system as it was at present administered.... There were thousands of insured persons who, although taxed to pay for medical benefit deliberately refrained from going to an insurance practitioner because, rightly or wrongly, they believed that they would get insufficient treatment."[21] Another spokesman, Mr. T. Lewis of the National Conference of Friendly Societies was even more blunt. Lewis claimed that "the service was not generally satisfactory."[22] Other more specific complaints were heard as well -- ranging from the lax certification of illness and the over prescribing of drugs to questions of surgery cleanliness and hours.

As the conference came to an end, its Chairman, Henry Brackenbury, congratulated those in attendance on their candor and offered suggestions for improving the panel medical service. Pointing out that the participants had agreed to establish a standing joint committee to pursue some of the questions raised, he added that it was his hope that a more intimate relationship among all those involved in insurance work would evolve. Brackenbury was merely being polite. He, as well as the society representatives, knew that the fundamental differences between them would never be bridged. Pleasant words could not hide the implacable hostility of the societies towards the continued independence of the panel medical service. Moreover, as the societies assumed a larger share of the act's financial burden their claim of authority over the medical benefit would grow more irresistable to the government. The government had refused to exclude the societies from panel service negotiations and it was highly unlikely that they would withdraw of their own accord. After the close of the January 1923 conference the profession was again reminded of its continuing political isolation. Doctors, though, were resolved not to be caught flat footed, as in 1912 and 1921. Should the expected assault be launched on either the independence of panel doctors or insurance remuneration, medical leaders intended to be prepared.

Phase Two: The Doctors On Their Own

Medical leaders could have had little real hope of either eliminating the societies from the panel negotiation process or of quieting their opposition. Still, to try was certainly consistent with the profession's experience under the act. The approved societies, however, were not the government. Peaceful cooperation and goodwill between themselves and the medical profession was only possible if the panel medical benefit was brought under their control. This, of course, was unthinkable for the medical men and after the January 1923 conference Alfred Cox and Henry Brackenbury began to prepare the nation's doctors for what was increasingly becoming a choice between capitulation and defiance.

The B.M.A. had learned a great deal since its attempted boycott of the panel system before the war. As a result of its constant dealings with the insurance bureaucracy, the Association had emerged as a fighting force.[23] During the war, it will be remembered, some preliminary steps had been taken to ensure that a political war chest was established and in 1916 the B.M.A. formulated a collective bargaining agreement.[24] These two steps ensured that if the B.M.A. chose to stand firm against the government, it would have a fighting fund and the backing of its membership.

In February 1923, largely as a result of the hostility shown by the approved societies at the plenary conference, Cox and the Insurance Acts Committee issued a general circular to all panel practitioners.[25] The circular calmly laid out the political and financial realities that would face the profession in January 1924 when the medical service regulations and the capitation agreement expired. Shortly after the circular appeared, Dr. Cox spoke before medical audiences at Crewe and Stockport on 21 March in order to explain personally the profession's position to medical men outside London.[26] The B.M.A.'s Medical Secretary informed his audience that the money to raise or hold the level of panel remuneration at 9s.6d. could only come from two sources f the government chose to end its subsidy. Increased contribuions from the insured and their employers were in all probability ut of the question so long as trade remained depressed. The nly other pool of money was the surplus fund so jealously uarded by the approved societies.[27]

In both cases, Alfred Cox told the nation's doctors that the rospects for the profession were not bright and might fade ompletely should the profession not maintain a united front gainst further capitation reductions or encroachments by the ocieties.[28] The only weapon the medical men had was resignation. However, withdrawal from the panel medical service was like a gun ith a single bullet. If not used effectively the first time, ll would be lost not only in the upcoming fight but in all those hat might follow.

It was a dangerous game and while Dr. Cox rallied medical pinion to the B.M.A.'s side he also set a cautious course that ould involve the most careful brinkmanship of his political areer. "I am quite convinced," Cox stressed to his Cheshire audiences, "that if we could get 3,000 men, judicially distributed, o resign the fight would be won ... At the Guildhall conference we said to the approved society representatives, point-blank, 'do you want to drop this system?' And reluctantly after some hesitancy, they said, 'No.' I think in the face of the wish of the approved societies to retain the medical benefit if the Government would be unlikely to withdraw it. But the time to put our foot down is not yet. It will be time enough when the Insurance Acts Committee gets from the government the very last offer."[29]

Realizing that there was little hope of pushing the approved societies to a more conciliatory position, Cox told his listeners that the best hope for panel doctors was to try to force the government to continue its financial underwriting of the capitation fee. Such a proposal was in direct violation to the principles established by the Geddes Committee but the medical leader felt that after ten years of national insurance, the government and public opinion would share the unwillingness of the societies to upset the system.[30]

As usual, as the deadline for the new panel agreement approached, the medical profession found that it had to deal with the government on two different levels: the conditions of panel service and the controversial remuneration issue. On 7 June 1923 a special conference of representatives of local medical and panel committees met in London to discuss the non-capitation side of panel medical work. A series of alterations were recommended and throughout the rest of the summer the Insurance Acts Committee hammered out the new benefit regulations for 1924 with the Ministry of Health.[31]

The general outlines of the issues were familiar to both sides after a decade of working the act. The medical spokesmen argued, as they had in the past, that the range of insurance medical service should be better defined. The doctors suggested that much of the profession's confusion about fees and additional payments might be ended if the Ministry would state those medical procedures that were specifically outside panel work. Not surprisingly the government negotiators refused this request because it might restrict unduly the insured population's right to <u>all</u> general practitioner care. The profession's representatives also asked the government either to alter or suspend the regulations concerning the number of assistants a medical man in panel service might employ.[32] The Ministry of Health steadfastly refused. To allow the hiring of more than two assistants per panel doctor would only further threaten the right of the insured to be attended by a particular practitioner. The Ministry pointed out, after all, that it was the B.M.A. that had always sought to maintain free choice of doctor within the insurance scheme.[33]

In addition to the above points, the Insurance Acts Committee raised several other issues. The profession was still not quite satisfied with the medical record keeping requirements. The medical spokesman proposed that doctors be allowed to overlook attendances for minor ailments but the Ministry stood firm upon its demand that complete records be kept. The doctors also proposed certain innovations in the medical paperwork of panel service. These included a reduction in the number of forms and permission for doctors to stamp rather than than sign sickness certificates. Neither of these recommendations were accepted but the Ministry did agree to lower the official panel limit from

3,000 to 2,500 patients.[34]

The negotiations with the Ministry concerning the conditions of panel practice may have turned on seemingly small issues but they were hardly trivial. The problems dealt with during the summer of 1923 touched the entire profession. One proposed major change in the medical benefit regulations concerned medical discipline. Since the beginning of the insurance scheme only insured persons, local insurance committees, practitioners and regional medical officers had the right to lodge official complaints against panel practitioners. This right had long been demanded by approved societies which wanted to be allowed to make complaints in the names of their members. For the profession, already convinced that many groundless complaints were inspired by approved society interference, the proposal was ominous. The Ministry of Health at first agreed to allow the societies a role in the act's disciplinary machinery but it was forced to back down when faced with strident medical opposition. Instead the Ministry said it would accept Dr. Brackenbury's suggestion that the societies be allowed to present evidence at formal disciplinary hearings but never to initiate them. For the medical profession, still facing the capitation issue during the summer of 1923, this victory over approved society interference was, doctors hoped, an omen for the future.[35]

The discussions concerning the draft medical benefit regulations were, of course, being carried on against the backdrop of the imminent announcement of the government's decision about the future capitation fee. In early August, the Insurance Acts Committee issued a memorandum outlining the profession's case for not further reducing the rate of panel renumeration. The memorandum, put together with the assistance of the statistician, Professor A. L. Bowley, had three central themes. The first was one that the profession had used since the beginning of the panel medical service. While recognizing "the necessity for every reasonable economy," the Insurance Acts Committee argued that "the remuneration of insurance practice must compare favorably with that of private practice and that of other branches of medical work. It must not be based upon the lowest level of private practice or public medical appointments, but on a relatively high level; otherwise the best type of practitioner will devote himself to these other branches, leaving only the relatively inferior for insurance work."[36]

The second argument employed by the B.M.A. was based on its dissatisfaction with the financial position of the approved societies under the act. In 1921 medical men had been forced to accept an emergency reduction in their panel income as a patriotic duty. The burdens of the nation's financial difficulties, the memorandum charged, had not been borne equally by all parties. The profession's "acquiescence would not have been so readily forthcoming if it had been realized that this sacrifice was not properly required to relieve the national burdens but that it would in effect augment a fund which is now found to have balances of well over one hundred million sterling and to be growing by means of a surplus of some seven or eight million each year."[37] These surplus funds held by the approved societies, the doctors pointed out, could have easily been used to shore up the overall finances of the act -- including their own remuneration.

Finally, the memorandum issued by the Insurance Acts Committee insisted that even at the current panel fee of 9s.6d. medical men were being forced to accept unreasonable financial losses. As compared to 1913 a doctors income would had to have risen to £1,228 in 1923 from £800 (153.5%) in order to maintain a professional standard of living. In order to reach this level a minimum capitation fee of 10s.9d. was necessary, according to the profession. Moreover, even with a 10s.9d. panel fee the most careful economy would be necessary so as not to lower the standard of life significantly.[38] "It can be achieved only by the most rigid and continuous personal and domestic economy, by an almost perfect household management, by curtailing holidays, and, worst of all by ceasing to make proper provision for the education of the children beyond sixteen years of age. Otherwise financial disaster is threatened or the conditions of living are so altered that earning power itself is jeapordized." Augmenting its position, the profession's memorandum cited a variety of figures concerning the "Estimated Middle Class Budget for Foods" and the "Estimated Annual Expenditure of the Average Doctor's Family."

Professor A. L. Bowley in his commentary attached to the memorandum, noted that his figures were in distinct contradiction to those of the Labour Gazette.[39] Using 1913 as a base of 100, the cost of living had been reported at 230 in March 1920 and 252 in July 1920. After that point the nation had undergone a significant deflation with prices falling steadily from a level of 241 in March 1921 to 169 in July 1923. Professor Bowley however disputed the official figures that reflected a significant drop in the cost of living. For those necessary consumer goods, food, clothing and shelter, the fall had been only 4% since 1920. Yet, medical men were perhaps going to be asked to endure a reduction in fees far greater than that figure.[40]

There is no doubt that to some extent Professor Bowley was correct in his evaluation of economic trends. The official statistics reflected the economy as a whole. Many goods and services never used by individuals were evaluated and often resulted in lower (or indeed higher) rates of inflation and deflation. Bowley, however, took as his standard of measure goods and services that were used on a daily basis, and therefore affected the individual's domestic budget far more than the cost of durable goods.

Whatever the merits of the profession's case there is another issue that deserves to be emphasized before proceeding because it was the linchpin of the doctors' financial claims. All of their economic statistics used in the capitation crisis of 1923-24 were based upon a middle class standard -- and a fairly comfortable one at that. It is not insignificant that practitioners when establishing their costs of living used 2.6 servants as a statistical mean. In addition, fuel costs had risen dramatically not because of the cost of coal but because the automobile had become a central fixture of medical practice. Private schooling for children too was not considered a luxury but rather a necessity.

Nowhere is this assumption of middle class identity more apparent than in the commentary supplied by Professor Bowley. It is, he noted, "impossible for doctors in a moderate practice to reduce in the same drastic fashion the standard at which they are obliged by the nature of their practice to live. They are fixed to the locality of their practice and in most cases even to the premises from which their practice has been carried on. Their professional success from the financial point of view is to some extent dependent upon their maintaining a social position in proper relationship to that of those among whom they work."[41] Even that the medical profession could make such a claim for all practitioners, and seriously think it would be honored is another mark of just how far the profession had come since its battle with the clubs. The middle class had once been a goal for the bulk of the nation's medical men. By 1923, it was assumed that most if not all practitioners had at least climbed to its lower reaches under the insurance act and now this foothold needed a stout defense.

The leaders of the medical profession were not foolish enough to believe that the government would accept the suggestions of the August memorandum. The nation's doctors had been negotiating with the government for far too long not to realize that they were only a small part of a larger political game. The legitimacy of the profession's case was of little real importance. What was crucial was the jockeying between the approved societies and the government. Both wanted medical service for the insured class for as little expenditure as possible and each wanted the other to pay the bill. This maneuvering was beyond the medical profession's influence but it was hoped that the government would not give into society pressure. All medical leaders could do was wait for a winner and then if the need arose use its single trump card -- a boycott of panel service -- if they were brave enough.[42]

It did not take long for the cards to fall. On 26 September 1923 the Ministry of Health invited Dr. Cox and the Insurance Acts Committee to discuss the final arrangements for the 1924 medical benefit regulations due on 2 October.[43] Cox, realizing that the struggle was now about to begin in earnest, convened a secret meeting of the Insurance Acts Committee in order to make the final preparations for a mass resignation from panel service should the Ministry's capitation offer be below the existing 9s.6d. rate. The doctors' meeting with the Ministry was delayed a day but on 3 October the Ministry finally issued its capitation offer for the coming year. The government offered the profession a choice. Either it could accept a rate of 8s.6d for a period of three years or a panel fee of 8s. for five years.

Speaking for the Ministry of Health, Sir Arthur Robinson informed the Insurance Acts Committee that while it wholeheartedly agreed with the profession's desire to ensure superior service, the Ministry had strong reservations about the financial claims made by doctors. Robinson conceded that insurance remuneration "should not compare unfavourably with that derived from private general practice."[44] However, little account had been taken of the important differences between private and insurance work. Most notably the medical men had not calculated the advantages of contract practice, such as regular payment, the collection of fees and bad debts. Robinson then went on to address the other main contentions of the profession's August memorandum.

As for the issue of society reserves, Robinson argued that these were not nearly as large as many thought. Surplus funds were not surplus at all, but the necessary component of a soundly based insurance system. "It is true that at present the contributions provide more than is necessary to meet current charges." Nonetheless, Robinson stressed it was the view of the government that "the liabilities under National Health Insurance increase with the ages of the insured persons and large reserves will ultimately be required to enable the claims to be met."[45] Therefore, the capitation fee for panel service could not be prudently met by drawing upon insurance reserve funds. This meant that the level of remuneration had to be judged solely on current economic grounds. In light of this, the government, Robinson asserted, could hardly be expected to protect medical men from the broader forces of the national economy. "If there is a tendancy for ... earnings to fall to the extent of a reduction of the standard of living, the medical profession, not through any act of the Government but through the operation of ordinary economic forces, must participate in the fall..."[46]

At the center of the government's case for its capitation offer were its own statistics of medical work and income. The Insurance Acts Committee had, according to Robinson, underrated the total value of medical practice by not taking into account opportunities for private patients. In order to show this, the Ministry had undertaken a study of 446 medical practices throughout England and Wales during 1922. The doctors examined had a total of 736,000 insured persons on their lists and of these, they inspected the records of 188,606 patients. The panel records revealed that the number of services per insured patient was slightly in excess of 3.5. According to the Ministry's figures, a medical practitioner with 2,000 panel patients gave 7,000 insurance services during the year. Using a total of 300 working days per year, this meant that a 2,000 patient list would entail an average daily visit/attendance rate of 24.[47] Assuming that private practice meant less work but a comparable income, a man with 2,000 patients could be expected to earn an annual income of Ł1,800 with a 9s. capitation fee. This, Robinson reminded the profession, was the income named by the Insurance Acts Committee as offering a fair reward for the whole time of a general practitioner in 1920 when the cost of living was at its peak. Now that the economy had deflated, the 8s.6d. was a more than generous offer.[48]

Not surprisingly, the Insurance Acts Committee immediately informed the Minister of Health that the panel medical men would reject both capitation offers as grossly inadequate. Despite this, the medical leaders realized that the government had resisted tremendous pressure by the approved societies for an even greater reduction.[49] In order to avoid exposing themselves to renewed society criticism, the profession's spokesman, Dr. Henry Brackenbury, suggested that the issue be submitted to an arbitration board as in 1920. If the government did not agree to this step then the medical spokesman warned that he would have no choice but to submit the signed but as yet undated resignations that the Insurance Acts Committee had been collecting.

The Minister of Health, Edward Joynson-Hicks, refused to consider an arbitrated settlement. The basis of remuneration, he argued, had been exhaustively studied in 1920 and all that needed to be done for 1924 was to reduce the capitation fee in accordance with current economic reality. Moreover, any further arbitration would lead, in the Minister's view, to "undignified disputes between the doctors and the approved societies, which are to be depreciated in the interests of successful working of the panel system."[50]

On 18 October, a special representative conference of panel men formally rejected the government's offer and voted its unanimous support for the actions of the Insurance Acts Committee.[51] Those inside the Ministry of Health, however, doubted the will of the profession to carry through with its threat to resign even though thousands of the nation's panel doctors had signed official resignations by mid-October.[52] The Ministry's skepticism was not surprising in view of the events of 1912, when thousands of doctors had also pledged to boycott panel service. Still, if the doctors finally did make good on their threat the entire insurance scheme might collapse into chaos. Parliamentary elections were expected soon and the Conservative government could ill afford such an embarrassment. At the same time, to concede openly to medical demands for more money or even an arbitration board would fly in the face of the government's own economic policies. Such weakness also threatened to spur the creation of a parliamentary combination of Liberals, Labour, and Unionists who always supported approved society interests.[53]

As always in such disputes the key to success was patience. Joynson-Hicks hoped to be able to weather the storm by simply waiting for the unity of the medical profession to dissolve. And, if it could be helped along by the liberal use of the approved society whip, so much the better. In a remarkable letter to Alfred Cox on

23 October 1923, the Minister tried to wean the doctors away from their threatened resignations. Appealing to the profession's sense of propriety, he pointed out that "This dispute is, if you will forgive me for saying so, both undignified and unprofitable, as I am quite convinced that you and I are really animated by the same desire, namely to do what is best for the country as a whole." As Minister of Health, Joynson-Hicks insisted that it was his duty to secure the best possible medical service without placing an undue strain upon the taxpayer, the employer, or the insured person. All were indeed partners in the work of the act. Therefore the Minister argued that if the question of medical remuneration were opened up all parties would be allowed to contribute to the ultimate decision -- including the approved societies. "Whether you like it or not," the Minister told Cox, in "refusing arbitration, I have in fact to a great extent been thinking of your standpoint." Finally, Joynson-Hicks, understanding the investment the profession had in the panel medical service, pointed out that he personally "was not enamoured of the panel system" and would, if the doctors insisted, ask for a Royal Commission to examine the working of the act -- before the capitation issue was decided.[54]

Such unveiled threats made little difference to the leadership of the profession as they watched the signed panel resignations climb to 94.69% of all those in panel service.[55] After ten years of working the act, the medical community had learned something of politics. Cox and Brackenbury had carefully prepared their course. Their timing was guided this time by calm deliberation, built upon a unity between the profession and its leadership that had been absent in 1912. Dr. James Smith-Whitaker, who, it will be remembered, was a central figure in the 1912 dispute, noted in a memorandum on 29 October 1923:

> "The important characteristics of this struggle on the profession's side are to my mind the calmness, deliberation and careful preparation with which it has been entered upon, and quite startling solidarity which has been manifest. At the end of 1912, a noisy minority who had captured the machine were relying on pledges, given in quite different circumstances some time before, as a means of coercing those who did not agree to stand with them. On the present occasion, they are relying on signed signatures obtained after the issue had been formally declared. Moreover, I think that the leaders know the mind of the rank and file much more intimately now than they did then.... Finally their tenacity and powers of endurance in the struggle which they would regard as a fight to the finish may prove much more considerable than you seem disposed to think."[56]

It was clear that the nation's doctors were not going to cave in. Therefore when the government met with the doctors on 31-31 October it had little choice but to accept the profession's demand for a board of inquiry. To do otherwise would be to risk the collapse of the panel system.[57]

After the agreement for an independent investigation of the capitation issue had been reached, attention immediately shifted to the interim settlement. At the late October meeting the medical spokesmen demanded that until the results of the inquiry were known, panel men should continue to receive the old capitation fee of 9s.6d. The Minister, though, insisted that the current dispute was not a normal trade union wage disagreement and that doctors could endure a temporary fee of 8s.6d. If medical men refused, the Minister told the Insurance Acts Committee they had better "send in their resignations in case no settlement could be reached."[58] The ensuing discussion was stormy and on several occasions the Insurance Acts Committee rose to leave the room. Finally, the Committee agreed in the name of concord and in order to avoid having to submit the resignations they held, when they had already won a significant victory in gaining an impartial inquiry.[59]

The profession's leaders felt that they had succeeded in removing outside political concerns from the capitation fee. Doctors hoped the promised board of arbitration would, unlike the government, be free to make its judgment based upon the legitimacy of the profession's case divorced from the larger demands of national economic policy. It would be madness to lose this anticipated advantage because of dissatisfaction with the interim settlement. Peace was clearly desired by Cox and Brackenbury and they felt confident they could bring their supporters into line. On 14 November, the leadership's evaluation of the profession's temper proved to be correct.[60] A special conference met at the Central Hall, Westminster, and despite some minor opposition, the representatives in attendance agreed to the government's amended terms by a vote of 141 to 29.[61] All attention then turned to the coming arbitration.

Phase Three: An Arbitrated Settlement

The court of inquiry met for the first time on 4 January 1924 and immediately ran into an obstacle. The approved societies refused to submit evidence because one of the members of the court, Sir Josiah Stamp, Honorary Secretary of the Royal Statistical Society, had served on the 1920 arbitration board and was therefore tainted in their eyes. Finally Stamp was removed and the court, now composed of Thomas Hughes, Chairman of the Welsh Board of Health, Frederick Goodenough, Chairman of Barclay's Bank and Sir Gilbert Garnsey, an accountant, began its deliberations.[62] The evidence submitted for the court's consideration was by now familiar to all who followed the internal politics of the insurance act. For the most part it was no more than a repetition of earlier statements. The medical profession presented its case for at least a 9s.6d. capitation fee based upon the costs of living and medical practice. For its part the government offered rival statistics showing that significant deflation had reduced the cost of living for the middle class some distance below 1919-1920 levels. The government spokesmen insisted that even at 8s.6d. per insured person, doctors would be turning a tidy profit from panel practice. Finally the approved societies demanded in their testimony that the capitation rate be reduced to at least 7s.6d.

At the same time they tried to enlarge the scope of the inquiry to include a discussion of the supposed defects of insurance medical care. The court rejected this ploy and on 23 January rendered its verdict. The arbiters ruled that doctors should receive a fee of 9s. rate until the end of 1927 when the issue would again be taken up.[63]

Given the type of evidence presented to the court of inquiry, its decision was equitable. Each group presenting evidence based its conclusions upon a different set of assumptions. The approved societies, seeking to preserve their financial position, simply stated that doctors had been over paid since the act's inception. The government, in contrast, used official statistics to argue for a reduction of 1s. per patient while asserting that doctors would not suffer in either social or financial standing when the value of private practice was calculated.[64] As for the medical profession, its representatives pointed out that panel men should not be expected to settle for less than a middle class standard of life. Excluding the testimony of the approved societies, the essential difference between the government and profession was one of definition. The government never challenged the doctors' expectation of being solidly middle class. What constituted a middle class lifestyle, however, was more an issue for individual bias than statistical measurement. In light of this, the Solomon-like decision of the court of inquiry, which forced the doctors and the government to meet halfway, was perhaps the fairest decision possible.

The capitation crisis had come to a peaceful end for Britain's medical practitioners. For the first time in their more than ten year relationship they had won a struggle with the government over a monetary issue. Doctors had not received all they had wanted but to lose only sixpence in the political atmosphere of the early twenties was not an insignificant feat. Financially the victory was only partial, but doctors could have lost far more. For many practitioners the successful maneuvers of 1923-24 marked an unmatched moral achievement. Britain's doctors had shown that with good leadership, careful planning and solidarity they could no longer be bullied by either the government or the approved societies. Reflecting this, Dr. Hubert Tibbits, Chairman of the Warwickshire Panel Committee, wrote to a disgruntled colleage even before the arbitration took place that "we have recently shown the country a united front upon a particular issue.... I am proud of the recent demonstration of solidarity and appeal to you to do nothing which might prevent such a demonstration upon any or every future occasion when we are threatened."[65]

This proven solidarity marks a watershed in insurance politics. The pattern for the remainder of the interwar years had been established. Just as the profession felt that it had become a partner in negotiations concerning administrative questions, after 1924 doctors gained new confidence in their ability to argue their financial claims peacefully and have them heard fairly. Both the government and the approved societies realized that the threat of a medical boycott of the panel system was no longer a fantasy, given the proper circumstances. Neither really wanted to see the insurance medical service destroyed or in fact even disrupted -- the nation had too many other pressing problems. Thus, once the medical profession proved the existence of its ultimate weapon, it was assured that it would never have to bring it into play. From 1924 onward the nation's practitioners became, within the scope of their interest, equal partners within the act. Never again would they seriously challenge the course of government policy with a boycott -- nor would they have to.

The Passing of the Society Threat

The new Labour government agreed to honor the court of inquiry's recommendation, even though it now had the responsibility of finding the money to pay the medical bill. On 24 March 1924 the government introduced a bill into Parliament that enabled the capitation fee to be paid from the general finances of the act. This was accomplished without raising the level of contributions from employers or the insured class. Approved societies were released from the responsibility, imposed in 1922, of paying for part of the capitation fee from their funds. The cost, estimated to be £1,350,000 per year for three years, was to be taken from heretofore unacknowledged funds derived from the sale of unclaimed insurance stamps and interest earned since 1913.[66]

The political and economic details of this scheme have been explored by Bentley B. Gilbert in his book British Social Policy 1918-1939, and lie beyond the scope of the present study. Nonetheless, it should be pointed out that for the medical profession the Labour government's financial wizardry represented a significant vindication. Since the immediate postwar period, the B.M.A. had stressed that the money to pay panel men an "adequate rate" had always been present within insurance act finances. The societies, they felt, had for too long hidden this money and now in 1924 the medical profession was satisfied that its case had been proved beyond all reasonable doubt. In their euphoria, the doctors, though, failed to realize that their settlement had come from funds that had been built up over a period of ten years and that the bulk of the newfound money was a result of war time surpluses, the unclaimed stamp fund in the post office and over cautious actuarial estimates. The doctors gave little thought to the question of how long the surplus pool would last.[67]

The medical leaders can hardly be blamed for their lack of foresight. The 1924 agreement had given them a three year respite from a problem that had dominated medical politics since 1912. Moreover, the settlement was seen as an important victory by the profession over the approved societies. Therefore, with understandable confidence, the profession's political leaders turned their attention to the Royal Commission on National Insurance which was appointed on 11 July 1924. The idea for a royal commission had been used as a club against the profession by Joynson-Hicks but medical leaders had actually welcomed the idea as a way to clear up accusations against the panel medical service. They pointed out that Lloyd George had promised a general review of the scheme after three years of operation. The war had delayed the investigation and in the immediate post- war period it was argued that the act should be allowed to reach a level of normality before a broad evaluation was undertaken. But, when it was evident that normality would be a constant trade depression, the profession jumped at the opportunity so casually offered by Joynson-Hicks.[68]

The appointment of a royal commission was delayed, however, by the fall of the Baldwin government in January 1924. But Labour, upon assuming office under Ramsey MacDonald, honored the previous government's pledge to sponsor a commission to examine the operation of the national insurance act. At first the medical leaders were not pleased with the appointments to the Royal Commission. They felt that its members did not all understand the nature of medical practice and that their own profession was under-represented.[69] Soon though, the Insurance Acts Committee, still chaired by Henry Brackenbury, threw itself into the process of providing the profession's views to the Commissioners. The doctors' evidence was based largely upon the material that had been gathered for the 1924 arbitration. It ranged over the broad landscape of insurance medical practice and not unexpectedly declared that, given the limitations of the act, health insurance had been a notable success. The Royal Commission never really questioned this conclusion but neither did it engage in a full-blown investigation of the medical benefit. Rather, the Commission became an arena for a concerted assault upon the industrial approved societies by the Labour Party because they were "both a center of power and a subversion of the old cooperative friendly society ideal."[70]

The Minority Report of the Royal Commission charged that the approved societies no longer represented the old friendly society ideal of voluntarism and self-government that its founders had invisioned.[71] The system had become dominated by the industrial approved societies while the older friendly societies were rapidly disapppearing.[72] Sir Alfred Watson, the government's Chief Actuary, pointed out that the societies controlled by the insurance industry did not afford their members any opportunities for self-rule. Their annual meetings were sparsely attended and their rules allowed organizations that held millions of pounds to be controlled by a small number of officials. Fully 50% of all insured persons were members of societies in which there was a "complete lack of any real opportunity for membership control."[73] The National Amalgamated Approved Society, for example, had a total membership of 2.25 million insured and had a quorum of 50 for its annual meeting. Only rarely were there more than 250 people in attendance and these were for the most part members of the society's full-time staff.[74] Because of these inequalities, the Minority Report of the Commission asked that the entire system be abandoned in favor of a scheme administered by the local authorities. However, the majority of the Commissioners refused to accept this proposal and declared that it "would create as much discontent as it would allay."[75]

For the medical profession, the deliberations of the Commissioners and their final reports signed 22 February 1926 were bitter sweet. Practitioners had hoped to be placed in the bright light of center stage and completely absolved of supposed sin. Instead, doctors were given good but only scant reviews while their great rival, the approved society system, drew all the attention. However, the medical community found it hard to hide its pleasure at seeing the societies' bad notices.[76]

The outstanding event of 1926 for the medical profession was beyond a doubt this Royal Commission's report. But the Economy Bill passed by the Baldwin government was perhaps of more real importance.[77] The bill called for deep cuts in domestic spending. For the health insurance scheme this meant a reduction of £2,750,000 annually in Treasury support. The approved societies were then required to pick up a larger share of the cost of benefits from their surplus funds. At the same time the government approved a step that the nation's doctors had always advocated. It required that the 13s. devoted to the medical benefit for the insured have the first call on the scheme's finances. This was an increase of

3s. over the amount previously available without having to appeal to the societies or the government for additional money. This extra margin was designed to raise the level of the drug fund but in effect it made the 9s. capitation rate impervious to approved society attack so long as the cost of prescribed medicines did not climb above 4s. per insured patient.[78]

The Economy Bill capped a tumultuous period for Britain's panel practitioners and their political arm, the B.M.A., that had begun in 1911. Since the introduction of national health insurance, politically minded medical men had perceived the profession as being in a life-or-death struggle against the approved societies.[79] This battle now seemed to be at least temporarily over. The approved societies had not been allowed to assume control over the insurance medical benefit nor had they been successful in forcing a drastic reduction in the capitation fee for 1924. At the same time their complaints about the level of care given by panel doctors had been declared to be unfounded by the Royal Commission. The Commission also subjected the societies themselves to intense criticism. Moreover, the passage of the Economy Bill all but guaranteed the doctors of the panel medical service a secure financial future.

Throughout the running dispute with the approved societies, medical men had seen the fight as one for medical independence. Unfortunately they could never persuade either the public, the politicians or, of course, the approved societies of the purity of their aims. Seemingly petty economic bargaining made medical men appear as just another narrow interest within British society. This contradiction had always been an embarrassment, albeit a necessary one, for a profession that had long sought to build up the mystique of its ethical and humanistic mission. Therefore, once free of the immediate fear of society control, medical leaders felt that the profession had an opportunity to extend the scope of medical politics beyond the monetary issues toward a larger discussion about future innovations in the nation's health services.

Towards A Common Health

The report of the Royal Commission on National Insurance and the 1926 Economy Act momentarily released the medical men from their need to defend themselves against economic and professional attack. With its enemies quieted, the profession was placed in a political vacuum. Its leaders were wise enough to realize the possibilities for medical men to polish up their public image by moving to guide rather than merely to follow health care politics.

The first step was to de-emphasize the importance of the capitation fee. Up to 1924, negotiations over the medical benefit regulations had been dominated by a disputed capitation fee. Significantly the profession decided not to challenge the continuation of the 9s. rate of remuneration in 1927 when the 1924 agreement expired. Admittedly, the medical leaders knew that they had little or no chance of success but this had never stopped the B.M.A. before.[80] Such an appeal was clearly recognized as being counterproductive if not unpatriotic given the continuing economic crisis. To be sure the capitation fee was to remain important. In 1931, panel doctors had to fight to receive only a 10% deduction and in June, 1935, they successfully regained 5% of their loss. The remaining 5% was restored in 1937 when the profession demanded and received a hearing before a formal court of inquiry.[81] Still, the leaders of the panel medical men after 1926 never again allowed the capitation issue to control medical politics.

Instead the B.M.A. leadership insisted that all doctors begin to look beyond immediate concerns to the future. Drs. Cox, Brackenbury and now H. Guy Dain, who replaced Brackenbury as Chairman of the Insurance Acts Committee in 1926, agreed that the profession would not survive the tensions of future political confrontations if it allowed the scope of health care politics and planning to be defined by others.

Already, deep seated structural changes in the British system of health care had been produced by the work of the insurance scheme. Specialty medical practice increasingly moved from the voluntary hospital to outpatient clinics as many panel practitioners sent insured patients with complex cases to clinics rather than providing treatment themselves. Panel men certainly had no incentive to treat such cases because extra payments for specialty work were not always easy to secure from local insurance committees. In response to this increased demand, the 1920s and 1930s witnessed an unprecedented increase in the capacity of out-patient facilities. While the old competition between such facilities and the general practitioner had disappeared, there was a real fear that the panel medical practice would eventually become nothing more than a halfway house between illness and the clinic.[82]

On another level the insurance act had created an underground health service that offered medical benefits beyond the mandated scope of the medical panel service.[83] In making the approved societies the guardians of the insurance sickness fund, the societies were responsible for seeing that surpluses were used to provide additional benefits to their members. After the first world war the large industrial approved societies such as Prudential and the Pearl began to offer dental and ophthalmic benefits to their members which were paid for by accrued surplus benefit funds. The smaller societies, especially the old friendly societies, found it difficult to compete because in general their surpluses were not as great. As a result, by the mid-1920s it was clear that the industrial societies were attracting new members at the expense of their smaller competitors. In turn, as their membership rosters grew, the larger companies were able to offer a wider variety of benefits.

The total value of additional benefits amounted to over £2.3 million by 1939 for dental and ophthalmic benefits alone.[84] In all, the government had approved sixteen additional benefits, including hospital care, convalescent homes, surgical appliances and nursing services.[85] The medical profession was not blind to this development. It appeared that one day the nation, not necessarily by design, would have an insurance financed health service whose benefits were administered by the industrial insurance industry. From this, it would only be a short step to greater society control over the profession. Equally serious was the threat posed by the Labour Party which had long advocated a full-time medical service in the pay of the government.

Neither prospect was particularly appetizing for the medical profession. It therefore seemed in the late 1920s that in order to forestall such developments and preserve the general practitioner, the profession had to begin to develop its own plans for future medical services. To do so would serve several purposes. Not only would it enable doctors to proclaim publicly their devotion to improving the nation's health, but a general discussion of health care issues offered a new political platform to the profession. No longer would doctors be in a defensive position. By looking beyond immediate problems, medical leaders hoped that the profession might help mold future innovations in health care services.

It was only natural that when medical men began to think seriously about the nature of health care services in the future they thought in terms of expanding the scope of the national insurance scheme. Certainly such ideas had been part not only of the profession's rhetoric, but of that of nearly all health-oriented organizations since the act first began to deliver benefits. Doctors had long complained that the insurance scheme was inadequate and illogical because it covered wage earners and not their families. Moreover, it did little to rationalize the jumble of public and private health services that had been built up since the early nineteenth century. In 1914, the B.M.A. and nearly everyone else had hoped that the budgetary proposals of that year for additional health facilities were the first step in the development of new comprehensive national health services.

The reconstruction of the 1914 budget and the coming of the war emergency diverted elsewhere the money that had been proposed to aid health services. But the idea of expanding and coordinating public health policies continued to hold the attention of the medical profession. It will be remembered that the 1917 Insurance Acts Committee report on medical opinion revealed that Britain's doctors favored broadening the scope of insurance benefits and extending the act to the dependents of insured laborers. Even the London Panel Committee proposed its own plan for the expansion of the national insurance scheme in 1917.[86] Health care planning was also engaged in by Christopher Addison, who in the midst of the struggle for a Ministry of Health, sponsored a series of conferences on the subject. At these, representatives from the Royal Colleges of Physicians and Surgeons, the Society of Medical

Officers of Health, the Local Government Board, the Board of Education, the Ministry of Pensions and the Chief Medical Officers of all departments met to discuss desirable innovations in health care policy. In April 1919, this consultative council issued its recommendations suggesting an expansion of clinical and diagnostic facilities and the coordination of institutions, specialists and general practitioner activities. Later this was to become incorporated within a more extensive document produced by the Consultative Council on Medical and Allied Services. This study, known popularly as the Dawson Report, was issued in 1920 and is sometimes mistakenly seen as a forerunner of the National Health Service.[87]

The medical profession cooperated in the planning of postwar health services. Nonetheless the profession's recommendations for additional services were always overshadowed by the dispute over the capitation fee.[88] Despite this, medical leaders never allowed the plans to be completely forgotten. When the opportunity arose in 1926 to dust them off, Cox, Brackenbury and H. Guy Dain were ready. The immediate product of this was the B.M.A.'s scheme, unveiled publicly in 1930, for a general medical service for the nation.[89] For the next ten years this plan represented the centerpiece of B.M.A. policy towards state sponsored health services and provided the Association with a counterweight to its political opponents.[90]

The underlying theme of the B.M.A.'s 1930 proposal was that the insurance principle had proven itself to be a successful and desirable basis for the delivery of health care. The time had come to extend its benefits to the dependents of those directly paying contributions and to create a comprehensive and coordinated national medical service. The foundation of this proposed new service was the general practitioner who, in his neighborhood surgery, was seen as being best suited to prevent as well as cure disease.

Auxiliary services were to be built upon the general practitioner base, with each family doctor acting as the agent for patients when specialty care was needed. Each insured person was to have access to nurses, midwives, masseurs and ophthalmic services in addition to technical facilities such as diagnostic laboratories. Institutional services too were outlined and included hospitalization, maternity, tuberculosis, mental and venereal disease treatment and access to convalescent homes. In addition, the B.M.A. suggested that a complete dental service be established. Finally, the Association sought the creation of a national maternity service to provide prenatal and postnatal care.[91]

The B.M.A. estimated that the number of people eligible to receive benefits under their plan would be 25-30 million, and except for the very poor, each person earning less than £250 would pay a weekly contribution. Participating medical men were to be paid a capitation fee for each insured patient and the entire scheme was to be fully integrated under the Ministry of Health. Local organization was to follow the pattern established by the insurance act, with the sole exception of the approved societies, which, not surprisingly, were to be completely abolished.[92]

In making this popular appeal for an expansion of insurance health services the leaders of the profession freely admitted among themselves that there was "nothing new in the medical profession's plan..."[93] Despite this, the scheme did represent a legitimate desire by Britain's doctors to help create an efficient and beneficial health care system while serving the medical profession's political and economic interests.[94] The proposal for a general medical service was an effort to institutionalize the success of the insurance act. Fearful of becoming a ward of the state or the approved societies, the Association's leaders hoped to guide the nation away from the concept of a full-time state medical service by entrenching the insurance principle and the existing part time status of panel practitioners.[95] Just as important, the B.M.A.'s proposal sought to fix the pattern of medical practice that the panel system had founded. Although the plan advocated an expanded program of continuing education, the separation between the general practitioner and specialist class was maintained if not accentuated. The technology and circumstances of the practice of medicine could change but given its preference the B.M.A. preferred to protect the traditional structure of medical practice that it found comfortable, beneficial and appropriate.[96]

In order to flesh out the 1930 scheme the B.M.A. published fairly complete outlines for the development of national nursing, maternity, consultant and specialist, hospital, ophthalmic and dental services throughout the 1930s.[97] In each case the Association's General Medical Services Committee worked closely with the different interest groups, so as to assure workability and political support for each aspect of what doctors called the nation's future common health. The medical profession even attempted to reach an understanding with the approved societies by holding joint meetings and exchanging speakers at annual conferences.[98]

As a public relations effort the B.M.A.'s planning activities were a success. Medical speakers could now point to the profession's positive efforts in fighting for new health services. Perhaps the best judgment of the value of the profession's work was that in 1932 the National Conference of Friendly Societies voted to develop their own suggestions on the nature of future health services.[99] Other groups, too, joined in, groups ranging from the Chartered Society of Massage and Medical Gymnastics to the British Dental Association.[100] For the profession it was satisfying to know that it was no longer a hapless follower but a leader capable of shaping a public debate.

The government, however, proved to be more difficult to manipulate than popular opinion. When the B.M.A.'s plan was first made public in 1930, the Insurance Department inside the Ministry of Health held an internal symposium in order to deal with the scheme.[101] The consensus was that the plan, while offering an acceptable basis for action, did not deal effectively with the practical problems of expense and administration. It completely lacked, in the Department's eyes, any understanding of the terrific burdens that would fall upon the shoulders of the local authorities if it was actually implemented. Because of this obvious weakness the Ministry responded only in the vaguest way to the profession's request for an opinion, hoping that the subject would die a natural death.[102] Sir George Newman, Chief Medical Officer of Health, noted in a private memorandum that he could not "escape the conviction ... that these proposals have about them an unmistakable appearance of the strengthening of the vested interests of a profession at the cost of the state and the patient ..." The scheme, however, was to Newman "quite clearly ... not unlike an advertising kite, and we need not be greatly disturbed by its ascent. It is too 'socialistic' for most of the medical profession, who are individualistic...."[103]

George Newman and his Ministerial colleagues, though, underrated the profession's enthusiasm for the scheme. Repeatedly the B.M.A. asked that a formal conference be called by the Ministry in order to debate the doctors' proposals. For the medical profession such a discussion would lend to their efforts an air of official credibility -- which was precisely what the Ministry wanted to avoid.[104] Still, it was apparent that in 1934 when approved societies began to call for such a conference, the government could no longer avoid the subject and it agreed to a meeting. However, the government stipulated that the subject would only come under formal discussion if the approved societies and the B.M.A. could agree on the specific topics to be explored. The government knew full well that such an agreement would be impossible because the societies would never assent to anything more than a discussion about additional specialty services. In contrast, doctors demanded that the wholesale expansion of medical and institutional benefits be the topic of any conference dealing with the nation's future health services.[105] As expected by the government, the proposed conference never met and the government was spared any embarrassment it might have caused.[106] Nonetheless, this did not discourage the profession from attempting to show that its proposals were workable.

The leaders of the B.M.A. fully realized that so long as the national economy was depressed no government was likely to embark upon an expensive expansion of the insurance act and the coordination of all health care services. Therefore, the Association felt that a basis for its envisioned common health program could be established without Treasury support. Considerable progress could be made, medical leaders argued, by creating voluntary public medical services at the county and municipal level until economic conditions and the political climate allowed the erection of a fullblown national medical scheme.[107] Moreover, while waiting for future developments, the public medical service offered the profession a way to counter further expansions of extra benefits being supplied by the approved societies.

The public medical service concept had long been in existence. Towards the end of the nineteenth century various private medical institutes, offering limited medical care for a small weekly payment, grew up alongside the friendly societies. These institutes employed staff practitioners on a contract basis and were the targets of abuse by the B.M.A. In order to maintain their independence many doctors with impoverished patients formed their own doctors' clubs. In these the poor paid a few pennies a week, as they would have to institutes, directly to a general practitioner in exchange for basic medical care. A more sophisticated system of private contract practice was promoted in the 1905 report of the B.M.A.'s Medico-Politics Committee. After a two year investigation the Committee suggested that in order to eliminate the friendly societies from the delivery of health services the profession should support the formation of local public medical services by individual or group practitioners.[108] Unlike the medical institutes these were controlled exclusively by their member doctors and clinical decisions could in theory be made without non-medical interference. Several of these were in fact begun, with the largest and most successful service in Leicester. However, the idea of doctor-sponsored public medical services received scant success and the few that survived the war remained small.[109]

Nonetheless, when in 1931 the B.M.A. was looking for a way to implement its suggestions for a general medical service for the nation, the public medical service was seen as an appropriate vehicle. Therefore, the Association reconsidered existing public medical services and drew up a model scheme based upon a 1922 plan put together by the Insurance Acts Committee.[110] The B.M.A. envisioned a national network of medical services to be financed by the contributions of subscribers who desired additional medical benefits for themselves and their dependents. Each of the services was slightly different. Some offered only general practitioner care to the insured but most supplied some specialty services such as dental care, limited outpatient hospitalization or ophthalmic benefits. Approved societies sometimes cooperated but in all cases medical services were established and operated by their member practitioners.[111] Most public medical services followed the lead of the B.M.A. and enforced a £250 income limit so as not to threaten private practice in their areas. The one exception was in London where medical men tried to attract the middle classes to their P.M.S. by allowing persons with incomes as high as £550 to enter.[112] But this experiment was not a great success. In January, 1933, only 15,000 members had paid their fees (an average of 33 per doctor) and most of these came from two Metropolitan boroughs, Paddington and Marylebone, which were hardly middle class areas.[113]

Nationally, public medical service doctors received an average fee of 11s.2d. in 1938, less the cost of medicines per contributor. This was not only an improvement over the insurance capitation fee which then stood at 9s. but a 1937 survey of 26 services revealed that the annual rate of attendance per member was only 1.9 -- far below the panel rate.[114] By 1938 there were 77 B.M.A. approved public medical services in rural as well as urban areas. Nearly 4,000 practitioners were actively engaged in these, caring for more than 650,000 subscribers.[115] There were, of course, critics of the rapid growth of public medical services. Liberal or socialist doctors accused them of being a sham, preying upon the poor in much the same fashion as the old club system.[116] More seriously though, at least from a political perspective, approved societies saw the services as a threat to their future because public medical services absorbed many juvenile contributors before they became eligible for national insurance benefits. It therefore was possible that the young would no longer feel it necessary to join an approved society and instead enter the insurance system as post office contributors.[117]

There can be little doubt that the approved societies were correct in seeing the rise of the public medical service as a threat. Public medical services, after all, had a political as well as medical goal. Together with the profession's plans for a general medical service for the nation, they were designed to thrust the B.M.A. to the forefront of medical planning and politics. The ploy worked. By the eve of the second world war the medical profession had transformed itself from the constitutional obstructionist group of 1912 to an interest that appeared to be engaged in important and innovative planing for the future. As selfserving as these plans may have been, they were widely accepted as legitimate by those outside the profession.[118]

More importantly, though, the work of the B.M.A., together with that of some approved societies and research groups such as Political and Economic Planning, illustrates a larger theme in development of modern British social policy. The idea of national health insurance cannot be written off solely as a halfway house on the road to the welfare state. The insurance principle had a life of its own and was seen by many in the interwar period as an effective basis for the future development of social services. To be sure there is a great deal of continuity.[119] The national health service borrowed heavily from the experience of the older panel system in 1948 but in the late 1930s informed opinion looked in a different direction. The B.M.A. and others saw a future of expanded benefits based upon the principle of social insurance, not social welfare. Hitler's bombs made such visions untenable and the prewar health plans in which the state played the role of the individual's partner gave way to the acceptance of the state as public guardian. The change is not inconsequential. It represents, after all, the difference between liberalism and socialism.

When considered as a whole, the activities of the medical profession from 1922 until the beginning of the second world war, three interrelated themes are evident. Each of these, the capitation crisis, the decline of the approved society threat and the B.M.A.'s planning for the future have been considered as part of the larger fabric of insurance politics. Underpinning these, however, is a pattern of intelligent leadership within the medical profession. Alfred Cox, Henry Brackenbury and H. Guy Dain provided temperate and politically astute guidance throughout the period. In itself, this was a notable achievement but it is an indication of far more fundamental change in the profession.

In 1912 when the medical profession was faced with national insurance, its political response was chaotic and amatuerish. Its leaders, men like Sir James Barr, were not politicians in the modern sense of the word. They had little idea of how to organize political opinion or pressure and were out of touch with the medical rank and file. For them, political activity was anathema to the ethical goals of the medical profession. The coming of the insurance act, however, bound doctors not only to the state but to politics. Men like Cox, Brackenbury, Dain and later Charles Hill understood the essence of this new situation.[120] The issues at hand were far too important to allow medical men to be buffeted from side to side by outside forces. The only way to secure success was never to cease playing politics. This is precisely what the leaders of the profession learned after 1921, if not before. They shaped a highly individualistic and conservative profession into a modern day pressure group.[121] In doing so, they deserve to be identified as the first of a breed with which the British public is now so familiar -- the full-time medical politician for whom the practice of medicine became secondary to its politics.

Notes

1. *The Times*, 15 July 1933.

2. Insurance Acts Committee, session 1921-1922. IAC 54, 20 March 1922.

3. Insurance Acts Committee, session 1925-1926. IAC 28, 28 January 1926. In 1921 a booklet was issued to all panel men who agreed to collect statistics. Few turned these booklets in to the Insurance Acts Committee. By 1924 the Committee reported that it had received only 200 and of these only 50 had been judged to be reliable.

4. Insurance Acts Committee, session 1923-1924. IAC 30, undated. Statistics as to Attendance on the Insured during 1922.

5. Insurance Acts Committee, session 1921-1922. IAC 83, 22 June 1922. Colin-Russ.

6. Bentley B. Gilbert, *British Social Policy, 1914-1939* (Ithaca: Cornell University Press, 1970), pp. 261-270.

7. Insurance Acts Committee, session 1921-1922. IAC 83, 22 June 1922.

8. H. A. Parker, "National Health Insurance," *National Insurance Gazette* (28 January 1933), p. 46. The Geddes Committee on National Expenditure was appointed to examine government spending. Its report issued in 1922 proposed deep cuts in the Treasury's support for all social problems.

9. *Ibid.*

10. Gilbert, pp. 271-273.

11. *BMJ* (8 April 1922), *Supplement*, p. 97.

12. *Ibid.*, p. 98.

13. *Ibid.*

14. *BMJ* (27 May 1922), pp. 185-189.

15. *Ibid.*, p. 189.

16. *Ibid.*

17. *Ibid.*

18. *BMJ* (24 June 1922), p. 55.

19. *The Lancet* (28 October 1922), p. 921.

20. *Ibid*.

21. *BMJ* (10 February 1923), p. 37.

22. *Ibid*.

23. *The Lancet* (28 October 1922), p. 921.

24. Alfred Cox to Local Medical and Panel Committees, 13 March 1922. Insurance Acts Committee, session 1921-1922. Cox defended the position of the Insurance Acts Committee which had refused to make use of these weapons in 1921. He argued that the time to stand firm had not yet arrived. However he promised to continue to fortify the unity of the profession so that in the future it would be better prepared to defend its interests. Cox pointed to the £46,000 in the defense fund as proof of the profession's growing interest in politics.

25. *BMJ* (7 April 1923), *Supplement*, pp. 105-107.

26. *BMJ* (28 April 1923), *Supplement*, pp. 161-163. Henry Brackenbury made a similar tour.

27. *Ibid*.

28. *Ibid*.

29. *BMJ* (7 April 1923), *Supplement*, p. 106.

30. Insurance Acts Committee, session 1923-1924. IAC 3, 7 August 1923.

31. *BMJ* (16 June 1923), *Supplement*, pp. 245-261.

32. Insurance Acts Committee, session 1923-1924. IAC 22, 12 September 1923.

33. *Ibid*.

34. *BMJ* (19 May 1923), *Supplement*, p. 194. The government did agree to allow appeals from individual practitioners who wanted to exceed the limit.

35. Insurance Acts Committee, session 1923-1924. IAC 22, 22 September 1923.

36. *BMJ* (11 August 1923), *Supplement*, p. 93.

37. *Ibid*., p. 94.

38. *Ibid*., p. 95.

39. *Ibid.*

40. *Ibid.*, p. 97.

41. *Ibid.*

42. Alfred Cox to Local Medical and Panel Committees, 14 September 1923. Insurance Acts Committee, session 1923-1924. IAC 20, undated.

43. Insurance Acts Committee, session 1923-1924. IAC 27 & 29, 26 September 1923.

44. *BMJ* (6 October 1923), *Supplement*, p. 149.

45. *Ibid.*

46. *Ibid.*, p. 150.

47. *Ibid.*, p. 151.

48. *Ibid.*

49. *National Insurance Gazette* (6 October 1923), pp. 469-470. The approved societies favored a capitation fee of 7s. 3d.

50. PRO. MH 62/149., 15 October 1923.

51. *BMJ* (27 October 1923), *Supplement*, pp. 190-195.

52. PRO. MH 62/149., 19 October 1923.

53. *Ibid.*

54. *Ibid.*, Joynson-Hicks to Cox, 26 October 1923.

55. Insurance Acts Committee, session 1923-1924. IAC 47, 30 October 1923. In a letter to the Minister of Health on 27 October 1923, Cox wrote that the profession was not striking but resigning in protest against the treatment of the medical service in general by the government. "This dispute is to maintain a good medical service for the industrial population and to have settled once and for all what is the relation of the approved societies to the medical service and the doctors who provide that service." Insurance Acts Committee, session 1923-1924. IAC 46, 27 October 1923.

56. PRO. MH 62/149., 29 October 1923.

57. *BMJ* (24 November 1923), *Supplement*, pp. 237-239.

58. PRO. MH 62/149., 1 November 1923.

59. BMJ (24 November 1923), Supplement, p. 239.

60. The Lancet (8 December 1923), pp. 266-267.

61. BMJ (24 November 1923), Supplement, pp. 243.

62. Gilbert, p. 274.

63. BMJ (2 February 1924), Supplement, p. 205.

64. Great Britain, Parliament, Parliamentary Debates (Commons) 5th Series, Vol. 59, Cols. 670-671.

65. BMJ (8 December 1923), Supplement, p. 267.

66. Gilbert, p. 274. Insurance stamps were issued to each contributor to be placed in an insurance book. Those that were paid for, but never claimed by the insured, resulted in a surplus in local insurance pools.

67. Parker, p. 46. By 1923 the insurance surplus amounted to £42,000,000. In 1928 however, the value of the surplus fund had fallen to £30,000,000.

68. Insurance Acts Committee, session 1923-1924. IAC 132, 29 May 1924.

69. Insurance Acts Committee, session 1924-1925. IAC 4, 18 September 1924. Sir Henry Rolleston was the only medical man appointed to serve on the Royal Commission.

70. Gilbert, Social Policy, p. 281.

71. Arthur Newsholme, International Studies: Prevention and Treatment of Disease vol. 3 (London: George Allen & Unwin, 1931), p. 113.

72. Gilbert, p. 280.

73. Great Britain, Parliament. Sessional Papers (Commons), Report of the Royal Commission on National Health Insurance Cmd. 2596 Reports of Commissioners, vol. 16, p. 304.

74. Gilbert, pp. 280-281.

75. Cmd. 2596, p. 102.

76. BMJ (30 October 1926), Supplement, p. 189. The report, which most notably suggested that the local insurance committees be abolished and the pooling of Approved Society surplusses, was never implemented.

77. Ibid.

78. Ibid.

79. Newsholme, p. 115.

80. Insurance Acts Committee, session 1925-1926. IAC 55, 1 July 1926.

81. BMJ (29 May 1937), Supplement, pp. 315-335.

82. P.E.P. (Political and Economic Planning), Report on the British Health Services (London: P.E.P., 1937), pp. 161-165.

83. Newsholme, p. 136.

84. Annual Report of the Chief Medical Officer of Health for the Year 1939, pp. 123-128.

85. Newsholme, p. 136.

86. The Panel Committee of London, "Memorandum of the Panel Committee Upon the Modifications and Extensions of the Medical and Sanatorium Benefits Under the Scheme of National Insurance," 22 May 1917.

87. PRO. MH 62/124., 9 April 1919. See "An Interim Report to the Minister of Health on Medical and Allied Services" (May 1920, reprint September 1950, King Edward's Hospital Fund for London).

88. The profession of course insisted that the two issues were not separate but tied closely together.

89. BMJ, "The British Medical Association's Proposal for a General Medical Service for the Nation" (26 April 1930), Supplement, pp. 165-182. Some minor alterations were made in 1933 and again in 1938, but the basic framework of the scheme remained the same.

90. General Services Committee, session 1929-1930. GSG 15, 29 October 1929. In a memorandum to the Committee, Alfred Cox wrote "I think we should definitely aim at making a popular appeal for it. Such a plan and such an appeal would forestall the Labout Party . . ."

91. BMJ, "A General Medical Service" (26 April 1930), Supplement, pp. 169-170.

92. Ibid.

93. General Services Committee, session 1929-1930. GSG 15. 29 October 1929.

94. Health Services Committee, session 1937-1938. HS 14, undated memorandum from H. B. Brackenbury.

95. Wand.

96. Herbert J. Patterson, "A Debate on a State Medical Service," *The Post Graduate Medical Journal*, 15 (April 1939), pp. 112-129.

97. Douglass W. Orr and Jean Walker Orr, *Health Insurance with Medical Care* (New York: Macmillan Company, 1938), p. 157.

98. See Joint Committee of the BMA and the TUC, BMA Archives.

99. Insurance Acts Committee, session 1932-1933. IAC 22, 17 November 1932.

100. Insurance Acts Committee, session 1933-1934. IAC 6, 3 November 1933.

101. PRO. MH 58/238, 6 August 1930.

102. *Ibid*., 4 July 1934.

103. *Ibid*., 6 August 1930.

104. *Ibid*., 20 February 1934.

105. *Ibid*., 11 November 1934.

106. Insurance Acts Committee, session 1934-1935. IA 14. 15 November 1934.

107. Wand.

108. Jeanne C. Brand, *Doctors and the State* (Baltimore: The Johns Hopkins Press, 1965), p. 198. See PRO. MH 58/240., Leicester Public Medical Service to Addison, 1 May 1918.

109. General Practice Committee, session 1938-1939, GP 19, 30 November 1938.

110. Insurance Acts Committee, session 1921-1922. Unnumbered, 12 May 1922.

111. Insurance Acts Committee, session 1932-1933. IA 22, 17 November 1932.

112. *BMJ* (25 June 1938), *Supplement*, p. 398.

113. PRO. MH 58/239, 12 August 1933.

114. BMJ (4 December 1937), Supplement, p. 334.

115. General Practice Committee, session 1938-1939. GP 19, 30 November 1930.

116. Colin-Russ.

117. General Practice Committee, session 1938-1939. GP 1, 9 September 1938.

118. P.E.P., pp. 133-135.

119. Charles Hill and John Woodcock, The National Health Service (London: Christopher Johnson, 1949).

120. Charles Hill (cr. Baron 1963, Life Peer) was Medical Secretary of the BMA from 1944 until 1950. He helped lead the BMA's resistance to the National Health Service. See Charles Hill, Both Sides of the Hill (London: Heinemann 1964).

121. Harry Eckstein, Pressure Group Politics: The Case of the British Medical Association (Stanford, California: Stanford University Press, 1960).

CHAPTER V

Facing the Slump: Over Prescribing and Lax Certification

To some degree all social welfare expenditures are subject to the criticism of those who see them as fiscally inefficient or a haven for the lazy. The national health insurance act was no different. From the outset, critics insisted that millions from the nation's treasury were being wasted by careless administrators and doctors, the lack of a means test and outright fraud by the undeserving insured. In the 1920s and 1930s, such accusations were endemic and represented perhaps the most enduring aspect of British social politics before the second world war.

One of the primary targets of the anti-wasters was always the panel medical service. Insurance practitioners potentially held the power of financial life and death over the entire health side of the insurance scheme because it was only upon their signatures that insured persons gained access to drugs and cash sickness benefits. Yet, panel doctors were not in 1913 made subject to any kind of clinical supervision and vast expenditures were based merely on the doctors' opinions of ill health. The approved societies, who were responsible for the soundness of insurance funds, objected to this lack of control and continually sought the administrative authority to curb what they saw as the kindhearted nature and natural inefficiency of the medical profession. Throughout the history of insurance administration, the arguments of the societies attracted many supporters but successive governments refused to forge an administrative link between sickness and medical benefits.[1] Despite this, neither government officials nor the B.M.A. could stand idly by and allow charges of widespread over prescribing and lax certification to persist unanswered.

In the past social historians have seen the problem of waste in the operation of the insurance act as a political issue debated in Cabinet and Parliament under the general topic of malingering.[2] Without a doubt this view from the top is an important key to understanding social politics during the depression years. From the perspective of the doctors working the act and the administrators overseeing the panel system's general operation, however, the incessant rhetoric of approved societies and politicians on the make had another dimension. Those in daily contact with the health insurance scheme had to do more than make angry speeches in the House of Commons about waste and malingering patients. They had actually to define such vague terms as over prescribing and lax certification and construct realistic methods of dealing with cases of waste and inefficiency. Such tasks not only provided the act's doctors and administrators with practical administrative dilemmas but moral choices as well. They were to discover that, unlike the building of public highways or the construction of ships, health administration was as inexact as the services it sought to deliver.

Over Prescribing

When the first medical benefit regulations went into effect in 1913, part of the panel practitioner's remuneration depended upon the possibility of saving some part of the amount provisionally set aside to meet the costs of medicines and appliances. As noted earlier in this study, if a particular area's expenditure did not exceed an average drug cost of 2s. per insured person, then panel doctors were granted all or part of the so-called floating sixpence. This gave medical service practitioners a personal interest in seeing that the value of drug prescriptions did not exceed an annual rate of 2s. per patient.[3] Some panel doctors continued to do their own dispensing but many chose to turn the responsibility over to the local chemists' panel.[4] When a prescription was issued by a panel practitioner, the chemist had to honor it and in turn charge the local drug fund according to an agreed drug tariff plus a small dispensing fee.[5]

From the act's first month of operation it was apparent that the charges against the drug fund were going to be more than anticipated. In part this was due to the higher than expected sick rate. But at the same time there was a widespread suspicion that doctors too readily supplied drugs and medical appliances to patients. Insured persons flooded chemist shops demanding such items as bandages, catheters, cotton wool, gauze, ice bags, lints, splints, eyedroppers and bath and hypodermic syringes.[6] Moreover, nearly all patients expected to be supplied with the traditional bottle of medicine which consisted of various malt mixtures or cod liver oil. There were even some scattered instances of panel men who prescribed food for their malnourished patients.[7] The prescribing of proprietary drugs, though, represented the largest drain upon the drug fund.[8] These were far more expensive, usually because of extra coloring or the addition of sugar or syrup, than their generic equivalents. Nonetheless, if a doctor specified a particular brand name, the chemist had no choice but to honor the prescription and, lacking any standard other than the doctor's judgment, local committees could do little to reduce drug costs.

Critics asserted that the root cause of the heavy drug fund expenditures was over prescribing by a few panel men who did not pay enough attention to the cost of medicines and appliances. On 6 March 1914 a special conference of Lancashire insurance committees was held at Blackburn in order to discuss high drug costs and the blame was placed squarely upon the shoulders of doctors.[9] The insurance commissioners announced that they too felt that doctors were at fault. In a 1914 memorandum they stated that "a considerable portion of the charges upon the drug funds could have been avoided without loss of efficiency." In large part, the Commissioners continued, over prescribing was due to "habit, either on the part of individual practitioners or of the practitioners in a particular district..." who prescribe "in excess of what may be regarded as necessary for the health of their patients."[10]

Doctors, though, pointed out with some merit that the act

demanded that they do their best for panel patients. It was not their job to cut corners in the name of economy. Most local insurance committees accepted these medical arguments for lack of any way to deal effectively with the high drug charges during the panel system's first years. Even in Salford, which had one of the highest prescription rates, the Insurance Committee decided not to surcharge any doctors who had been accused of prescribing too generously.[11] Nonetheless, the London Local Insurance Committee, with its responsibility for the nation's largest insurance area, could not afford to be so casual about the heavy costs to its drug fund.

In 1913, the London Insurance Committee began a program of spot investigations of the prescribing habits of the local medical service doctors.[12] The London medical community, however, complained that the investigation of prescription records was a direct threat to medical independence and asked that it be ended. Despite this objection, the Local Insurance Committee insisted that their scheme be allowed to continue until the end of 1914. By mid-1914, though, the spot checking of panel medical service prescriptions was brought to an end. After many hours of work and a total expenditure of £2,400 the net savings for the drug fund was only £500.[13]

In the first scheme's place the Insurance Committee established a Local Pharmaceutical Committee, composed of chemists, whose own drug capitation fee was threatened by over prescribing. This new committee was given the responsibility of referring suspected over prescribers to the Local Panel Committee for disciplinary action.[14] The new plan rarely resulted in measures being taken against insurance doctors, because of the hostility between the local medical leaders and the spokesmen for the London chemists. Medical men charged that the Pharmaceutical Committee was not selective enough and complained especially loudly when in April 1914, the chemists submitted 500 names for investigation.[15] It is therefore not very surprising to find that London's drug charges continued to be high. In the first quarter of 1914 alone the total claims against London's £150,000 fund amounted to £60,000.[16] At the end of the second year of the act's work the final drug bill came to £188,236 with an average cost per prescription for 1914 of 9.3d, in contrast to 7.4d. the year before.[17]

The inability of London and nearly all other panel areas to reduce drug charges was disturbing to the Insurance Commissioners. In response to the steadily rising costs they issued a circular in September 1914 to all insurance commitees in an attempt to lay down guidelines for prescribing. Doctors were warned about a heavy reliance upon proprietary drugs and stock mixtures but as in London the Commissioners had to leave the powers to curb any abuses in the hands of the local panel committees because neither chemists or local administrators were able to exercise any "therapeutic judgment."[18] Any other decision would clearly have worked against the insured class and angered the medical community.

Following the issue of the Insurance Commission's circular, drug charges did begin to fall but this was due more to the effects of the war than any action by the act's administrators. By the end of 1915 claims against London's drug fund had fallen to £142,615 and the value of the average prescription dropped to 7.8d.[19] Still, as a result of this decline, the accusations against panel men for over prescribing were momentarily put to rest in London as well as the rest of the country. Despite this, by 1917 doctors serving within the panel medical service were again asked to be more careful in their prescribing habits because the costs of drugs again began to rise.[20]

Medical men insisted that the reasons for the increasing costs were not quite as simple as critics liked to think. The wartime drug fund was at greater risk due to the continual withdrawal of the good lives from the insured population. No amount of corner cutting and patriotism would set these new actuarial realities right. But practitioners were also faced with a cultural problem. Long before the coming of the panel system, the bottle of medicine habit among the laboring classes had been a topic of concern among doctors. The bottle was sometimes filled with little more than colored water but usually one of several stock mixtures of vegetable nutrients and flavoring agents were used. Patients had grown to expect the dispensing of these mixtures. Therefore doctors, before and after the creation of the panel system, were often faced with patients who were not satisfied until a filled bottle was given.[21]

The cost of the bottle of medicine was usually minimal and in most cases less than the 2d. dispensing fee allowed chemists. The refusal of a panel practitioner to prescribe such all-purpose remedies could well lose him the patient to a more generous doctor. As a result, many medical men decided not to risk the potential loss. In any event, it was pointed out that the bottle of medicine habit was not all that insidious. In many instances the nutrients made up for insufficient diet and possibly prevented serious disease that could arise from chronic anaemia.[22]

Medical technology too, helped to assure that drug costs would remain high. The late nineteenth century marked the beginning of the modern patent drug industry. Heavily advertised, the new remedies ranged from simple laxatives to complex chemical based drugs. Admittedly many of these proprietary medicines were little more than the accustomed tonics, adding only expense, but it cannot be denied that the growing drug industry provided practitioners with effective weapons against sickness.[23] As drug research continued, doctors had available new, complex and increasingly expensive medicine. Medical spokesmen complained that the profession could not be faulted for trying to provide the best possible care for the insured class. Thus, it was pointed out with some pleasure by doctors that critics could not have both low cost and good medical service.[24]

Clearly, at its core, over prescribing was a matter of

medical standards and the framers of the insurance act's medical benefit had chosen not to apply any. As with excess sickness, over prescribing was less a fact than an opinion. After all, there was nothing sacred about the actuarial basis of the drug fund. Nonetheless, as the war came to a close, one of the first items to be discussed was the cost of panel supplied drugs which in 1920 stood at £1,247,137 for England and Wales.[25]

Despite the concern for rising drug costs in the immediate postwar period the reforming zeal of the new Ministry of Health overshadowed narrow economic concerns. The 1920 medical benefit regulations abandoned the floating sixpence when the panel capitation fee was raised. Social liberals and even some approved societies had long asserted that the original system encouraged some panel doctors to withhold prescriptions for medicines or appliances from needy insured patients so that the floating sixpence would be credited to themselves.[26] After 1920, though, the Ministry of Health still recognized a need to hold the panel medical service doctors accountable for their prescribing habits. To offset any lack of caution, the Ministry gave the newly appointed regional medical officer corps the responsibility for carrying out investigations of doctors suspected of over prescribing. However, appropriations to carry out these investigating duties were held up pending the Geddes Report.[27]

It was not until 1922 when charges against the insurance drug fund in England and Wales rose to £1,337,300 that the

Ministry decided to reopen the possibility of assigning its RMOs the task of investigating alleged cases of over prescribing.[28] The Insurance Department within the Ministry of Health complained that since the abandonment of the floating sixpence, panel committees had all but ceased to grapple with the over prescribing issue. Writing to L. G. Brock, James Smith-Whitaker noted that the Ministry of Health's Medical Benefit Committee revealed that there was a "marked inactivity on the issue of over prescribing by a large number of Panel Committees. The present system of depending on Panel Committees is not effective - it has broken down and a new system must be devised."[29] Clearly self-regulation by each individual doctor had to come to an end. Nonetheless at the same time Smith-Whitaker reminded his colleague that any plan of RMO inspections had to be light-handed enough to avoid jeopardizing the insured population with enforced under prescribing. In view of this, the Ministry in June 1922 created local pricing bureaus that were given the responsibility of collecting data on the cost of drugs prescribed by each individual practitioner within the panel medical service.[30]

Panel areas with exceptionally high costs were to be targeted for attention by the regional medical officers, who were to confer with the local panel committee and prepare cases against medical men with excessive prescription costs. Any doctor formally charged was first privately interviewed and allowed to defend himself. If an adequate defense was not provided then formal, but confidential, disciplinary hearings were begun. The first prescribing investigations began in late 1922 but due in part to the lack of enough full-time RMOs, panel committees were not required to undertake inquiries. In addition the B.M.A. was not entirely comfortable with these arrangements and in light of the ongoing capitation dispute the Ministry felt that it should not force the issue.[31] The profession's leaders feared all non-medical interference and Smith-Whitaker warned his colleagues that the B.M.A. was "not fully supporting the new procedures."[32]

The B.M.A., though, was prepared to accept the ministerial appointment of a Drug Advisory Committee. This Committee, made up of both medical practitioners and chemists, was given the responsibility of determining what drugs and appliances ought to be included or excluded from the scope of the medical benefit. The findings of this Committee were to serve as a basis for the provision of guidelines to panel doctors. In turn, the Advisory Committee could also hear evidence concerning new drugs and advise the Ministry of their medical value. In order to complement this structure on the national level, local insurance committees were asked to appoint their own drug advisory committees. In this way localities could draw up their own drug formularies and include items that were of specific importance to a particular panel area.[33]

These measures of the early twenties may seem halfhearted but it must be remembered that, for the Ministry, the problem of prescribing costs was one of propaganda. By making panel doctors aware of their economic impact upon the finances of the act it was hoped that practitioners would be cautious when precribing. Moreover, ministerial officials understood that no one, least of all themselves, knew the actual extent of the so-called over prescribing. To be forced to act rashly by the scheme's political critics would almost certainly damage relations with the medical profession and might very well cost lives. Therefore, a 1922 ministerial circular to RMOs reminded them that they must be on guard against "underprescribing too, that will jeapordize the insured person."[34]

The over prescribing issue continued to force its way to the surface as the cost of panel prescribed drugs and appliances continued to rise. By 1926 expenditures in England and Wales had grown to Ł1,729,073 from a 1921 level of Ł1,189,450 and the per head cost had advanced from 2s.22.1/4d. to 3s.1.4d.[34] To be sure there were more insured persons by 1926 but the sharp increase in cost was in the face of a general decline in the wholesale value of average ingredients.[35]

The rising drug expenditures were attributed to several factors. Panel doctors, it was claimed, had not been sufficiently careful to see that their directions were always clear to patients. As a result those receiving the drugs sometimes took larger than necessary doses. Practitioners had not always heeded the warnings about the prescription of proprietary drugs and there also seemed to be a bias towards new and expensive medicines. In addition dangerous, narcotic-based remedies were increasingly called for by panel doctors. Moreover, despite repeated warnings, practitioners and chemists alike still seemed to be including expensive flavoring agents which at times cost more than the drug itself. A report by the Dundee Panel Committee noted that "a number of prescribers are not content to add a simple syrup to a mixture but require this syrup to be flavoured with Virginian prune or tolu and frequently to be conveyed in a vehicle of chloroform water. The addition of chloroform water to a prescription containing syrup of squills adds 1 1/2d. to its cost."[36] There were other complaints too. Some doctors were accused of prescribing various malt mixtures and cod liver oil in huge quantities and there were reports that similar ingredients were combined unnecessarily.[37] Finally, not all panel committees had prepared drug formularies in order to aid panel doctors when prescribing for insured patients.

In February 1926, the Ministry of Health received the results of a comparative study that it had carried out in Leeds and Bradford.[38] The two similar industrial towns, only nine miles apart, were not at all similar in their prescribing costs. Leeds had experienced an average cost per prescription of 8.6d; the Bradford charges were 8.1d. The most significant difference, however, was in the average number of prescriptions per patient. The Leeds panel patient received an average of 4.5 prescriptions during the survey; the insured population of Bradford averaged only 3.1. The difference, the Ministry's staff concluded, was that the doctors in Bradford were "far more interested in their work" and their own panel committee, in contrast to the one in Leeds, provided "active leadership and constant propaganda about insurance issues."[39] Moreover, Leeds and Bradford were not alone in having greatly differing prescription costs. Places such as Gateshead, Middlesbrough, Kingston-Upon-Hull and Grimsby, though neighbors geographically, were far apart in their panel drug charges.[40] Such wide variations could hardly be tolerated and in the words of L. G. Brock, "the sooner action was taken the better."[41]

In July 1926, James Smith-Whitaker prepared and issued a memorandum dealing with the Ministry's limited investigations of the rising drug costs.[42] The memorandum, distributed in August, informed each panel committee that disciplinary procedures and RMO investigations were going to be given new life. Still, it was clear to the Ministry that it needed to provide more direction for panel doctors and be more specific about what was expected of them with regard to the prescription of drugs. Reliance on local initiative to construct formularies had clearly failed. Some of these were far too restrictive and others did little but list every imaginable medicinal mixture. It was therefore proposed to the Insurance Acts Committee that it cooperate in the creation of a drug formulary. The B.M.A. readily accepted this responsibility and with the approved society threat diminished the Insurance

Acts Committee also agreed to help develop a workable disciplinary procedure.[43]

The structure of the disciplinary machinery for over prescribing was placed, as were all disciplinary matters, in the hands of the local panel committees. Their judgments were based upon a system of comparative analysis. Panel practitioners in each area were divided into three groups by the local pricing bureaus. At the end of each quarter chemists were required to bundle the prescriptions issued by each medical man and send them to the local pricing bureau.[44] A form was then prepared, listing the frequency of prescribing and the average cost per head for each panel doctor. These forms were then sent to the practitioner, the local pharmaceutical and medical committees and the Ministry of Health.[45] Should the cost of an individual man's prescriptions seem abnormally high when compared to others in the same area, then the RMO was to seek an explanation. If none was offered or if proof of special conditions was not presented, then the RMO could ask for a more formal disciplinary hearing by the panel committee.

The national formulary was not completed until 1929 and therefore the scheme of comparative analysis of prescribing patterns did not go into effect until 1930. In mid-1927 however, chemists had been told that they were to substitute generic drugs for proprietary drugs, unless panel doctors specifically stated that this should not be done.[46] The B.M.A., too, moved to honor ts promise to the government to cooperate fully with the efforts o reduce drug expenditures. In January 1928 the Insurance Acts ommittee issued a memorandum to all panel doctors cautioning hem to be careful.[47] This was the beginning of a full-fledged ropaganda campaign aimed at waste and the Ministry was so impressed y the B.M.A. memorandum that it ordered seventy-five copies for tself.[48] Panel committees were exhorted to work closely with he regional medical officers and even before the 1930 formal egulations took effect, prescribing investigations increased.[49]

The number of panel practitioners charged with over prescribing as never large but example rather than punishment was the main oal of those concerned with the escalating cost of drugs. In 928 forty-five doctors had deductions made from their panel hecks for abuses such as ordering 520 pounds of cod liver oil nd malt for only 179 insured patients. By the end of 1929, ,369 men had been investigated by regional medical officers. Of hese, 147 received warning letters following an investigation nd twenty-nine of thirty men referred for formal hearings suffered eductions in their panel incomes. In 1930, the first year of oth the national formulary and a systematic comparative analysis f prescribing costs, 1,885 doctors were investigated but only hirteen panel men were punished for excessive prescribing.[50]

Considering the millions of prescriptions issued, this was small return for all the time and effort devoted to over prescribing by the Ministry of Health. Thus, it is apparent that over prescribing was never more than a minor abuse within the panel medical service, even though as late as 1937 a Minister of Health, Sir Kingsley Wood, claimed that increased drug costs were "out of all proportion to the increase in the insured population."[51]

To be sure a minority of medical men new to industrial practice had prescribed proprietary drugs for their panel patients when generic equivalents would have done just as well. This difficulty was quickly resolved as practitioners were informed by official circulars, the medical press and the RMO corps that patent medicines were to be used only when there were no alternatives.[52] Moreover, if a question arose, most panel men had the national formulary on their desks by 1930. All of this no doubt resulted in some savings but in all probability charges against the insurance drug fund were stimulated by far more complex forces than over prescribing.[53] From 1928 until 1930, when the anti-prescribing compaign was at its most earnest, the value of the average panel prescription did indeed fall. Nonetheless, the average cost of each panel prescription was stable during 1931 and 1932 but from 1933 through 1937 prescription values rose steadily each year.[54] Despite this, the number of medical men who actually had deductions from their panel checks for over prescribing never exceeded ten per year after 1930.[55]

Panel drug costs were therefore controlled by forces other than medical carelessness. As in the discussion of the sickness rate in 1913, no one really knew the quantity of medicine that would be needed to meet the legitimate demands of panel patients. The actuarial estimates used to determine drug costs had been based on the experience of friendly societies, who had tightly regulated their own expenditures on medicines. The government had felt in 1911 that the 2s. per head devoted to drugs by the insurance fund was more than adequate. Studies had shown that many societies actually spent less than 1s. per patient.[56] The difference was that practitioners under the insurance scheme had been told to do their best for patients. Without the oversight of penny-pinching club officers, most doctors prescribed drugs according to the medical needs of patients. As George Newman, Chief Medical Officer of Health, noted in 1933, increasing drug costs were "undoubtedly due to the necessity for prescribing expensive forms of treatment (e.g. insulin, liver extract, etc.) which have been introduced in recent years."[57]

Weather, too, played an important role in determining the value of average prescriptions as well as the total cost of panel medicines. Severe winters raised the charges against the drug fund significantly as did national bouts with influenza.[58] These were of course beyond the control of doctors and administrators alike. But there is one final factor that seems to have determined the amount of medicine prescribed by panel doctors. The English as a people, were clearly, "medicine drinkers."[59] Throughout the history of the insurance act, doctors in Scotland prescribed only half as much medicine as their English colleagues. Yet this was not reflected in the national sickness rate.[60] The reason for the difference was apparently cultural. As pointed out earlier, the bottle of medicine habit had long been the hallmark of industrial private practice. English patients expected to receive one every time they visited a doctor and medical men, by custom, fully expected to give them a "fill-up."[61] In contrast, Scotland had no similar tradition and there was little anyone could do to change the habits of Englishmen overnight.[62]

Given the administrative limits imposed by an act that guaranteed the clinical freedom of practitioners, there was really no precise way of determining the scope of the over prescribing problem. At any rate, even the most vocal critics of medical prescribing habits conceded that the potential savings were small. At the most, ten to twenty thousand pounds might have been saved nationally if strict administrative measures had been taken. However, the cost of inspection and perhaps of health would, as in London in 1914, have made any return negligible at best. The Insurance Department of the Ministry of Health was fully aware of this and although it engaged in occasional propaganda campaigns, it never moved to strengthen its investigative procedures after 1930.

Lax Certification

Over prescribing was an irritating but minor problem for the insurance medical service. The same, however, cannot be said of what became known as the lax certification of illness. This issue was at the center of the political antagonism between the approved societies and the medical profession and it cut to the heart of the administration of the health benefit. At stake were not thousands but millions of pounds that could be the difference between financial ruin and stability for national health insurance.[63]

The societies had a vested interest in seeing that the rate of medical sickness certification was kept to a bare minimum. They had the responsibility of administering the cash sickness and disablement benefits to most of the insured class. Should the claims exceed the allotted reserves, the societies were required to make up the difference from their private funds. Despite this, panel doctors and not the societies had the power to decide who would receive the sickness benefit.

When it became apparent in 1913 that the scheme's sickness experience exceeded its actuarial estimates, societies began to complain loudly that the sickness rate was not a matter of actuarial error but due instead to widespread malingering among the insured class.[64] Panel patients, the societies said, were attempting to make good on Lloyd George's promise of ninepence for fourpence. It was conceded, though, that the fault did not lie with the insured, who were expected to be lazy and naturally prone to malingering. The societies pointed their fingers at the doctors of the panel medical service who, they charged, carelessly issued national insurance certificates to perfectly fit patients in order to build up the size of their lists. The government too, was guilty because it, in the eyes of the societies, had failed to enforce a high standard of certification in order to safeguard the insurance fund.[65]

Throughout the first year of the scheme's operation, the approved societies almost daily increased the volume of their complaints. Finally, the London Local Insurance Committee agreed to appoint six medical referees to investigate the charges. Beginning on October 1913, thirty societies sent the London referees over 700 cases of alleged malingering. After beginning their examination of referred individuals, the referees issued their first report in December. It revealed that of the 471 persons already examined, 208 had been declared capable of work. Most of these had originally been furnished with certificates for debility, anaemia and general weakness but 15% of those declared fit were listed as suffering from varying degrees of rheumatism and dyspepsia.

The ability to work with such chronic illnesses was certainly a matter of disagreement among medical men. Therefore despite the action by the London referees to remove nearly half of those examined from the sick list, their report did not lend its support to the societies' accusations that the insurance scheme's doctors harbored malingering on a vast scale. Instead the referees pointed out that their findings revealed a high degree of low vitality and mental inertia that was caused by lack of proper nourishment. The difficulty, of course, was that while many people among those examined could not be regarded as physically fit, they could not be certified as completely incapable of work either.

The few cases of discernable malingering uncovered were generally among the lowest paid workers, who it may be assumed, received nearly as much or more from their sickness benefit than from their pay packet.[66] Moreover, as The New Statesmen pointed out in its commentary on the London report, the societies selected the cases to be examined and "it is indeed remarkable that only 208 of 471 were pronounced capable of work."[67]

With the coming of the war the sickness claims among the insured population fell and by the end of 1917 it was reported that claims were 25% below 1914 levels.[68] After the war, it did not take long for the rate of certified illness to begin to rise. Seeing this the societies again began to accuse the panel medical doctors of failing in their duty. "We appreciate the doctors' difficulties" The National Insurance Gazette stated in February 1923, "and we ask for nothing unreasonable. But every approved society is getting certificates every week which ought not to be given."[69] For the societies the evidence seemed overwhelming. One approved society, the National United Order of Free Gardeners, reported that while the number of individual claims rose only slightly, the average number of sick days claimed rose from 5.25 in 1914 to 7.6 in 1923 for its male subscribers and from 7.74 to

12.96 for women. By 1927 though the society experienced an average length of illness of 9.14 days for men and 15.42 for its female members.[79]

Each approved society had its own experience with rising sickness claims. Some were far less affected than others but nationally claims upon the sickness funds of all societies rose rapidly after 1921.[71] A statistical study completed by Sir Alfred Watson, the Government Actuary, revealed that the sickness experience of the insured class from 1921 to 1927 showed that for men the number of sickness claims had risen by 51% and the disablement claims by 85%. The rates for women revealed an even more dramatic increase. For unmarried females the increase in sickness benefit claims had been 60% and certified disablement was up by 98%. Claims made by married women rose by 106% and disablement claims increased 159% between 1921 and 1927. The report, however, did not show a general rise in the length of insured illness. These rates for men and unmarried women had actually decreased from the 1921 level. Only married women increased their average duration of illness during the period.[72]

From the vantage point of 1920 or 1921 it was difficult to be sure of the nature or causes of the increasing sickness claims. Before 1918 the act had never functioned under normal conditions. Furthermore, the influenza pandemic of 1919 had destroyed any hope of accurately measuring the sick rate among the insured until the act had time to work in less extraordinary times. The societies however, fearing for their newly acquired surpluses, kept up their political rhetoric against malingering and careless doctors. "We can say to the doctors," noted The National Insurance Gazette, "that there is positively wholesale certification of a nature which needs their immediate attention ... The false certificates given by the doctors to persons who are not ill, are in fact robbing persons who are ill of services which they need."[73] In 1923 Denton Woodhead, speaking for the National Federation of Rural Approved Societies, charged that "a certain number of doctors - not a negligible number - issued certificates which were not reliable, or were even dishonest."[74] For the societies, the lack of care shown by doctors had only served to increase the natural level of malingering by the insured and if the medical profession would not control its members then the Ministry of Health, charged the Amalgamated Monthly, must see that the "funds of the approved societies are also protected."[75]

While the societies found many eager allies in the postwar Parliament the medical profession claimed that whatever the sickness rate, doctors could not be blamed. Speaking before the members of the Faculty of Insurance in York, Dr. J. C. Lyth, Honorary Secretary of the York Local Medical and Panel Committee, put the profession's position squarely before the societies. Noting the fundamental lack of precision in medical science, Lyth pointed to the one question that he felt the societies had lost sight of.

> "Medical practitioners as a profession are not trained to regard the issuing of medical certificates as their main object of life, nor even as an important part of it. The Hippocratic oath, which still forms the ideal after which every medical student is trained to strive, contains no mention of medical certification. Yet we must recognize the fact that we have come to live in a bureaucratic age; more and more our lives are governed by rules and regulations. But the practice of medicine is essentially difficult to tie up into parcels with red tape; all sorts of unforseen side issues crop up. However good rules may be, if too rigidly applied they may become a tyranny."[76]

Dr. Lyth's comments, however, had little impact upon those society officials who feared for the funds in their possession. To them, malingering was a national scandal and the medical profession was the primary contributor to the problem. No matter how much evidence the medical leaders mustered to show that the rising demands upon the act were products of increasing medical standards and familiarity with the panel service, the societies were not going to be satisfied.[77] Nothing short of the complete domination of the medical benefit and panel doctors was likely to make the societies happy and this would have been intolerable for the profession.

On the surface the approved societies' criticisms of the certification habits of the profession may seem legitimate. This view was certainly accepted by the friends of the societies in Parliament and the press.[78] Still, the problem of lax certification was far more complex than critics admitted. Just as in over prescribing, it was not a problem that could be defined accurately by statistics. To be sure, there were kindhearted medical men who could always be counted on for an insurance sickness certificate. Some doctors, too, sought to build their panel lists by acquiring a reputation as soft touches. At the same time, medical men were aware that malingering patients did sometimes shop from doctor to doctor for certificates.

Still, as the profession correctly asserted, medical work was far from a precise art and the diagnostic skills of its practitioners varied greatly. Moreover, what appeared as illness to one doctor was easily interpreted as good health by another. The framers of the act recognized this difficulty but chose to accept it rather than open the panel system to the abuses of the old clubs and the stigma of a Poor Law means test. Thus, each doctor was allowed to determine for himself his own standards of sickness and certification. Quite properly, health and sickness retained their individual nature under the insurance act. Therefore, as long as the independence of the insurance medical service remained intact, lax certification would remain an elusive question, one that the insurance bureaucracy could never come to grips with despite the intense political pressure applied by the approved societies.

The Insurance Department of the Ministry of Health was in the uncomfortable position of having to reconcile the differences between the approved societies and the medical profession. In order to reduce the friction between the two groups the Ministry gave its regional medical officers the primary responsibility for the investigation of cases of lax certification and malingering in 1920. This plan was immediately accepted by both doctors and the societies as a suitable middle course. The societies now could refer all suspected malingerers to an independent medical referee and panel practitioners were assured of continued independence and medical privacy.[79] The RMOs though were immediately swamped by referrals and every year the number of persons investigated rose. In 1921 RMOs had 69,544 referrals; in 1922, 113,685; and by 1928, 372,324.[80]

The majority of referrals resulted in the suspension of the sickness benefit. In England and Wales 59% of those summoned for RMO examination between 1922 and 1925 were declared fit for work. For the same years the Scottish rate was only slightly lower with 57%. For their part, spokesmen for the panel medical service argued that the high rate of off benefit declarations was only the natural outcome of what doctors saw as a campaign of harassment against their panel patients.[81] Practitioners stressed that many insured persons were intimidated by the official summons sent by the regional medical officer. As a result genuinely ill people failed to report for their examination and were prematurely forced to return to work because their sickness benefit was automatically suspended. "Experience" a British Medical Journal pointed out, "seems to show that the proportion of such patients to those who are actually summoned to attend referee sessions may be as high as 4 or 5 percent ... Such persons often do not seek a final certificate and resume work at once."[82] Doctors also noted that the RMO examination usually took place ten to fourteen days after referral, which itself was often not made immediately after the original diagnosis. Judgments about the certification practices of medical men under such circumstances were hardly creditable.[83]

Other problems remained as well. The insurance medical and sickness benefits did not extend to pregnancy. Yet, pregnancy often aggravated other chronic but not serious disabilities. In such cases most panel doctors felt fully justified in issuing sickness certificates and it is apparent that many insured pregnant women were placed on the sickness list sometime during their pregnancy.[84] Doctors defended this as good medical practice. Some medical men even asserted that women, upon reaching their eighth month of pregnancy, should automatically be granted a sickness certificate.[85] Still, there could be little doubt that such attitudes, no matter how laudable, contributed to the rising benefit claims. On a broader level, the difficulty over pregnancy again pointed to the central problem in the certification issue. Sickness was a matter of personal interpretation with a basis in intuition as much science.

Officials inside the Ministry of Health were sensitive to the arguments of medical men for caution when considering the experience of the RMO service in the early twenties. The Ministry was, however, under an almost constant attack by approved societies and their anti-waste allies to reduce the assumed but far from proved level of malingering. In addition, as the economic situation worsened after 1921, the Treasury became increasingly suspicious that the sickness benefit fund was being drained of its resources by kindhearted doctors who certified the unemployed as ill or disabled.[86]

Still the Ministry of Health's Insurance Department did not show any willingness to grapple seriously with the issue of lax certification. Not only was there some doubt about whether lax certification actually existed on a broad scale, but it was recognized that it would be expensive, time-consuming and perhaps futile to prove cases against individual doctors. However, beyond the enormity of the task, the ministerial officials realized that they would have to define lax certification administratively, which could only rest upon an administrative definition of fitness to work and acceptable sickness. The prospect of developing such standards bordered on a civil servant's nightmare.

In the mid-1920s, the Ministry sought to avoid the quicksand of the certification issue by relying on propaganda and minor administrative changes rather than discipline. In 1924 new certification rules were brought into force.[87] The new guidelines made it the panel doctor's responsibility to see that his patient's name and address on the sickness certificate were accurate and clearly written. This, it was hoped, would make it easier for societies to keep track of their members. The regulations also required a practitioner to state as precisely as possible his diagnostic opinion of the patient's condition.[88] Accompanying the 1924 medical benefit regulations, the Ministry issued a series of new circulars advising medical men to be more careful when certifying illness. Finally in 1925 the Ministry of Health sought to establish a central medical index, in order to consolidate the government's information about each panel doctor, but this plan was never adopted. The scheme fell through because the Scottish Insurance Office and the Admiralty refused to make their records on medical practitioners available to the Ministry of Health.[89]

For the most part, the Ministry of Health's Insurance Department agreed with the profession's assertion that lax certification was, where it existed, a personal rather than national problem. Reflecting this, the activities of the Ministry in the mid-twenties were aimed at propagandizing the profession. It was hoped that this would help to reduce any abuses that existed and also appease the societies even though benefit claims continued to climb steadily. Two unconnected events, however, forced the Ministry to adopt a more assertive policy by 1928.

During the 1926 general strike, many approved societies nervously referred all sickness claims to regional medical officers.[90] Long before, the strike society officials had watched the rate of illness rise steadily. The greatest increases in the rate of certification furthermore had been in the nation's coal districts.[91] It was apparent that many panel medical men were finding the back pains of miners especially debilitating and that they were in some cases attempting to ease the hardship of unemployment as well as sickness.[92]

Nonetheless the connection between increasing unemployment and the rising rate of certification was not as firm as the societies liked to assume. To be sure many insured men and women who lost their jobs sought relief through their panel doctors and some of these could certainly be legitimately accused of malingering. Still there is little evidence that these people were not, in general, certifiably ill. Statistically there is no correlation between sickness claims and unemployment when looking at the period as a whole. The rate of unemployment fluctuated but insurance claims rose steadily. Yet the rate of off benefit declarations never strayed far from 60% of those summoned, even though the number of referred patients also rose yearly. Two factors, much more important than malingering, seem plausible explanations for the level of sickness. First, as the system became a fixture of English life, the insured became more familiar with its benefits and were more willing to make use of the services offered by the act. Second, unemployment may have in fact encouraged sickness claims but not in the way envisioned by the societies. Unemployment made it easier for individuals to seek medical advice about illnesses, chronic or otherwise, that would have been ignored in more prosperous times. After all, the members of the insured class were at the bottom of working society. The loss of a day's pay in order to visit a doctor's surgery was a hardship that most patients liked to avoid. Due to unemployment this economic barrier no longer existed and this no doubt led to increased claims, but this made the sickness claims of the unemployed no less legitimate.

During the winter of 1926-1927 the rise in the rate of sickness claims was even sharper than it had been in the preceding years due to an increase in the incidence of influenza.[93] This only raised the level of anxiety among the approved societies and it was clear that the Ministry of Health had to take a firmer position. In order to devise a scheme to investigate and reduce the increasing insurance benefit claims, the Ministry of Health asked the B.M.A. for its assistance in the spring of 1927. The medical organization, now resolved to improve its image in the wake of its political success, readily agreed to help and in April the Insurance Acts Committee was placed at the disposal of the Ministry. Together, the doctors and the Ministry hoped the issue of lax certification could be at last laid to rest.[94]

The first step was to review those factors that could lead to lax certification. Foremost among these were the regulations concerning change of doctor. Originally the insurance scheme's regulations let panel patients change practitioners once a year with seven days formal notice. In 1920, this was revised to allow insured persons to choose a new panel doctor every six months. This procedure was again altered in 1924 when all panel patients were allowed to remove their name from a doctor's list anytime without prior notice.[95]

The medical men had encouraged the adoption of the 1924 regulation, arguing that it moved the panel scheme one step closer to private practice. In spite of this expanded freedom, few patients ever removed themselves from a practitioner's list for any other reason than the doctor's death, retirement or their own departure from the panel area. The approved societies, however, were never happy with the 1924 regulation. They suspected that the ability to change doctors freely would encourage shopping around for sickness certificates. In addition, the societies pointed out that panel doctors, knowing that patients could easily leave, might be tempted to give into the demands of malingerers rather than risk the loss of income.[96]

Clearly the potential for such abuse was present so the Insurance Acts Committee agreed that some slight restrictions on the free movement of patients was a relatively harmless step in light of the obvious political goodwill which the profession might gain.[97] Therefore the Committee recommended to the Panel Conference, which met in October 1927, that fourteen days' notice be given before a patient changed doctor. The Conference readily accepted the new regulation and at the same time promised the Ministry its full cooperation in devising a method for dealing with lax certification.[98]

On 15 January 1928, the Ministry of Health began a series of four conferences with the Insurance Acts Committee that were to last into the late spring. At these dicussions the Ministry and the profession's representatives carried on a dialogue concerning the causes of the rising sickness rate.[99] The approved societies were allowed to voice their opinions about the medical profession's supposed contribution to the problem but the Ministry wisely kept them at arms length so as not to upset its friendly relationship with the B.M.A.[100]

The B.M.A. was at first wary of anything that smacked of outside interference with professional control over medical practice and discipline. Unlike over prescribing, the controversy surrounding certification was not as simple as eliminating flavorings or reducing the use of proprietary drugs. The issue was a doctor's right to diagnose and treat his patients according to his best professional judgment.

The Ministry of Health realized that it could not rest disciplinary procedures upon the existing certification regulations. As James Smith-Whitaker reminded L. G. Brock, a Principal Secretary within the Ministry, "the problem is how to establish the difference between failure to exercise sufficient care in forming an opinion in order to justify withholding a grant. Some guidance may be found in the regulations for prescribing," but noted Smith-Whitaker, "the two are not the same."[101] The Ministry, he asserted, had to be very cautious not to destroy the flexibility of panel doctors to deal with sickness effectively. Smith-Whitaker's colleagues inside the Ministry accepted his advice and the B.M.A. was quickly reassured that the government did not intend to limit the freedom of the individual panel practitioner. All disciplinary and investigative powers would be shared by the government and the profession. Under no conditions would these powers be delegated to either approved societies or local insurance committees. This put to rest any uneasiness the profession's leaders may have had and the process of establishing certification guidelines moved ahead quickly.[102]

On 15 August 1928, L. G. Brock wrote a lengthy letter to the Insurance Acts Committee in order to clarify some of the central issues surrounding the giving of sickness certificates. Doctors were told that the yardstick for certification was the ability of the patient to perform "the physical and mental process which constitute work."[103] Work, Brock argued vaguely, should not be interpreted, as it had been in the past by some doctors, as the ability to carry on the usual occupation. "Work means all work - not just ordinary occupation ... The patient should not be declared to be incapable of work unless the practitioner is satisfied that he is unfit to undertake remunerative work of any kind ..."[104] Only pregnancy was dealt with specifically in the Ministry's letter and here too, the Ministry did little to clarify the issue. Practitioners were reminded that pregnancy was not within the scope of the sickness benefit unless "real sickness" was diagnosed or that work would seriously injure the woman.[105] The meaning of "real sickness" however, was still to be defined by the panel doctor.

There is little doubt that Brock's August letter left most insurance practitioners as confused as ever about the certification guidelines. The Ministry had attempted to appease its critics while preserving the clinical independence of the panel medical service. To apply too rigid a standard or indeed any standard of sickness would have violated the interests of the insured population and thrust non-medical bureaucrats into a very delicate position. This arrangement, however, must have caused the Insurance Department of the Ministry to wonder more than once whether its principles did not effectively doom its efforts to define lax certification, let alone discipline guilty doctors.

It was hoped that the difficulties of definition would be circumvented by allowing the panel practitioners themselves to set the standards for certification. As in prescribing, it was decided to compile statistical averages of each medical man's rate of certification. The RMO corps, however, instead of a separate bureau, was given the job. The Ministry believed that each RMO would be able to spot men with disproportionately high rates of certified illness among their patients. If a closer examination of medical records revealed to the medical officer that a particular doctor had been careless in certifying illness and the problem could not be handled privately then the case was referred to the local panel committee. If the panel committee believed that there was sufficient evidence after examining individual cases of lax certification then, failing all informal warnings, a full report was sent to the Ministry of Health for disciplinary action. At the ministerial level, a special Medical Advisory Committee was established to advise the Ministry upon the technical aspects of each case and to determine whether negligence was proved.[106] Should the Ministry find that reasonable care had not been taken by a panel practitioner when certifying illness, then it had the power to deduct money from the guilty doctor's next quarterly check. As in other disciplinary cases, the Ministry could also order the accused medical man removed from the panel.[107]

Finally in July 1929, the B.M.A. formally accepted the establishment of the disciplinary machinery designed to deal with lax certification.[108] The plans for the new procedures had been delayed because the Ministry had come under attack from the National Association of Local Insurance Committees who demanded a role. Unlike the approved societies, the local insurance committees were not going to be allowed even to refer suspected cases of malingering and lax certification. The problem was more than one of administrative pride.[109] The approved societies were using the insurance committees as a way to become involved in panel discipline.[110] Three-fifths of all local committees were made up of representatives from the societies. Since they had been denied a formal role, the societies were trying to force their way into the process from another direction. If the Ministry allowed this ploy to work, it could be sure that the medical profession would withdraw from the negotiations. Facing this prospect, Arthur Robinson, Permanent Secretary to the Ministry of Health, noted that "we have spent the last 18 months in persuading the Insurance Acts Committee, not that any doctor ever gives certificates which he ought not give, but that, if there were such a doctor, it would be right to take money off him. The thrust of departmental policy is to get disciplinary standards ... and we are plainly lucky to have the Insurance Acts Committee support."[111]

Robinson's argument was accepted by the Ministry but the administrative infighting did not end once the Ministry had made its decision clear. Michael Heseltine, an Assistant Secretary to the Minister of Health, reported in August 1929 that "more and more Insurance Committees are upset with their exclusion from the lax certification negotiations and proceedings under the proposed regulations."[112] In addition, the autonomous Scottish Insurance Department also caused problems by refusing to allow the plans to apply in Scotland. (While the Welsh Commission was generally dominated by the decisions of the English Commission, Scotland had a long tradition of independence.) The Scottish Department argued that since 1922 it had carried out its own investigations of lax certification and these were handled at the local level by the insurance committees. Throughout August, 1929 Arthur Robinson tried to convince his Scottish counterpart, John Jeffrey, to accept the new procedures. He informed Jeffrey that unless Scotland agreed, the B.M.A., which was demanding uniformity throughout the United Kingdom, promised to withdraw its approval of the new discipline procedures.[113] Jeffrey, however, stubbornly refused to concede his department's independence. Finally, though, the B.M.A. agreed not to hold up the new regulations that were scheduled to go into effect in January 1930.[114]

The Scottish Insurance Department never relented but the new disciplinary procedures for lax certification came into force on schedule for England and Wales.[115] As in prescribing, the creation of an administrative mechanism to deal with lax certification was intended to serve more as a warning to doctors than an actual way of cutting down on malingering. Careless doctors were still to be dealt with politely, quietly and privately. Despite this, by early 1931 the Ministry had before it several petty cases against panel doctors that it felt should never have reached the ministerial level.

The most notable and certainly the most troublesome case involved the complaints of Mr. Denton Woodhead, Secretary of the Yorkshire Rural Friendly Society. Woodhead charged that not only were there doctors not conforming to certification rules but that local authorities refused to act against them.[116] When the

Ministry of Health refused to become involved, Woodhead angrily wrote to Sir Walter Kinnear, the Minister of Health, that he had been accorded a "lack of courtesy in connection with your department... I am exceedingly sorry to have to trouble you but we shall not tolerate such irregularities either by the Middlesbrough Insurance Committee or your department... I am coming up to London."[117] Once in London though, Woodhead found that Kinnear refused to receive him. Michael Heseltime noted that in the Ministry's view Mr. Woodhead had been the cause of "trouble out of all proportion to the importance of the case. This case is one in which in any other society ... a few minutes conversation on the telephone to the insurance committee on one hand, and between the clerk and the doctor on the other, would have settled the whole matter."[118]

Woodhead finally returned home but he as well as others continued to believe that lax certification was causing an immense amount of malingering.[119] The release in 1931 of an investigation of sickness on 5 May 1930 only served to add fuel to the anti-wasters' campaign against the act. The study by Sir Alfred Watson revealed that on that single day fully 12.5% of all certified patients were capable of work. Few of these people, though, the report insisted, were malingerers. Most were doing little more than waiting for their sickness certificate to expire and therefore following their doctors' advice before returning to work. Doctors, it seemed, had to be more precise in their dating of sickness certificates, although Watson noted practitioners could hardly be expected to pinpoint the exact day of recovery on a certificate.[120] In response to the findings of Alfred Watson and the rising political pressure that ignored the difficulties in administering a huge health care delivery system, the Ministry again revised the change of doctor regulation in March 1931. From 31 March insured patients were allowed to remove themselves from a panel practitioner's list only once each quarter and then only after a month's notice had been given. The Ministry also attempted to streamline its disciplinary procedures by regrouping panel committees into larger districts. This was done in order to relieve medical men of the embarrassing task of judging close friends and colleagues. By reducing the personal element in panel committee administrative duties it was hoped that doctors would be more stern with each other when examining evidence of lax certification as well as over prescribing.[121]

Despite all its effort, the national insurance bureaucracy appreciated that all attempts aimed at defining and reducing lax certification had proven to be cosmetic at best by August 1932. Michael Heseltime, in a candid departmental minute, wrote that, "the difficulties attendant on these investigations have been much greater than we anticipated when we first began interviewing practitioners on the subject..." The problems, Heseltine concluded, are "almost all traceable, I think, to the fact that the causal relation between the error we seek to demonstrate - the lack of reasonable care in the issue of certificates - and the facts we are able to adduce in evidence - chiefly derived from statistics of results of reference - is neither so direct nor so obvious as in the case of extravagant prescribing."[122]

The Ministry of Health's Insurance Department had never been eager to tackle the certification issue but the task had been forced upon it by politicians and approved societies. Clear-cut abuses were nearly impossible to detect but in the aftermath of the 1931 economic crises the Ministry's insurance officials felt that they had to begin to consider more formal and visible disciplinary actions. No longer would critics be appeased by a new memorandum or conferences with the Insurance Acts Committee.[123] Moreover, in light of the bankruptcy of the unemployment insurance fund in 1931 the Insurance Department was understandably nervous. As a result, the Ministry began to look for a case of alleged lax certification that could be used to underline its concern and placate some of the insurance act's critics.

The Ministry hoped to find a solid case of lax certification quickly but it was not until the end of 1934 that a seemingly indisputable one was discovered.[124] A Welsh practitioner, Dr. MacQuillian, was charged by his local panel committee with violating the rules of certification. The evidence was overwhelming, if circumstantial. In all of Wales, 49% of referrals to regional medical officers were declared off benefit. Dr. MacQuillian's region had a rate of just above 49% and the five medical practices adjoining his in Aberoycham experienced a 51% rate. In contrast Dr. MacQuillian had over 71% of his referred patients declared fit for work. Based upon this evidence, the local panel committee recommended that Ƅ10 be deducted from MacQuillian's next capitation payment. The Welsh practitioner refused to accept this verdict and in December 1934 he challenged the committee's recommendation. In his appeal he wrote that "I have never given a national health certificate to any insured person whose illness, in my opinion, did not merit one."[125] He went on to ask the Ministry to show which of his patients did not deserve a certificate. The Ministry had desired a test case to show its vigilance but now it was faced with an almost insurmountable defense. The judgment by the panel committee was based entirely upon comparative statistical averages but now the Ministry had to prove, case by case, that the decision to withhold money was correct.

The whole matter was full of potential political complications. Dr. R. Peterson, one of the Ministry's Senior Medical Officers, noted that "cases of this kind are obviously liable to be politically dangerous. Lax practitioners can make out a very plausible case to Parliament and the public, and it is easy to conceive the raising of a storm of protest against what might be construed as attempts to defraud insured persons of their rights."[126] At the same time failure to take up MacQuillian's challenge would give the approved societies, which were already disenchanted with the

Ministry's efforts, fresh ammunition for their attacks on civil servants and doctors. Therefore it was with a great deal of caution that the Ministry moved ahead on its investigation of the MacQuillian case.

It was hoped that specific examples might be found to confirm MacQuillian's lack of care when issuing insurance sickness certificates. Arthur McNalty, the Chief Medical officer, studied the case personally but what he found was not abuse. Instead, all the individual patients examined were shown to have been genuinely ill despite MacQuillian's ready admission that he gave his patients the benefit of doubt. "Most," McNalty reported, "seem to have benefited from prolonged convalescence and on one case Dr. MacQuillian seems to have been better than the RMO as the patient two weeks after being declared fit needed an operation." Cases such as MacQuillian's, McNalty advised, should never be allowed to "reach the judicial stage."[127]

Doctor MacQuillian never lost the £10 from his panel check. Instead, the Ministry issued a polite letter of warning, more to save its own face than to warn the Welsh doctor.[128] After years of attempting to define lax certification and devise a disciplinary procedure to deal with it, the Ministry had to admit complete failure. Writing to his colleagues, Dr. Peterson stressed that, "statistics from any source can at best afford only presumptive evidence of lack of care on the part of the doctor in issuing certificates... The line between illness and good health is not clear and cannot be on a single day. We can't hope, under present circumstances, to produce from individual cases convincing evidence of lack of reasonable care..."[129] The time and expense involved in collecting and collating statistics had not produced anything more than superficial evidence that, as in the MacQuillian case, could always be challenged by a case by case evaluation. The Ministry of Health had in a sense come full circle without ever really arriving at a definition of the problem it was supposed to solve.

Over prescribing and lax certification drew more attention than any other issues associated with the national insurance panel service. Nonetheless, those most intimately associated with the working of the act could neither prove nor disprove their existence. After forty years, historians can do no better. There was of course some over certification but as the Ministry of Health found, proving it, was and remains an impossibility. The story of the effort to come to administrative grips with the two questions, though, represents more than an interesting but frustrating sidelight to the operation of the panel medical service. It in fact further illustrates several important points concerning the medical profession and its relationship to the insurance act.

On the political level it was hardly a coincidence that the B.M.A. did not join with the government to deal with over prescribing and lax certification until after 1926. As argued in the previous chapter, the medical profession emerged from the 1923 capitation crisis and the Royal Commission Report with a new sense of security and political optimism. The threat posed by the approved societies had faded as the societies themselves went on the defensive. For the most part, prior to 1926 the profession's spokesmen had denied all allegations of panel abuse so as not to give the societies' accusations against insurance doctors even the slightest credit. After 1926 the B.M.A.'s leaders, safe in the knowledge that the panel service would remain independent, became active agents in the attempt to reduce over prescribing and lax certification.

This attitude served to strengthen the relationship between the medical profession and the insurance bureaucracy that since 1912 had been strained by the capitation issue. As a result, the Insurance Acts Committee became almost an arm of the Ministry of Health. It not only advised the Insurance Department, but sought to do its best to see that practitioners were conscious of their importance to the financial stability of the act's medical and sickness benefits. The value of this cooperation is hard to measure but its psychological advantages were immense. Doctors, observing the close working relationship between their leaders and the Ministry, could feel fairly certain that the profession's views were receiving a fair and usually friendly hearing. The medical profession appeared to have a role in shaping policy and to panel practitioners this was a much appreciated advantage.

As important as the political side of over prescribing and lax certification is the picture of the act's administration that has emerged from this discussion. Plainly the act's administration was marked by a great deal of good sense. Given the economic situation and prevailing fiscal conservatism, it would have been easy for the act's administrators to undertake a ruthless investigation of waste within the panel service.[130] Fortunately the insurance bureaucracy, under successive Ministers of Health, appreciated that medicine was not a perfected science and that it shared nothing with a production line. At their hearts, over prescribing and lax certification were problems of individual standards.

In both cases the Ministry of Health was faced not with abuse but rather varying definitions of adequate medical care. Doctors had no financial interest in either the stability of the panel drug fund (after 1920) or the number of sickness claims. Therefore fraud was not a question. Because of the capitation method of payment, medical men had only to be concerned about the health of their patients. Thus, the problems that did exist, did so usually because an individual doctor honestly felt that the nutrients in the bottle of medicine or a few days off work would benefit the patient. To be sure, medical men made mistakes and no doubt some may have been too easy with sickness certificates or drugs. Nonetheless over prescribing and lax certification could not have eliminated by anything short of a strict means test and hundreds of sick visitors. Such measures would have reduced the panel system to little more than an expanded Poor Law Medical Service. The act's national administrators consistently refused to impose such measures despite intense political criticism by the approved societies. To do so would clearly have destroyed the panel medical service, which was constructed upon a foundation of medical independence. Health and sickness are intensely personal experiences and a definition of each was moral and clinical territory that the act's administrators did not want to invade. The potential savings were greatly outweighed by the possible cost in health. Thus, by the mid-thirties the Ministry of Health's Insurance Department conceded, at least to itself, the limits of health care administration rather than encumber insurance medical care with non-medical considerations.

Notes

1. William J. Braithwaite, *Lloyd Georges' Ambulance Wages* Henry Banbury ed. (Portway Bath: Cedric Chivers Ltd., 1940), p. 141.

2. Bentley B. Gilbert, *British Social Policy 1914-1939* (Ithaca: Cornell University Press, 1970), pp. 284-299.

3. *BMJ* (4 January 1913), *Supplement*, p. 454.

4. T. M. Tibbets, *The Panel Doctor: His Duties and Perplexes* (London: John Bale, Sons, 1918), p. 26.

5. *Ibid*.

6. G. F. McCleary, *Memorandum on the English Scheme of National Health Insurance, with Special Reference to its Medical Aspects* (London: Wyman & Sons, 1929), p. 15.

7. Herman Levy, *National Health Insurance* (Cambridge: Cambridge University Press, 1944), p. 189.

8. *The Lancet* (8 January 1927), pp. 88-89.

9. *BMJ* (14 March 1914), *Supplement*, p. 150.

10. *The Lancet* (26 September 1914), p. 828.

11. *BMJ* (30 May 1914), *Supplement*, pp. 401-402.

12. The Panel Committee of London, minutes, 28 April 1914.

13. *Ibid*.

14. *Ibid*., 13 July 1914.

15. *Ibid*., 20 April 1915.

16. *Ibid*., 18 April 1916.

17. *Ibid*.

18. *The Lancet* (26 September 1914), p. 828.

19. The Panel Committee of London, minutes, 18 April 1916.

20. *Ibid*., 27 March 1917.

21. Colin-Russ.

22. _Ibid_.

23. Charles Singer and E. Ashworth Underwood, _A Short History of Medicine_ (Oxford: Oxford University Press, 1962), pp. 671-693.

24. _BMJ_ (9 January 1915), _Supplement_, p. 1.

25. _Annual Report of the Chief Medical Officer of Health for the Year 1920_, p. 38.

26. _The Lancet_ (26 July 1919), p. 170.

27. PRO. MH 62/107, 19 June 1922.

28. _Annual Report of the Chief Medical Officer of Health for the Year 1922_, p. 45.

29. PRO. MH 62/107, 19 June 1922.

30. _Ibid_., "Extract From the Instructions Issued to the Regional Medical Staff, Investigation of Prescribing," undated.

31. _Ibid_., 5 June 1924.

32. _Ibid_.

33. _BMJ_ (10 February 1923), pp. 38-40.

34. PRO. MH 62/107, 19 June 1922.

35. _Annual Report of the Chief Medical Officer of Health for the Year 1927_, p. 134.

36. _The Lancet_ (8 January 1927), pp. 88-89.

37. Levy, pp. 188-195.

38. PRO. MH 62/109, 8 February 1926.

39. _Ibid_.

40. _Annual Report of the Chief Medical Officer of Health for the Year 1933_, p. 108.

41. PRO. MH 62/109, 4 May 1926.

42. _Ibid_., 11 July 1926.

43. Insurance Acts Committee, session 1927-1928. IAC 5, 26 October 1927. The Insurance Acts Committee feared that the local pharmaceutical committees might be given more than referral power, thus creating another level of non-medical interference within the insurance act's administration.

44. PRO. MH 62/111, "Memorandum on Pricing of Prescriptions and Investigation of Prescribing," June 1933. The statistics were based upon a single day's prescriptions.

45. Ibid.

46. Insurance Acts Committee, session 1926-1927. IAC 68, 23 June 1927.

47. Insurance Acts Committee, session 1927-1928. IAC 23, 30 November 1927.

48. PRO. MH 62/110, 1 January 1928.

49. Annual Report of the Chief Medical Officer of Health for the Year 1931, pp. 37, 39.

50. Ibid., p. 36.

51. BMJ (30 October 1937), Supplement, p. 275.

52. Colin-Russ.

53. BMJ (30 October 1937), Supplement, p. 275. One complaint that was often heard but is difficult to assess is that doctors ordered too much medicine on a single prescription form. Since chemists were paid in part by the size of the bottle that the prescription was placed in, the larger the bottle the larger the fee. In their own defense, medical men asserted that it was in the long run cheaper to order a single large bottle of medicine rather than several smaller ones. The suspicion lingered though that much of the medicine was poured down the drain or taken needlessly.

54. Annual Report of the Chief Medical Officer of Health for the Year 1930-1938.

55. Ibid.

56. Great Britain, Parliament, Parliamentary Debates (Commons), 5th series, vol. 59 (1914), cols. 670-671.

57. Annual Report of the Chief Medical Officer of Health for the Year 1933, p. 107.

58. *Statistical Review of England and Wales for the Year 1937*, New Annual Series (No. 17), *Text* (H.M.S.O. 1940), Table 47.

59. *Annual Report of the Chief Medical Officer of Health for the Year 1933*, p. 107.

60. *Ibid*.

61. Colin-Russ.

62. *Annual Report of the Chief Medical Officer of Health for the Year 1933*, p. 107.

63. Arthur Newsholme, *Medicine and the State* (London: George Allen & Unwin, 1932), pp. 123-127.

64. *The National Insurance Gazette* (20 January 1917), p. 46.

65. Great Britain, Parliament, *Parliamentary Debates* (Commons), 5th series vol. 59 (1914), cols. 638-648.

66. *The Lancet* (3 January 1914), p. 77.

67. *The New Statesman* (6 December 1913), p. 263.

68. *The National Insurance Gazette* (2 February 1918), p. 49.

69. *The National Insurance Gazette* (17 February 1923), p. 44.

70. *The National Insurance Gazette* (24 November 1928), p. 560.

71. PRO. PIN 4/39, 4 May 1931. To some degree this judgment must be tempered by the lack of a normal sickness experience before 1921. The first years of the act had shown that the actuarial estimates that the finances of the act were based upon were inaccurate in that they did not account for enough sickness. The war can hardly have supplied the level of expected sickness claims as did the higher risk due to war time losses. Thus what was normal illness among the insured class was a matter of opinion rather than fact.

72. *Ibid*., pp. 10-14.

73. *The National Insurance Gazette* (4 August 1928), p. 367.

74. *BMJ* (10 February 1923), *Supplement*, p. 38.

75. Quoted in *The National Insurance Gazette* (29 January 1927), p. 51.

76. *BMJ* (12 May 1928), *Supplement*, p. 206.

77. BMJ (19 March 1927), Supplement, p. 94.

78. See The Daily Mirror, "Robbing the State," 16 June 1931. Also "Malingerers Who Regard Sickness Benefit As Pension," 15 July 1930.

79. BMJ (6 December 1919), Supplement, p. 146.

80. Annual Report of the Chief Medical Officer of Health for the Year 1921-1928. The medical profession in general was not happy with this trend but it was pleased that they were not open to direct society inspection. Moreover, the doctor of a suspected malingerer did not have to answer any inappropriate questions posed by the society clerk.

81. BMJ (20 June 1931), pp. 1078-1080.

82. Ibid., p. 1079.

83. Insurance Acts Committee, session 1932-1933. IA 1, 23 September 1932.

84. Insurance Acts Committee, session 1933-1934. IA 38, 29 March 1934.

85. BMJ (1 November 1930), Supplement, pp. 189-190.

86. The National Insurance Gazette (6 October 1928), p. 475. Sir Walter Kinnear in a speech before a conference of friendly society officials claimed that the government was concerned that there were far too many doctors who did not take anough care when certifying their patients ill. He went on to make note of the government's concern about the potential financial implications for the societies.

87. The National Insurance Gazette (24 May 1924), p. 243.

88. BMJ (22 March 1924), Supplement, pp. 145-147. This again raised the issue of the privacy of the doctor-patient relationship. But as in the past the Ministry had neither the will nor the means to enforce such precision.

89. PRO. MH 62/134, undated.

90. The National Insurance Gazette (6 November 1926), pp. 516-519.

91. BMJ (5 November 1927), Supplement, pp. 44-46. In a speech Dr. H. B. Brackenbury claimed that according to the statistics that the Insurance Acts Committee had gathered there had been a 300% increase in these areas.

92. The Times, 23 February 1928.

93. Annual Report of the Chief Medical Officer of Health for the Year 1927, pp. 58-61. The total number of deaths from influenza in England and Wales for January through March of 1927 was 17,931. The year before only 8,963 persons died from the disease. In contrast the pandemic of 1918-1919 was responsible for 156,130 deaths.

94. Insurance Acts Committee, session 1926-1927. IAC 52, 21 April 1927. The Insurance Acts Committee used the opportunity to solicit complaints from all local panel committees so that it could present a variety of issues to the Ministry.

95. PRO. MH 62/40, 12 February 1932. In 1932 the Insurance Acts Committee suggested a return to the system of only 14 days notice that had been in force from October 1927 until April 1931. But the Ministry refused and continued the once a quarter system throughout the remainder of the thirties.

96. The National Insurance Gazette, "Medical Certification of Incapacity of Insured Persons to Work" (24 September 1927), p. 465. The Gazette asserted that the change of regulations was brought about by the certification crisis. While economic forces played a role the issue, it was pointed out, was simple. Patients were shopping for certificates and doctors were doing nothing to stop this abuse of the system.

97. Insurance Acts Committee, session 1926-1927. IAC 70, 23 June 1927.

98. BMJ (29 October 1927), Supplement, pp. 171-173. There was some objection to the form of the new regulation. Dr. G. A. Roue of Aundee, objected because he felt that six months was a more appropriate interval.

99. PRO. MH 62/55, 1930-1931.

100. PRO. MH 62/46, 12 August 1929.

101. Ibid., 13 March 1928.

102. Insurance Acts Committee, session 1927-1928. IAC 108, 4 July 1928. The medical profession, from the beginning, asserted that its members were not at fault for the high sickness claims. Normal sickness, it argued, was not all that clear. Therefore terms like excessive illness meant very little.

103. PRO. MH 62/45, 15 August 1928.

104. Ibid.

105. Ibid.

106. PRO. MH 62/139, 5 January 1928.

107. Ibid., "Functions of the Medical Advisory Committee," undated.

108. Insurance Acts Committee, session 1929-1930. IAC 27, 6 March, 1930.

109. Cmd. 2596, pp. 165-174. The Royal Commission on National Insurance had in its 1926 report recommended that the local insurance committees be abolished. They were therefore defending their own existence in this certification dispute. Obviously the fewer their powers, the less likely the local committees would be to survive.

110. PRO. MH 62/46, 30 July 1929.

111. Ibid., 12 August 1929.

112. Ibid., 14 August 1929.

113. PRO. MH 62/46, 23 September 1929.

114. Ibid.

115. PRO. MH 81/115, 26 June 1931.

116. Ibid., 24 June 1931.

117. Ibid., 3 July 1931.

118. Great Britain, Parliament, Parliamentary Debates (Commons), 5th series, vol. 238 (1930), cols. 65-171.

119. PRO. PIN 4/39, "memorandum 329/I.C." 4 May 1931.

120. Newsholme, p. 124. Approved societies as a rule did not challenge the initial certificate issued by the panel doctor. The friction occurred when the doctor issued an intermediate certificate. These, as did the originals, had a life of a week and few doctors were willing to issue them for any shorter period.

121. PRO. MH 62/55, 28 May 1931.

122. PRO. MH 62/47, 18 August 1932.

123. Newsholme, pp. 124-126.

124. PRO. MH 62/47, 18 August 1932.

125. *Ibid*., Dr. J. D. MacQuillian to Monmouthshire Panel Committee, 12 December 1934.

126. *Ibid*., 3 September 1935.

127. PRO. MH 62/46, 23 September 1935.

128. *Ibid*., 4 October 1935.

129. PRO. MY 62/47, 25 September 1935.

130. Alan Deacon, *In Search of the Scrounger: The Administration of Unemployment Insurance in Britain, 1920-1931*, Occasional Papers on Social Administration, No. 60 (London: Bell and Sons, 1976). In contrast to health insurance, where the insured were eligible for benefits up to a year after they ceased to be employed, claims for unemployment insurance benefits were often subjected to a means test of bureaucratic red tape and narrow standards.

CHAPTER VI

The Manchester and Salford Experience, Fee-for-Service 1913-1928

In 1912 local insurance committees were established as independent bodies with the power to oversee the work of the insurance act within each administrative district. These committees were responsible for administering the local insurance fund and for distributing payments to participating medical men. Nonetheless practitioners could decide the basis for allocating their own panel fees. In the vast majority of areas the capitation system was accepted by local doctors but in Manchester and Salford local medical men adopted a fee for service scheme.[1] This method of remuneration was to endure as a unique situation within the working of the act until 1927 and 1928 when Salford and then Manchester doctors chose to conform with the rest of the nation. Despite its eventual rejection, however, the story of the fee-for-service scheme in the Lancashire cities was an important experiment within the insurance act and deserves close attention. Moreover, even with its limitations, the system of payment used in the two cities presents an opportunity to examine some of the problems associated with a non-capitation method of paying for medical care.

Payment per attendance within state sponsored medical services had long been promoted by the B.M.A. as a defense against club control. As early as the 1905 B.M.A. representative meeting, the Association declared that payment by attendance should be the goal of the profession.[2] In 1911 the B.M.A. continued to support the fee-for-service principle and at the outset of the insurance struggle it seemed as if the profession was immovable in its desire to see the payment system adopted.[3]

The government's position on the issue was ambivalent. Its concern was simply to get the needed 10,000 men to join the panel medical service. So long as payments did not exceed the allotted insurance benefit pool, each locality could divide available money among practitioners as they pleased. At the same time, the government did not encourage the adoption of the attendance system because it feared that it would lead to excessive clerical work, disputes among doctors over billing practices and costly over attendance. Speaking before a special representative meeting of the B.M.A. on 31 May 1911, Lloyd George insisted that "any attempt to demand payment on the number of attendances would break down. There are, I believe, one or two societies who carry on business on those lines, but they are generally in healthy districts. To doctor the whole working class on that basis," Lloyd George told his medical audience, would be "quite impracticable."[4] Still, the Chancellor was willing to allow doctors to try the system as long as local insurance funds were not exceeded.

This less than enthusiastic approval by the government probably dissuaded many panel committees from demanding the attendance system. In addition many local insurance committees avoided the problem by suggesting to practitioners that the capitation method of payment should be tried first.[5] Nonetheless, thirteen areas, including Newcastle, Manchester, Salford, the Isle of Man and Lancashire County adopted the attendance system in January 1913. But of these thirteen, only three -- Manchester, Salford and the Isle of Man -- survived the first year of the act.[6]

In January 1913 the Salford Insurance Committee agreed to accept the attendance system. Shortly afterwards Manchester insurance officials followed suit. These agreements between doctors and their local committees made the transition to panel work among the smoothest in the nation.[7] Local doctors, it appeared, had gotten precisely what they had wanted. In both cities, formal panel patient lists were eliminated and absolute free choice of doctor was maintained. Insured persons had only to present their benefit card to a qualified practitioner in order to receive care. After providing treatment, doctors submitted bills calculated according to a prearranged medical tariff to the local insurance committee. However, according to the local agreement, if the medical benefit funds were inadequate to meet the charges against them, doctors would be subject to a uniform reduction in panel payment.[8]

Initially the attendance system was adopted for only a three month trial period in each city.[9] Before the close of its third month though, it became apparent that payment by attendance had special problems that did not seem to be occurring in those areas using the capitation method of payment. One of the great fears of opponents of the act had always been that limited funds for the payment of panel practitioners would lead to inadequate medical care. It was in the doctor's financial interest to have a large list and few attendances. Mr. J. U. Smith, a member of the Manchester Insurance Committee representing the approved societies, charged that doctors were, "jerrying their work and not diagnosing the complaints of patients properly." Those medical men with large lists, he asserted, could not "give efficient service under present conditions..."[10] Just as dangerous as the threat of too little attention was the possibility of too much. Because medical men were paid by the attendance, patients often found during the first months of the panel scheme that Manchester and Salford doctors were always at hand, eager to give their advice.[11]

Doctors argued that they were only being careful but realists within the profession were not so sure. The absolute free choice of doctor by patient meant that patients tended to shop around more in the Lancashire cities than elsewhere. Panel patients lacked even the limited anchor provided by official registration upon a doctor's panel list. Malingering patients therefore had an extra degree of leverage that was not shared by the insured population under the panel system.[12]

As anticipated by the government, the relative freedom of

the Manchester and Salford schemes resulted in rising hostility among medical men. All doctors had a stake in the insurance fund and many men worried that unnecessary or even fraudulent over attendance by their colleagues would rob them of money. A practitioner who saw his patients more often than others, even if the visits were necessary, was likely to be subjected to personal abuse for claiming too high a share of the insurance pool. In a report on the Manchester/Salford situation The British Medical Journal noted that "By far the greatest difficulty arises when there is nothing like unfair attendance ever contemplated... It is not wholly theoretical, for several cases have already arisen of two practitioners practicing in the same neighborhood with about an equal number of patients and on the average a similar class of illness to deal with, where the bills sent into the Committee by one practitioner have been almost double those sent in by the other..."[13] Doctors therefore found that their incomes were in the hands of colleagues. In both Manchester and Salford, the result was an atmosphere of suspicion that was enhanced by accusations of the open canvassing of patients.[14]

After the first quarter's operation, payments for insurance medical work were distributed to Manchester and Salford doctors. In spite of their suspicions, most practitioners anticipated receiving the full value of their panel fees. In both cities, however, though, this was not the case. Due to over attendance, competition for patients, too many kind-hearted doctors or a high rate of sickness, the benefit fund could not meet all the charges made upon it for early 1913. Therefore, in accordance with the act's regulations and the January agreement with panel doctors, the Manchester insurance committee reduced all payments by 1/3 of their billed value.[15]

In Salford, the situation was even worse. Practitioners there received only 56% of their claims.[16] Medical men rationalized the discounting of their bills by blaming patients and weather. "The present system," they argued, "cannot have had a fair trial yet. The novelty of free medical attendance has induced a large number of patients to seek advice for mere trifles which in the future may be disregarded. Moreover, January to March are normally perhaps the busiest months of the year for general practitioners, and a pool that may be quite insufficient for the last three months may possibly be sufficient for the next three months."[17] Indeed practitioners could certainly make out a case to prove their point. In Manchester the average daily attendance figures during January showed 1,451 panel patients seeking medical advice and in February the average was 1,414. For the two months a total of 64,274 insured persons, out of 240,000, consulted one of the 260 panel doctors at least once.[18]

Many practitioners hoped that these totals would fall once patients became familiar with the panel system but Dr. J. D'Ewardt, the Treasurer of the Manchester Local Panel Committee was not so sure. He pointed out that in his view his more optimistic colleagues were wrong. "The remarkably small drop in the daily average in February seems to dispose of the idea that there was a considerable rush in the early days of the medical benefit. Even if we do not add those numerous insured persons who consulted doctors not 'on the list,' these astounding figures support very strongly the assertions of the profession as to the incidence of disease, and dispose very effectively of the inept optimism of Mr. Masterman as to the amount of sickness to be expected."[19]

Local medical leaders and the members of the insurance committees were hardly surprised when the first payment checks were met with uneasiness. Doctors who had been careful charged that they were being punished for the habits of their colleagues. Some demanded that disciplinary action be taken but this was never entertained seriously in either Manchester or Salford. Manchester's Medical Service Subcommittee stressed that "it is definitely and distinctly understood that the reductions made do not carry in any sense a reflection on the <u>bona fides</u> of the practitioner whose account is reduced. The reduction is a regrettable necessity owing to the lack of funds and not a condemnation. A few errors in bookkeeping have occurred, as was to be expected, but in subsequent accounts these will no doubt be eliminated."[20]

In spite of the reduction in the first quarter's medical checks, doctors in both Manchester and Salford agreed in late March 1913 to continue the fee-for-service scheme until 15 July

1913.[21] These decisions, though, were not made without some reservations. "The feeling," reported the British Medical Journal, "has been expressed that the present system lends itself to certain abuses which are extremely difficult to deal with... The cases in which there is over-attendance merely to obtain a greater share in the pool will be few and far between, but unfortunately, if they occur at all, they cannot generally be known and inquiry cannot be undertaken into them until a month or perhaps several months after the patient has been discharged and returned to work, when satisfactory evidence of over-attendance can hardly be obtained."[22] Nonetheless it was clear that a remedy had to be found.

In order to avoid the odious duty of investigating colleagues, the Manchester Panel Committee devised a system of averaging, to determine if the scheme could be made to work more equitably. The idea was to take the average number of daily attendances per medical man for the whole panel service and allow each doctor to charge fees for only that number.[23] While this protected the fee-for-service tariff, it was hoped that the revised system would also keep panel fees within the bounds of available funds. The Salford Insurance Committee accepted the new averaging scheme as well, but it also asked doctors to submit a full account of each attendance including drugs prescribed and the diagnosis. Should specific doctors be challenged, the Salford officials felt that they would have a basis for either accepting or disallowing each bill.[24]

To be sure, the imposition of these new controls severely limited the freedom of the fee-for-service system. Nonetheless, the Salford and Manchester Panel Committees argued that they had managed to avoid what was seen as the dead uniformity of the panel scheme elsewhere. Still, it was apparent to County of Lancashire doctors that, with the link between work and pay further circumscribed, the rationale behind the attendance system had been destroyed. Therefore, the county doctors abandoned the fee-for-service scheme for the capitation system in mid-1913, leaving their urban brethren to continue the battle.[25]

Manchester and Salford medical men refused to give up the attendance scheme so easily. At a meeting on 20 June Salford doctors formally agreed to continue the fee-for-service system until 1914. Several days later, on 24 June, the Manchester Local Panel Committee announced that doctors in that city had also agreed to continue work under the fee-for-service system through a postal vote.[26] Those who voted to maintain the fee-for-service principle argued that it still held the greatest hope for medical freedom despite the increased paper work and the regular discounting of medical bills. As long as patients were free from the bonds of formal panel lists, doctors too would be able to avoid the feared hazards of contract practice.[27] Moreover, Manchester and Salford men felt that they were also doing a service for the rest of the profession which was trapped by what was seen as the inflexible capitation fee. For them, their experiment of the first quarter of 1913 had not shown that doctors were over billing but that the size of the insurance pool was too small to meet the needs of the insured class.[28] This was an idea that gave the supporters of the attendance scheme a sense of mission and pride in their independence.

It had been optimistically hoped that warmer weather and familiarity with the working of the scheme by patients and doctors alike would reduce benefit claims. Unfortunately, no such decrease occurred. In Manchester practitioners performed 100,006 panel attendances in February. In spite of better weather in July, medical men were called upon for 113,071 attendances. In August the first decrease was achieved (by 5,000) but in September doctors were called upon 115,382 times for their services. As a result of this high attendance rate medical bills continued to be discounted. Manchester panel practitioners found their expected incomes reduced by 50% for the second quarter of 1913, when the charges exceeded the insurance benefit fund by £18,817. The third quarter in Manchester, though, showed an improvement and all billing doctors were paid at a rate of 60% of their total charges. Salford practitioners found that their bills continued to be discounted even more than in Manchester. There doctors averaged less than 50% of billed value for the first nine months of insurance work.[29]

Despite the imposition of averaging and panel fee deductions, some doctors did very well under the attendance system. In

Manchester there were three hundred doctors registered with the Local Insurance Committee by the end of 1913. Of these men who did panel work, forty-five received about a third of all payments and thirteen earned over £1,000 for their efforts, even after discounting. One man's panel income even approached £2,000.[30] This kind of inequality angered doctors who attended only a small number of insured persons. They felt that it was unfair that their bills were discounted at the same value as those of men with thousands of panel patients. Moreover, disgruntled doctors charged that such large panel practices could only lead to low quality of care for patients. Despite this hostility, nothing was done to reduce the opportunity for abuse, perhaps because little proof was ever presented, and at the end of 1913 doctors voted by more than 3 to 1 to continue the attendance system in 1914.[31] The vote, however, was hardly a vote of confidence.[32] Rather, medical men in Manchester and Salford were drawn together by a force more powerful than money -- the approved societies. The societies in the area had launched an attack upon doctors and the attendance system, charging that it had led to widespread abuse that threatened the financial stability of society funds.

The societies asserted that the fee-for-service system had shown what could happen if doctors were left to their own devices. Mr. E. Lloyd Jones, an approved society official on the Manchester Local Insurance Committee, insisted at a Committee meeting on 25 November 1913 that the system had failed. The doctors in Manchester had "not given their best to the insured, but had shirked their work, and the people had not been properly treated. How was it possible for a doctor to give proper attention whose bill for treatment for three months came to Ł1,000 for attendances costing on the average from 2s. to 2s.6d. each?"[33] Mr. W. Mellor, another society spokesman, asserted that some societies had experienced claims 40% higher under the fee-for-service scheme in Manchester than in areas with a capitation fee in force.[34] In place of the fee-for-service system, Jones, Mellor and a few other society representatives proposed a fulltime contract medical service. The Local Insurance Committee could, they suggested, hire 180 to 190 doctors at salaries of Ł400 a year to care for the insured population. The entire scheme would cost only Ł100,000, far less than the panel medical service.[35]

In response, however, Dr. McGowan, representing the Local Medical Committee, took issue with the charges of the societies. Nowhere, he asserted, had the act been administered "more successfully than in Manchester... the capitation system favoured the approved societies, the Manchester system favoured the health of the patients... In London under the capitation system there had been a large number of complaints by insured persons against the doctors, but in Manchester there had been none." Some of the speakers, he noted, "had attributed defects to the Manchester system which were really defects of the act itselt."[38]

Agreeing with the profession's arguments, the Manchester

Local Insurance Committee rejected the societies' proposal by a vote of 39 to 3 and approved the continuation of the attendance system. However, the more vocal societies were in no mood to surrender and they continued to argue for a full-time service.[36]

Not surprisingly the hostility of some societies placed Manchester and Salford medical men on the defensive. As a result, it was apparent that doctors themselves had to see that the most glaring defects of the attendance system were repaired. Therefore, the Manchester Local Panel Committee agreed to allow the establishment of an £800 limit upon panel incomes for 1914.[37] It was thought that by imposing a maximum income, costs could be controlled and a redistribution of panel patients would occur. Moreover, the approved societies might be satisfied by the elimination of the largest panel practices. Nonetheless, for many Manchester doctors in 1914, the £800 limit must have appeared to re-make their fee-for-service system into a complex variation of the capitation system.

The attendance system, circumscribed by the use of averaging and income limits, continued throughout 1914, as did the discounting of medical bills. The effects of the adopted method of payment, however, extended to the cost of drugs as well. As in the rest of the country, high drug charges plagued the Lancashire cities. But in Manchester and Salford the cost of drugs per patient was the nation's highest. For 1913 Salford's average rate was 2s.7.3/4d. and Manchester's was even higher, with an average expenditure of 3s.2.5/5d. These rates were in excess of those experienced by other towns even in the same county and far greater than cities in other regions.[39] There was little doubt that the high drug costs were a direct result of the equally high rate of attendance per insured worker. Unlike excess attendance, though, prescription costs beyond an average of 2s., robbed chemists. As a result, drug bills submitted by dispensing chemists were reduced by 30% for the first nine months of 1913.[40] Needless to say, chemists in both Manchester and Salford were angered by this unexpected turn of events and they encouraged their local pharmaceutical committees to push for more rigorous control of medical prescribing habits.

The chemists' complaints against doctors were similar to those voiced in other parts of the country. In Manchester and Salford the crisis, though, was of far greater proportions. Chemists complained that the high costs were, "due to no small extent to the large quantities of extract of malt with cod-liver oil and emulsion of cod-liver oil that have been ordered, and also to the fact that many practitioners have ordered drugs under proprietary names which might just as well have been ordered under their scientific chemical names at a fraction of the cost."[41] In view of the discontent among local chemists the Salford Pharmaceutical Association wrote to the Insurance Commissioners for England on 31 October 1913, demanding payment in full. If this was not forthcoming, the Association threatened their own boycott of panel work.[42] The Commissioners saw the problem as a local dispute and while they refused to make any guarantees, they suggested that the chemists consult the Local Insurance Committee or local doctors. Any plan for reducing the demands upon the drug fund would be agreed to by the Commissioners, so long as all parties consented.[43]

With the issue returned to local hands, a meeting between chemists and panel doctors was held in Salford on 2 December in order to devise a plan to reduce drug charges.[44] The result of the conference was a new and novel scheme. Doctors and chemists agreed that the root of the difficulty under the original system for providing drugs was that the doctors who prescribed drugs and appliances were not at financial risk beyond the floating sixpence. Chemists who filled the prescriptions, however, were. To shift this burden, it was decided that the economic risk should be taken by doctors alone.

Under the terms of the insurance act in 1913, 9s. per head were available for the total medical benefit. Rather than dividing this amount into medical and drug funds, panel men agreed that all money should be first credited to their accounts. Before final payment, though, the cost of each doctor's prescriptions up to 2s.6d. per head would be subtracted. In this manner chemists would be assured of most if not all of their dispensing fees. Thus chemists might not always be paid the full value of their services but the new plan in Salford guaranteed that those doctors who over prescribed would directly suffer from their actions.[45] The British Medical Journal noted that "at first sight this would appear to leave the pharmacists no better off than they are at present, but they are willing to accept the arrangement, because they are so confident that every doctor will prescribe more carefully and less lavishly when he has the constant reminder at every pay day that he must be debited with the whole cost of his own prescriptions."[46]

As promised, the Insurance Commissioners accepted the Salford plan despite some opposition from local doctors who charged that the outcome would be too little rather than too much prescribing.[47] These dissenting doctors may have been correct although proving under prescribing was as difficult as proving over prescribing. Each was ultimately a matter of opinion. Nonetheless, the number of prescriptions in Salford fell sharply after the institution of the new scheme in 1914. During 1913 the cost of drugs and appliances had been £12,064 and the number of prescriptions dispensed had been 405,748 with an average cost of 9.1d. In 1914 with the new system of debiting doctors, the charges against the Salford drug fund fell by £4,789 to £7,275. The number of prescriptions written for panel patients dropped to 344,554 and the average cost for a single prescription declined to only 5.1d. As a result the area's chemists who in 1913 had been paid only 66% of their claims found that in 1914 they were awarded 90% of their charges.[48] Nonetheless the scheme was criticised. Miss Heygate, Lady Superintendent of the District Nurses in Salford, decried the new system. She said that "in 1913 dressings were supplied in such quantities that they had actually been used for washing floors, but during the last year patients had even been told to use old rags for dressings and the district nurses had often had to supply even the most necessary dressings." Another member of the Local Insurance Committee, Mr. Speakman, noted the sudden fall and suggested that the Committee ought to see if "the insured were getting what the law said they ought to get -- proper and adequate care."[49]

Medical men naturally rejected the suggestion that doctors had been denying the insured the full value of their services. Dr. J. H. Taylor, a prominent Salford medical leader, pointed out to the Local Insurance Committee that the dramatic fall in charges against the drug fund could be accounted for in several ways:

> "There had not been actually any decrease in the amount of sickness, and though it was true that a number of men had been away part of the year on war service they were the healthiest part of the population, who required but little medicine. By far the greatest cause of the drop in the number of prescriptions was to be found in the Salford system, under which each doctor is debited with the cost of each prescription he gave, and, if it were only in order to save the dispensing fee... the doctors were tempted to give medicines out of their own stocks. That had been done to a great extent, and had considerably reduced the number of prescriptions sent to the chemists."[50]

Whatever the cause, though, the scheme seemed to be contrary to the interests of patients and doctors alike. Therefore the Salford Panel Committee abandoned the scheme in 1915 as "too drastic."[51]

Salford chemists complained that this was unfair, but without medical cooperation they could do little. Doctors, however, were conscious of the uneasiness on the part of chemists and after abandoning the 1914 payment system, medical leaders asked chemists to accept the responsibility for reporting cases of over prescribing. Chemists agreed, even though they doubted that few of the doctors reported would be dealt with effectively. The scheme, however, never got a trial. In September 1915 chemists throughout the nation were guaranteed payment in full by the Insurance Commissioners and as a result the Salford Pharmaceutical Committee lost all interest in the question of over prescribing.[52]

When the war came to an end, Manchester and Salford panel practitioners could look back upon five years of a fee-for-service system and consider its future. Doctors in Manchester were paid 77% of their submitted bills in 1918 while Salford medical men received 88% of their claims. Only once, in Manchester in 1919, did either city pay 100% of submitted medical charges.[53] Nevertheless, Manchester and Salford doctors were paid about as much as their colleagues who worked on a strict capitation basis. At the same time, the number of attendances, though always high by national standards, was reduced during the wartime period.[54] However, while doctors felt that under the attendance system they were free from non-medical interference, clerical work took more time and the panel committees had tremendous power to reduce individual medical incomes and to discipline doctors. But the number of formal complaints against doctors was fairly low, with Salford reporting only nineteen after seven years of insurance work.[55]

For Manchester and Salford doctors, their system, in spite of its limitations, seemed to be a closer approximation to private practice than the capitation-based panel scheme. The capitation fee, from their perspective, enslaved doctors. Therefore, with a great deal of local pride that sometimes blinded them to the facts, practitioners in both cities voted to continue payment by attendance after 1920.[56]

Nowhere is this quality of local pride more evident than in the controversy in 1920 concerning the views of Dr. J. Charles of Durham. In response to an article by Dr. J. H. Taylor in the British Medical Journal that generally favored the attendance system, Dr. Charles asserted in a letter to the journal that the evidence did not support the "superiority" of the fee-for-service system "over the ordinary capitation system, whether it be from the point of view of the doctor or the insured persons... At best it is only a very important adaptation, and a mere approximation to the private practice system."[57] Charles went on to criticize the working of the system for paying too little, overburdening the doctor with paper work and greatly increasing the instability of the scheme as a whole. The attack by Dr. Charles was met by several letters from Salford doctors questioning the Durham man's judgment. One of the most defensive was penned by Dr. Stanley Hedgson, Chairman of the B.M.A.'s Salford Division.

> "I have had sixteen years' experience of capitation practice at 8s.6d. and 9s. per head and seven years of payment-per-attendance insurance practice, and I am a whole-hogger for the latter. Dr. Charles's experience is one-sided. As I say, let him remain unconverted, but let him also refrain from rhetorical flights into the realms of imagination. We Salford practitioners do not want to join those who are thronging the main road. They are always howling and protesting at their discomforts of that road, and their efforts to make the peace have been crowned with singularly small success. We prefer the 'by-path,' the 'secluded path' along which we travel in comfort and peace."[58]

The attendance system may at times have been tedious and irksome but clearly it was their system and therefore worth defending. But as we shall see a succession of events in the twenties finally forced Manchester and Salford doctors to abandon their experiment.

In 1924 the rest of the nation adopted the practice of allowing patients freely to change doctor. This was a severe blow to the Manchester and Salford practitioners who had always argued that they put up with heavy clerical work in order to maintain absolute freedom of choice. The two Lancashire cities no longer could claim to represent an ethical ideal. Thus a large part of the rationale for their system disappeared. The supposed intrinsic tie between fee-for-service and medical freedom no longer could be supported. Moreover, in the early twenties, practitioners increasingly felt isolated as other areas considered and then rejected adopting payment-by-attendance. Cheshire doctors, for example, "vigorously rejected" a payment-by-attendance plan drawn up by the local insurance committee in 1923.[59] For many non fee-for-service doctors the system had failed. Writing in the British Medical Journal, Dr. G. C. Garratt of Chichester, asserted that:

> "a system which necessarily discourages preventive medicine, which must foster the fussy incompetent doctor at the expense of his more busy and capable neighbour, and which renders malingering and invalidism not only easier for the insured, but profitable to his medical attendant, is not likely to commend itself either to the student of public health or to the educated laymen... I do not anticipate its extension beyond its present home."[60]

Manchester and Salford doctors apparently were the only ones in the profession who appreciated the moral superiority of the fee-for-service principle after ten years of working the act.

Wounded professional and regional pride was not nearly as serious as scandal, involving both fraud and the breach of professional ethics. In early 1924 a Salford medical man, Dr. Sandelson, was accused of stealing patients and defrauding the insurance fund by charging the cost of prescriptions for non-insured members of a family in the name of a member who was insured. Dr. Sandelson was also accused of padding his day books.[61] This was a serious offense in Salford because after 1922 the straight averaging system was dropped in favor of a scheme that tied payment closer to attendance records. The old scheme had become inflated as doctors tended to bill for each attendance, no matter how minor. In order to eliminate this, a "bogey system" was developed. Doctors were still allowed to submit bills but they were paid according to a fixed rate per treated patient. Little more than a convoluted capitation scheme, the "bogey award" for practitioners was 16s. in 1923 and 15s. in 1924 for each patient seen, regardless of the number of treatments provided to the individual throughout the year. Therefore, under the new scheme doctors were encouraged more than ever to see patients only once.

Dr. Sandelson was ultimately removed from the Salford panel service but the case was not free from controversy. As a young doctor, in his first year of practice in 1923, Sandelson was apparently well enough off to have purchased his own practice. In his appeal, Sandelson claimed that he had only followed the advice of more experienced men. There is little doubt but that the young doctor was correct, and he was not the only Salford practitioner who falsified records. Unfortunately Sandelson was to some extent a victim of his own excessive nature and the jealousy and conservative nature of his fellow medical men. As a young Jewish doctor, he only heightened the dislike of colleagues when he was elected a Labour member to the Salford Council with posters proclaiming himself "The People's Friend." Given his religious and political preferences, it is not difficult to imagine the level of resentment felt by other Salford medical men.[63]

The Sandelson case provided ample grist for the Salford medical profession's gossip mill and no doubt it served as an endless source of entertainment. However, because of the special circumstances surrounding the charges against Dr. Sandelson, the case did not pose a threat to the attendance system in Salford. For many, Sandelson had gotten precisely what he deserved.

The same cannot be said of another case of fraud in 1925. This was to leave little doubt that the attendance scheme was in crisis. Drs. J. G. Hill and J. Smyth, who were partners in Salford, were charged with wanton fraud. The Local Panel Committee discovered that their day sheets for 1923 and 1924 were kept without regard to the actual services rendered. The names of patients were placed on the day sheets randomly and from the records it was impossible to identify the treatment that patients had received or when they had been attended. After interviewing many of the partnership's patients, the Local Panel Committee declared that the records of the practice were hopelessly unreliable. This alone did not constitute fraud, even though it was a violation of the record keeping provisions of the medical benefit regulations. But upon a close examination of the day sheets it was apparent that many entries had been made long after the actual delivery of medical service. Work done on 30 February, 31 April, 31 June, 31 September and 31 November represented more than the lack of a calendar. Even more damaging was the fact that during January

1924 a total of 944 separate names had been listed, with each patient receiving nine attendances and then disappearing from the partnership's medical records.[64]

The case against Drs. Hill and Smyth was scandalous but unlike Dr. Sandelson both men were respected and established practitioners in Salford. Dr. Hill was even a member of the Local Panel Committee, which was responsible for adjudicating his case. Clearly the two doctors should have known better. Neither doctor, though, was removed from panel practice but they were required to pay the cost of the proceedings against them. In addition the Ministry of Health suggested that they be censured, although there is no record of such local action. The Hill and Smyth case was widely publicized and a full description of it was sent to every panel doctor in Manchester and Salford. To reinforce this, a meeting was held in Salford Town Hall to discuss the working of the attendance system on 20 December 1925.

Doctors from both Salford and Manchester were invited to attend the meeting. Those present engaged in a lengthy discussion of insurance medical service and the fee-for-service system. Although no record of the actual debate remains, a report in the British Medical Journal reveals that the medical men engaged in a wide ranging comparison of the capitation and attendance methods of payment.[66] This was reflected in the memorandum issued by the Panel Committee. In this it was pointed out that clerical work was heavier and more complex under the attendance system. In the capitation areas record cards were issued by the insurance committees but in Manchester and Salford day books and cards were kept that required much of the doctors time. The total administrative cost for this in Manchester alone amounted to ₤1600 in 1924. In addition, each medical man in Manchester and Salford had to surrender his day book for annual inspection whereas under the capitation system medical records were only periodically inspected by the regional medical officer.[67]

The primary difference between the two systems, though, was their financial structure. Under both systems there were limits upon a single doctor's income. Under the attendance system in 1925 no doctor was allowed to earn more than ₤1,125 from insurance work in Manchester. In Salford the bogey scheme also placed limits on income. In contrast, the capitation system limited medical incomes by allowing doctors no more than 2,500 panel patients. The amount received from panel work, however, could vary depending on the number of unallocated persons. Therefore medical men with panel lists could earn as little as 8s. and as much as 11s.5d. per patient under the capitation scheme. As a rule of thumb, though, the practitioners conceded that under the attendance system each patient was worth an average of 1s.11d. per service while in the capitation areas their colleagues earned about 2s.7d. per attendance.[68]

In general the practitioners attending the meeting agreed that under the attendance system, "more attendances and more prescriptions are given than necessary." At the same time, however, it was asserted that "under the capitation system attendances and prescriptions are fewer than are desirable."[69] Yet neither system really worked against the general health of the insured class. The memorandum issued by the Panel Committee noted that "the attendance system lends itself to grave irregularities by unscrupulous practitioners, such as false entries in the daysheets of attendance, and insertion of names of persons never attended." Still, under the capitation system, "equally contemptible canvassing and touting are known to take place."[70]

Clearly medical men in Salford and Manchester were not entirely happy with the fee-for-service scheme wherein, even accounting for fraud, doctors worked harder for their insurance fees. Nonetheless local pride was as intense as ever and the doctors present at the meeting in December 1925 decided to await the report of the then sitting Royal Commission on National Insurance before taking further action.[71]

The Royal Commission paid only scant attention to payment by the attendance scheme. The Commissioners did little more than confirm what the Manchester and Salford profession already knew.[72] What had begun as an experiment had evolved into an unwanted aberration. The scheme was so over-regulated to protect against fraud that doctors actually had more clerical work than those men paid by capitation. Patients, in addition, had little more freedom, and income for Manchester and Salford practitioners had consistently fallen short of 100% of the value of medical bills. By the late twenties, payment by attendance no longer made sense, even to those doctors for whom it had always been a distinct point of pride. Therefore, following the Royal Commission's Report in 1926, Salford medical men voted to abandon the scheme at the end of 1927. Manchester panel practitioners decided to give the scheme one more year but they too adopted payment by capitation in 1928.[73]

With the abandonment of the attendance system by Salford and Manchester doctors it would seem that the system was a complete failure. Still this may be too harsh a judgment when the peculiar circumstances under which the system operated are considered. Doctors in both cities had always argued that they were victims of a naturally high sickness rate that made the medical benefit fund inadequate. Indeed, they may have been correct. Of the twenty areas with the highest drug costs, ten were in Lancashire, and Manchester and Salford lead the list.[74]

Average total cost of prescribing for 1933 per head of the insured population included in the Prescribing Lists in each Insurance Committee Area.[76]

(Areas arranged in order of decreasing costs.)

Area	Average Cost Per Insured Person (in pence)
1. Manchester	58-139
2. Salford	57-863
3. Rutland	50-027
4. Barrow-in-Furness	49-031
5. Kingston-upon-Hull	47-892
6. Oldham	46-673
7. Preston	45-887
8. Leeds	44-654
9. Southend-on-Sea	44-558
10. Blackburn	44-000
11. Gateshead	43-194
12. Stockport	43-112
13. Liverpool	42-500
14. South Shields	42-475
15. Bury	41-604
16. Birkenhead	41-217
17. Newcastle-upon-Tyne	40-987
18. Birmingham	40-849
19. Lancashire	40-362
20. Cheshire	40-224
21. Rotherham	39-594
22. Burnley	38-976
23. York	38-890
24. Huddersfield	38-759
25. Sheffield	38-629
26. Essex	38-592
27. Stoke-on-Trent	38-366
28. Bootle	38-804
29. Isle of Wight	38-267
30. Bristol	38-171
31. West Ham	38-094
32. West Hartlepool	38-009
33. Hastings	37-887
34. Warrington	37-739
35. Chester	37-679
36. Brighton	37-335

37.	Devon	37-234
38.	Isle of Ely	37-055
39.	Blackpool	36-948
40.	Bxeter	36-840
41.	Yorks, West	36-812
42.	Durham	36-479
43.	Nottingham	36-434
44.	Derby	36-418
45.	Lincs, Lindsey	36-402
46.	Wallasey	36-399
47.	Portsmouth	36-323
48.	Bradford	36-300
49.	Rochdale	36-287
50.	West Bromwich	36-188
51.	Bolton	36-053
52.	Bedfordshire	35-882
53.	London	35-751
54.	Sigan	35-734
55.	Great Yarmouth	35-723
56.	Kent	35-542
57.	Halifax	35-461
58.	Westmorland	35-172
59.	Tynemouth	34-852
60.	Northumberland	34-678
61.	Bath	34-196
62.	East Ham	34-083
63.	Bournemouth	34-025
64.	Herefordshire	34-003
65.	Reading	33-984
66.	Somerset	33-941
67.	Smethwick	33-859
68.	Dorset	33-833
69.	Norfolk	33-676
70.	Middlesex	33-562
71.	St. Helens	33-554
72.	Wakefield	33-512
73.	Worcester	33-448
74.	Cornwall	33-438
75.	Wiltshire	33-338
76.	Salop	33-328
77.	Croydon	33-111
78.	Sussex, West	33-033
79.	Doncaster	32-828
80.	Lincs, Kesteven	32-648
81.	Norwich	32-423
82.	Wolverhampton	32-356
83.	Lines, Holland	32-288
84.	Yorks, East	32-119
85.	Eastbourne	32-069
86.	Sussex East	32-008

87.	Barnsley	31-894
88.	Worcestershire	31-728
89.	Yorks, North	31-516
90.	Suffolk, West	31-502
91.	Sunderland	31-435
92.	Derbyshire	31-321
93.	Gloucester	31-250
94.	Nottinghamshire	31-233
95.	Northampton	31-233
96.	Southport	31-140
97.	Coventry	31-129
98.	Gloucestershire	31-100
99.	Plymouth	30-995
100.	Warwick	30-930
101.	Soke of Peterborough	30-875
102.	Hertfordshire	30-737
103.	Buckinghamshire	30-576
104.	Staffordshire	30-478
105.	Leicester	30-351
106.	Hampshire	30-202
107.	Surrey	30-116
108.	Huntingdonshire	30-057
109.	Cumberland	29-942
110.	Southampton	29-725
111.	Grimsby	29-614
112.	Leicestershire	29-198
113.	Middlesbrough	29-193
114.	Lincoln	28-966
115.	Dudley	28-873
116.	Walsall	28-804
117.	Suffolk, East	28-723
118.	Dewsbury	28-490
119.	Carlisle	28-323
120.	Northamptonshire	28-148
121.	Darlington	27-820
122.	Oxfordshire	27-613
123.	Berkshire	27-570
124.	Canterbury	27-362
125.	Burton-on-Trent	26-996
126.	Cambridgeshire	26-958
127.	Ipswich	25-785
128.	Oxford	21-992

In 1935, long after the adoption of the capitation system, Manchester and Salford not only remained the most expensive prescribing areas but they led the nation in the frequency of prescriptions issued to the insured. Salford had an annual rate of 7.125 per person and Manchester was not far behind with an average of 6.85. Oldham and Blackburn had the next highest prescription rates with averages of 5.969 and 5.864 respectively.[76]

Doctors argued that these high Lancashire drug costs reflected a much greater degree of illness, although this sickness did not necessarily show up in the area's benefit claims. This was of course an important point because if medical men could prove it then undoubtedly their argument would be won. However, because the approved society system had no tie to geographic boundaries it was, according to L. G. Brock, "very difficult if not impossible to establish from their records the sickness experience among insured persons in a particular locality."[77] Broader health statistics, however, are of some help. The Registrar General's Report for 1933 shows that influenza was responsible for 465 deaths per million in greater London and for the area including Manchester and Salford the rate was 657.[78] The incidence of diptheria follows a similar pattern. For each 100,000 persons, Manchester had 134 notified cases of diptheria, Salford 350 and Liverpool 340 in 1933. In contrast, London's Administrative County had 118 cases per 100,000 reported while Birmingham had a rate of only 83 for the same year.[79] Finally infant mortality, often an indication of general health, reveals that the northern region that included Manchester and Salford had an overall mortality rate of 77.9 per 1,000 live births. Greater London's rate was 54.2 for 1933 and for all of England and Wales the annual rate of infant mortality was 63.7 for each 1,000 live births.[80] Finally, these figures have a historical precedent. Since the mid-nineteenth century Lancashire's health statistics have consistently shown a higher incidence of disease and mortality than other regions.[81]

In light of this evidence, it does appear that Manchester and Salford practitioners did work under adverse conditions. The incidence of sickness was not spread evenly throughout the nation. Climate and industrial environment joined to establish illness zones, where people endured high rates of bad health. For anyone who has visited the northern industrial towns of England, it is no surprise that doctors from Lancashire to Birmingham to the West Riding had to treat more illness than colleagues elsewhere. Moreover, while Leeds, Wakefield and Wolverhampton all had high levels of illness, it was Lancashire that led the way. Rochdale, St. Helens, Bolton and Burnley panel practitioners always had prescription and illness rates in excess of the national average and in the center of this area are Manchester and Salford.[82] Thus, given the limitation of the local benefit fund, a worse place to test the principle of fee-for-service could not have been found. Nonetheless, the high incidence of sickness only contributed to the failure of a system that was doomed from the beginning.

The local benefit fund placed a limit upon the amount that could be earned by medical men for treating insured persons.

Manchester and Salford practitioners therefore had to live under this financial roof and very quickly they discovered that they could not. As a result they were forced to destroy the great advantage of the insurance medical service -- the simplicity of its administration. Unlike other insurance areas, Manchester and Salford had to create layers of regulation that were designed to protect doctors from their own excesses. As each year passed the guidelines became more convoluted. In the end this imposed more work upon doctors, afforded them less freedom and resulted in less money per attendance. What began as an experiment to secure medical independence by maintaining the link between work and pay ended in bondage to clerical work, discounted checks, mutual suspicion among colleagues and no advantage for the insured.

The attendance system as practiced in Manchester and Salford was never a true fee-for-service scheme. It existed as only a limited experiment under the worst possible conditions. Nonetheless, the story of these cities' experiences provides a valuable insight into the critical weakness of an unregulated fee-for-service system. Apart from simple fraudulent billing, payment for state sponsored medical care on the basis of each service has a significant psychological disadvantage. Under the normal conditions of private practice medical fees are to some extent established by the patient's ability to pay. Practitioners with poor patients may ask for high fees but logically they can expect to receive only a portion of the total bill. Therefore doctors historically simply reduced charges to meet the patient's financial capabilities. The intrusion of public money into this relationship, however, removes all restraint. Instead of the poorly dressed and ill patient, doctors see nothing but a tremendous pool of money to draw upon. A few extra pennies added to each bill or casual over attendance may seem insignificant. But multiplied by several millions, the cost can be a crippling burden upon a national treasury which, while usually large, is not inexhaustible.

On another level, fee-for-service, in theory and perhaps in fact, encourages too much medical care. The human body is not a machine, nor are doctors mechanics. The practice of medicine is an intensely personal and emotional art. There is a natural and quite understandable tendency by doctors to tinker, whether or not there is any legitimate hope of a satisfactory return. Of course in any publicly sponsored health care scheme the clinical decisions must remain with the individual doctors and patients. Yet, the state has an equal responsibility to see that public resources devoted to health care are not exhausted by the ever rising demands of medical men and their patients. Fee-for-service does nothing in this regard because, at least in principle, payment upon this basis makes it in the doctor's economic interest to have ill rather than well patients. The capitation fee can and did sometimes lead to under attendance but in the long run this was less damaging to the public's purse and perhaps the patient's health.[83]

None of these arguments about the hazards of the fee-for-service system of health care in any way singles medical men out as being greedy, selfish and unconcerned with the welfare of their patients. In the vast majority of cases precisely the opposite was true. The crucial point, however, is one that the B.M.A. itself constantly stressed. Medical men are also business-men with a direct financial interest in the economic return of their medical practices. For any society considering the provision of health care it is absolutely critical that this economic fact not be blurred by the profession's humanistic calling. To allow this would only condemn state sponsored health care to spiralling costs.[84] No government official would responsibly give a blank check to road builders, printers or other contractors. Doctors should hardly expect to be treated any differently once they consent to harness their skills to the public welfare.

Medical practitioners in Britain recognized the necessity of this relationship with the state in 1913. Even in Manchester and Salford strict limits from the outset were placed on the fee-for-service system. The success of the British system of national health insurance is ample evidence of the wisdom of choosing payment by capitation over the fee-for-service system. The panel service remained flexible and responsive to the individual needs of insured patients. Perhaps more importantly, the medical benefit of the national insurance act was not curtailed in an atmosphere of continuing economic crisis and tightfisted government fiscal policies. To be sure the panel medical service had its critics. Still, because of its continuing financial solvency, few beyond approved society clerks ever contemplated its elimination.

Notes

1. D. S. Less and M. H. Cooper, "Payment Per-Item of Service, The Manchester and Salford Experience, 1913-1928," Medical Care 2 (August-September 1964), pp. 151-156.

2. Jeanne L. Brand, Doctors and the State (Baltimore: The Johns Hopkins Press, 1965), pp. 197-199.

3. Lees and Cooper, p. 151.

4. BMJ (3 June 1911), Supplement, p. 357.

5. Ibid.

6. Because the Isle of Man had a small native population and was a resort area, it counts as a special case. The large number of temporary residents meant that the fee-for-service system there made economic sense. As a result of this there was a complete lack of controversy surrounding the system employed.

7. The Manchester Guardian, 28 March 1913.

8. BMJ (10 May 1913), Supplement, p. 428.

9. BMJ (5 April 1913), Supplement, p. 302.

10. BMJ (7 February 1914), Supplement, p. 66.

11. Ibid.

12. BMJ (5 April 1913, Supplement, p. 302.

13. Ibid.

14. BMJ (7 February 1914), Supplement, p. 66.

15. Ibid.

16. Ibid.

17. BMJ (5 April 1913), Supplement, p. 302.

18. BMJ (10 May 1913), Supplement, p. 429.

19. Ibid., p. 428. There was a total of 520 doctors practicing in Manchester. This total includes specialists, and all others listed on the Medical Register.

20. Ibid., p. 429.

21. Ibid.

22. BMJ (5 April 1913), Supplement, p. 302.

23. Ibid.

24. Ibid.

25. BMJ (3 May 1913), Supplement, p. 402.

26. BMJ (28 June 1913), Supplement, p. 592.

27. Ibid.

28. BMJ (14 March 1914), Supplement, pp. 149-150.

29. BMJ (3 January 1914), Supplement, p. 6.

30. BMJ (6 December 1913), Supplement, p. 515.

31. Ibid., p. 514.

32. Ibid., p. 515.

33. Ibid.

34. Ibid.

35. BMJ (14 March 1914), Supplement, p. 149.

36. BMJ (6 December 1913), Supplement, p. 514.

37. BMJ (7 February 1914), Supplement, p. 66.

38. BMJ (6 December 1913), Supplement, p. 515.

39. BMJ (14 March 1914), Supplement, p. 150. Also see (3 April 1915), Supplement, p. 123.

40. BMJ (20 December 1913), Supplement, p. 561. In Hull, for example, chemists were paid an average fee of 7d. per prescription for the first quarter. This had to be discounted to about 75% of value. But by the end of the year it was reported that the local drug fund was balanced. The Lancet (27 September 1913), p. 955.

41. Ibid.

42. Ibid., p. 562.

43. Ibid.

44. *Ibid*.

45. *BMJ* (27 February 1915), *Supplement*, p. 76.

46. *BMJ* (20 December 1913), *Supplement*, p. 562.

47. *BMJ* (27 February 1915), *Supplement*, p. 76.

48. *Ibid*.

49. *Ibid*.

50. *Ibid*.

51. J. W. Lowe, "The Manchester System of National Health Insurance Medical Service," *The National Insurance Gazette* (25 March 1922), p. 142.

52. *BMJ* (25 September 1915), pp. 476-477. The dispensing fee was raised from 0.8d. to 1.0d. with stock mixtures carrying a value of 1-1/2. After the war the fee rose to 2d. In addition the fee for the largest bottles was eliminated. Also see Great Britain, Parliament, *Parliamentary Papers* (Commons), 1914-1916, vol. 1 (Reports), vol. 2. 29, Cd. 8062, "Report of the Departmental Committee on the Drug Tariff Under the National Insurance Acts."

53. Insurance Acts Committee, session 1923-1924. IAC 39, undated.

54. *Ibid*.

55. J. H. Taylor, "National Insurance: The Payment by Attendance in Salford," *BMJ* (28 August 1920), *Supplement*, pp. 70-71.

56. *Ibid*., p. 71.

57. *BMJ* (18 September 1920), *Supplement*, p. 79.

58. *BMJ* (19 October 1920), *Supplement*, p. 122.

59. Lees and Cooper, p. 151.

60. *BMJ* (9 October 1920), *Supplement*, p. 91-92.

61. PRO. MH 62/73, 4 February 1924.

62. PRO. MH 81/116, 15 January 1920.

63. PRO. MH 62/73, 14 March 1925.

64. *BMJ* (9 January 1926), *Supplement*, p. 17-18.

65. *Ibid.*, pp. 18-19.

66. *Ibid.*

67. *Ibid.*, p. 19.

68. *Ibid.*

69. *Ibid.*

70. *Ibid.*

71. *Ibid.*

72. Cmd. 2596, p. 431.

73. Lees and Cooper, p. 155.

74. *Annual Report of the Chief Medical Officer for the Year 1933*, p. 108. Lancashire was singled out by the Chief Medical Officer for having a long-standing tradition of heavy medicine use. The fault was the bottle of medicine habit according to Newman.

75. *Ibid.*

76. Insurance Acts Committee, session 1936-1937. IA 36, 11 March 1937.

77. Cmd. 2596, p. 634.

78. *Statistical Review of England and Wales for the Year 1933*, New Annual Series, no. 13. Tables part 1 Medical (London: H.M.S.O., 1935), Table 41.

79. *Ibid.*, Table 38.

80. *Ibid.*, Table 6.

81. F. B. Smith, *The Peoples Health* (London: Croom Helm, 1979), pp. 106, 137.

82. Insurance Acts Committee, session 1936-1937. IA 36, 11 March 1937.

83. Smith, pp. 414-425. Smith argues that too much medical care has as many hazards as too little. He points out that improved nutrition, sanitation and housing have done far more than medical science to improve the state of health. Indeed, he suggests that medicine in many cases throughout its history has often retarded progress.

84. Brian Inglis, "Breaking the Health Monopoly," *The Spectator* (28 July 1979), pp. 14-15.

CONCLUSION

In 1912 when the loudest medical critics of national health insurance stirred the profession's ranks with visions of clinical and economic bondage, few doctors would have believed how advantageous insurance practice would become for the average general practitioner. In spite of their initial opposition medical men did indeed do well under the insurance act and this study has measured that success politically, administratively and professionally.

On the political level the relationship between the profession and the health insurance act altered the organized arm of the nation's doctors. Before the passage of the insurance scheme the B.M.A. had a narrow base among the profession as a whole. While it claimed to speak for all doctors, the B.M.A. clearly did not. The Association was dominated by Fellows of the Royal Colleges and its leadership, composed or primarily Harley street specialists, knew little of the lot of the general practitioner who scratched a meager living from rural, industrial or club practices. For these impoverished medical men, who made up the bulk of the profession, medicine was not working in hospitals or among well-to-do society patients. Instead it was usually a cramped surgery, filled by too many dirty and destitute patients who could barely afford food, let alone medical fees.

The opposition to the insurance act in 1912 by the B.M.A. made the sharp divisions within the profession clear for all to see. The Association had become an outmoded relic of the nineteenth century that was illsuited to meet the challenges of the twentieth. In the wake of the 1912 defeat it became apparent to many of the B.M.A.'s leaders that if the Association was to survive it would have to broaden its base of support and convince the lowly general practitioner that it held his interests as dear as those of the specialist class. The process was slow but by the mid-twenties the position of the B.M.A. as the natural leader of the profession was no longer questioned.

Reflecting this change in the nature of the B.M.A., the Association became much more adept at political organization than it had ever been before the act. The B.M.A. was thrust into the center of politics and national social administration and became an effective fighting force under the direction of Alfred Cox, Henry Brackenbury and H. Guy Dain, who themselves emerged as Britain's first full time medical politicians. These men and others streamlined the profession's internal organization without altering its fundamental democratic qualities and guided it through the perils of high level negotiations with the government. The results were not always successful but as shown during the 1923 capitation dispute, organized medical opinion had developed a political power that could no longer be swept away casually.

No where are the effects of this transformation in medical organization and its leadership more apparent than in our consideration of the approved society question. Throughout this study the societies have been presented the medical profession's great political nemises. Prior to the coming of the insurance act the clubs and doctors had carried on an often bitter struggle. Although under a different guise, this battle, that had begun in the late nineteenth century, continued under the act. The societies and their spokesmen clearly animated the medical profession's political activities and the government adeptly exploited the doctors' fears to create a taught balance within the insurance scheme's administrative machinery. As long as medical men failed to stand united they, as did the government and the approved societies, knew that they would never be able to defend their own interests without the support of the government. But in 1923 the profession's rebuilt political organization was tested and doctors showed their adversaries that they were able to stand firm when they felt that their position within the act was threatened. Ths notable success effectively ended the advantage held by the government and the societies, who had always doubted the medical profession's willingness to back up their claims with unified political action. Thus for the doctors of Britain, the 1923 capitation fight was an important turning point in their relationship with the national health insurance scheme.

After 1923 it was evident that the profession as a whole had a new sense of confidence in itself, its institutions and its leaders. The Royal Commission and the Economy Bill of 1926 added to this feeling of political security within the insurance system. This new confidence was reflected on two levels. Politically the profession's leaders sought to reshape medical politics by launching their campaign for a general medical service for the nation. On another level after 1926 the profession's leaders actively involved themselves in the efforts to reduce over prescribing and lax certificcation -- two problems that they had earlier either ignored or denied.

This willingness to cooperate though, was a sign of more than the political success of the medical profession. Equally it reflects satisfaction with the nature of insurance administration. Rather than entering a new form of medical bondage, the medical profession became a full partner in the administration of the act's medical benefit. In general, administration was light handed and non-medical bureaucrats respected the difficulties of providing medical care. Despite intense outside political pressure, over prescribing and lax certification were dealt with cautiously and local variations, such as those in Manchester and Salford, were allowed to run their course. On the national level, the Insurance Acts Committee worked closely with the Ministry of Health's Insurance Department to resolve administrative questions and to iron out special difficulties that arose. Local administration was usually open to medical opinion and it had the advantage of being flexible and casual. At the same time, doctors at both the national and local levels were given by statute a firm grip upon problems involving medical ethics and discipline within the insurance medical service.

Finally, from the perspective of the history of medical practice in Britain, the act was a significant force in improving the lot of the general practitioner. Many of the privileges of professionalism were extended downward to all medical men. But professionalism is a luxury built upon a secure financial base and there is no doubt that the act was responsible for placing the British general practitioner upon a firm economic foundation. Never before had the practice of medicine at the primary care level been so profitable. For most doctors with industrial practices a middle class income was no longer a dream, it was a reality. The image of the starving medical man, reliant upon an impoverished working class population faded rapidly as insurance income shielded doctors from economic dislocation and bad debts. Also dependents of the insured added extra money to the pockets of medical practitioners and there is no doubt that the relationship between doctors and their patients was vastly improved by the elimination of the link between work and pay.

National health insurance in Britain was an attempt to dull the rough edges of a capitalist economy and within its limits it was a success. The scheme did not include maternity services or hospital care and was only the largest of many uncoordinated state sponsored health welfare activities. There were also abuses and inequalities within the system. Some patients received rushed and at times inadequate care and to be sure mistakes were made. In this, however, health insurance differed little from private practice and it was certainly a significant improvement upon the health services available to the laboring poor before 15 January 1913.

Finally the work of the insurance act has a wider importance for British society as a whole. To most, the 1911 scheme remains a discarded relic that has been completely obscured by the present National Health Service. For Aneurin Bevan and his Labour colleagues in 1945, the nation's health services needed to be based upon a simple principle of social faith. All those in need deserved medical attention by right and it was the state's responsibility to organize and provide adequate medical care. This was a new principle that had little in common with Lloyd George's 1911 health scheme. Nonetheless, when the Labour planners moved to construct their health service, they did little to alter the insurance act's system of primary care.

Approved societies disappeared and were replaced by a huge state bureaucracy. Hospitalization and specialist care were introduced. Still, for the general practitioner in 1948, the differences were hardly noticeable. Patients continued to register themselves on a list and payment was made according to a fixed capitation fee. Furthermore, the basic administrative structure remained essentially unchanged. Local panel committees were simply renamed local medical committees. The general practitioner service was placed under the direction of local executive councils, which were no more than the old insurance committees without the approved societies. Administrative boundaries and duties remained largely unchanged and throughout the general practitioner service, money continued to dominate internal medical politics.

In 1972 the National Health Service underwent a thorough reorganization. More direct local control was allowed and administrative districts were reduced in size. But the general practitioner service continued much as it had been since the medical profession was stampeded onto the panels in early 1913. Now a new Royal Commission has completed a study of the Health Service (Cmd. 7615, July 1979). The Commissioners heard evidence concerning the admittedly top heavy bureaucracy and proposals ranging from a voucher system for patients to ways of increasing the efficiency of the service's specialty care and hospitals. But few in Britain have seriously suggested that the general practitioner service be disbanded in favor of private practice upon the American model. This is perhaps the most lasting testimony to the wisdom of the framers of the national insurance act and the work of those doctors who became part of its medical service.

BIBLIOGRAPHY

PRIMARY SOURCES

1. Unpublished Private Documents

   a. Archives of the British Medical Association

   General Practice Committee, Official Reports and Committee Minutes.

   Health Services Committee, Official Reports and Committee Minutes.

   Insurance Acts Committee, Official Reports and Committee Minutes.

   Medico-Political Committee, Official Reports and Committee Minutes.

   State Sickness Insurance Committee, Official Reports and Committee Minutes.

   b. Archives of the Secretariat for the London Local Medical Committees

   Panel Committee of London, Minute Books 1913-1939.

2. Personal Interviews

   Dr. E. Colin-Russ. Interviewed by author, Bournemouth, 1 July 1978. Dr. Colin-Russ was active in BMA politics from the late thirties and still serves occasionally as an advisor to the government on health matters. He had a medium sized panel practice in London from the mid-twenties.

   Dr. Frank Gray. Interviewed by author, London, 10 July 1978. Dr. Gray was a prominent member of the London Panel Committee and was active in BMA politics throughout the thirties. He is still active in the Association and is a sometime contributor to the _Daily Telegraph_ on medical issues. His panel practice was near Clapham Junction.

   Dr. Solomen Wand. Interviewed by author, Birmingham, 15 July 1978. Dr. Wand served as a member of the Insurance Acts Committee in the mid-thirties and was intimately involved in many of the Committee's negotiations with the government. His panel practice was in Birmingham, where he has now retired.

3. Unpublished Government Documents

A. Public Record Office (Kew)

Administration of National Health Insurance (Ministry) of Health), Series I, II MH. 62-81. PIN. 2-5.

B. Wakefield Public Health Authority

West Riding Insurance Committee, Minute Books 1913-1939.

4. Published Government Documents

A. Official Report, House of Commons Debates

B. Parliamentary Papers

Papers by Command

C. Ministerial Publications and Departmental Reports (Ministry of Health and Social Security Library, Elephant and Castle)

An Interim Report to the Minister of Health by the Consultative Council on Medical and Allied Services, 1920. (The Dawson Report).

Annual Reports of the Chief Medical Officer of Health, 1920-1939.

Explanatory Statement as to Medical Benefit as Affecting Medical Practitioners, undated memorandum.

Memorandum on the English Scheme of National Health Insurance, with Special Reference to its Medical Aspects, 1929.

Ministry of Health and Scottish Office Court of Inquiry into Remuneration of Insurance Practice, 1923.

National Health Insurance Bill, 1920. Report by the Government Actuary Upon the Financial Provisions of the Bill, 1920.

National Health Insurance Circular A. S. 278. Control of Expenditure on Sickness and Disablement, May 1931.

National Health Insurance Joint Commission, Memorandum of Discussions on Certain Questions of Provision of Medical Services, at five of Members of the Medical Profession, 1918.

National Health Insurance Joint Commissioners. The Statutes, Regulations and Orders Relating to National Health Insurance, 1916.

National Health Insurance Memorandum 329/I.C. Memorandum on Certification if Incapacity for Work, Giving the Results of Recent Investigations as to the Causes of Increased Claims to Sickness and Disability Benefit, May 1931.

National Insurance Commissioners (England). Reports of Inquiries and Appeals Under the National Benefit Regulations, 1919.

Outline of National Health Insurance, unpublished pamphlet, 1935.

Registrar General's Annual Statistical Review of England and Wales, 1920-1939.

Reports of Inquiries and Appeals Under the National Health Insurance Medical Benefit Regulations, 1917-1924.

Reports of Inquiries and Appeals etc., Under the National Health Insurance Benefit Regulations, 1924.

Reports of the Committee Appointed by the Minister of Health to Consider the Distribution Amongst Insurance Committees of the Funds Available for Remuneration of Medical Practitioners for Treatment and Mileage, 1919.

Royal Commission on National Health Insurance, Minutes of Evidence, 2 vols., 1925. I Oral Evidence, II Appendix. 1925.

5. Letter Collections

A. Christopher Addison Papers (Bodleian Library)

Box 24 Correspondence with Ministry of Health Staff 1919.

Box 33 White Paper on Public Social Services.

Box 36 Correspondence with Geddes 1920.

Box 53 Correspondence with Morant 1920-1921.

Box 60 National Health Insurance Correspondence 1920-21.

Box 135 National Health Insurance Diary Notes.

6. Contemporary Pamphlet Literature

A. Ministry of Health and Social Security Library

Brend, William. An Examination of the Medical Provisions of the National Insurance Act. London: 1912.

Burnam, C. Clark. The Responsibilities, Rights, Duties and Privileges of Insured Persons and Medical Men Under the Insurance Act. London: 1913.

Burrows, Roland. Legal Problems Relating to Medical Services Under the National Insurance Act. London: 1912.

Dawson, Bertrand. (Lord Dawson) The Nation's Welfare--The Future of the Medical Profession. London: 1918.

Faculty of Insurance. Report of the Commission of Investigation into National Insurance. London: 1917.

Gray, A. Some Aspects of National Health Insurance. London: 1923.

Harris, R. W., and Sack, L. Shoeten. Medical Insurance Practice. London: 1924.

Hilton-Young, Edward. National Health and Pensions Insurance in Great Britain. London: 1932.

Hoffman, Frederick. An Address on the Methods and Results of National Health Insurance in Britain. New York: 1920.

________. More Facts and Fallacies of Compulsory Health Insurance. Newark, New Jersey: 1917.

________. National Health Insurance and the Friendly Societies. Newark, New Jersey: 1920.

________. Poor Law Aspects of National Health Insurance. Newark, New Jersey: 1920.

Joint Advisory Committee on Public Health. National Health Insurance Medical Benefit. London: 1923.

Newman, T. S. A Practical Guide to Medical Benefit: A Practical Guide to Medical Benefit for the Use of Insurance Persons, Agents and Branch Secretaries. London: 1923.

Tibbets, T. M. The Panel Doctor: His Duties and Perplexes. London: 1918.

Tixier, A. A Social Insurance Medical Service. London: 1934.

Watson, Alfred. National Health Insurance (A Statistical Review). London: 1927.

Wood, K. Policy of the British Government on National Health Insurance. Undated.

7. Contemporary Books, Memoirs and Biographies

"AGP". This Panel Business. London: John Bale, Sons and Danielson Ltd., 1933.

A Panel Doctor. On the Panel. London: Faber and Gwyer, 1926.

Addison, Christopher. Politics From Within, 1911-1918. 2 vols. London: Herbert Jenkins Ltd., 1924.

Armstrong, Barbara. The Health Insurance Doctor, His Role in Great Britain, Denmark and France. Princeton, New Jersey: Princeton University Press, 1939.

Banbury, Henry, ed. Lloyd George's Ambulance Wagon, Being the Memoirs of William Braithwaite. Portway: Bath: Cedric Chivers Ltd., 1970.

Booth, Charles. Life and Labour of the People of London. London: Macmillan, 1903.

Brand, W. A. Health and the State. London: Constable and Co., Ltd., 1917.

Brown, E. and Wood, K. The Law of National Health Insurance: The National Insurance Act 1911-1918. London: The Insurance Publishing Co., 1929.

Cox, Alfred. Among the Doctors. London: Christopher Johnson, 1950.

Cronin, A. J. The Citadel. Boston: Little Brown and Company, 1937.

Falk, I. S. Security Against Sickness. New York: Da Capo Press Reprint, 1972.

Forster, W. J. and Taylor, F. G. National Health Insurance. London: Sir Issac Pittman & Sons, Ltd.

Harris, Robert. National Health Insurance in Great Britain, 1911-1946. London: G. Allen & Unwin, 1946.

________. "National Health Insurance Medical Service in Great Britain." Canadian Journal of Public Health, 22 (February 1931), pp. 55-69.

Hill of Luton, (Lord). Both Sides of the Hill. London: Heinemann, 1964.

Hill, Norman. War and Insurance. London: Humphrey Milford, 1927.

International Labour Conference Report on Sickness, No. 7, 10th session. Geneva: International Labour Office, May 1927.

Lesser, H. The National Insurance Acts, 1936-1938: With Explanatory Notes, Reported Cases, Decisions of the Minister of Health and Statutory Rules and Orders. London: Stone and Cox, 1939.

McCleary, G. F. National Health Insurance. London: H. K. Lewis and Company, 1932.

Morgan, Gerald. Public Relief of Sickness. London: Allen and Unwin, 1923.

National Health and Unemployment Insurance, Complete Information for the Employer. Liverpool: T. H. Woodrow & Co., 1920.

National Insurance Yearbook, 1913. London: The Insurance Publishing Company, 1913.

Newman, George. The Building of a Nation's Health. London: Macmillan & Co., 1939.

Newman, T. S. The Insurance of Women Under the National Health Insurance Act. London: Wyman & Sons Ltd., 1933.

Newsholme, Arthur. Fifty Years in Public Health. London: G. Allen and Unwin, 1935.

________. International Studies: Prevention and Treatment of Disease. 3 vols. London: George Allen & Son, 1931.

________. Medicine and the State. London: George Allen & Unwin, 1932.

________. Public Health and Insurance, An American Address. Baltimore: Johns Hopkins Press, 1920.

Newsholme, Arthur. The Last Thirty Years in Public Health. London: George Allen & Unwin, 1936.

________. The Story of Modern Preventive Medicine. Baltimore: The Williams & Wilkins Company, 1929.

Orr, Douglass and Orr, Jean Walker. Health Insurance with Medical Care. New York: Macmillan Company, 1938.

P.E.P. (Political and Economic Planning). Report on the British Health Services. London: P.E.P., 1937.

The Panel Doctor's Pocket-Book. London: J.C. Eno, 1933.

Roberts, Harry. A National Health Policy. London: Labour Publishing Co., 1923.

Stamp, Winifred. The Doctor Himself: An Unorthodox Biography of Harry Roberts, 1871-1946. London: Hamish Hamilton, 1949.

Willis, Addington. National Health Insurance Through Approved Societies. London: University of London Press, 1914.

8. Contemporary Newspapers and Periodicals

British Medical Journal

Contemporary Review

Daily Express

Daily Mail

Daily Mirror

Daily News

Daily Sketch

Daily Telegraph

Economist

Evening Standard

Glasgow Evening Citizen

Glasgow Herald

Insurance Mail

John Bull

Journal of the American Medical Association

Journal of the National Association of Clerks to Insurance Committees

Journal of the National Association of the Officers of Public Health

Lancet

Liverpool Daily Post

Manchester Guardian

Medical World

National Insurance Gazette and Sickness Review

National Insurance Weekly

New Statesman

Nineteenth Century and After

Post Graduate Medical Journal

Practitioner

Spectator

Sunday Pictorial

The Star

The Times (London)

Westminster Review

SECONDARY SOURCES

1. Monographs and Articles

Abel-Smith, Brian. *The Hospitals in England and Wales 1800-1948*. Cambridge: Harvard University Press, 1964.

Brand, Jeanne L. *Doctors and the State*. Baltimore: Johns Hopkins Press, 1965.

Bruce, Maurice. *The Coming of the Welfare State.* London: Batsford, 1961.

Collier, Richard. *The Plague of the Spanish Lady: The Influenza Pandemic of 1918-1919*. New York: Atheneum, 1974.

Deacon, Alan. In Search of the Scrounger: The Administration of Unemployment Insurance in Britain, 1920-1931. Occasional Papers on Social Administration, No. 60. London: G. Bell and Sons, 1976.

Department of National Health and Welfare, Research Division. Health Insurance in Britain, 1911-1948. Social Security Series, Memorandum No. 11. Ottowa: Department of National Health and Welfare, March 1952.

Eckstein, Harry. The English Health Service. Cambridge: Harvard University Press, 1958.

________. Pressure Group Politics: The Case of the British Medical Association. Stanford: Stanford University Press, 1960.

Frazer, W. History of Public Health, 1834-1934. London: Harrison and Sons Ltd., 1950.

Freeden, Michael. The New Liberalism. Oxford: Clarendon Press, 1978.

French, Richard. Antivivisection and Medical Science in Victorian Society. Princeton: Princeton University Press, 1975.

Gilbert, Bentley. British Social Policy 1914-1939. Ithaca: Cornell University Press, 1970.

________. "David Lloyd George: The Reform of British Landholding and the Budget." The Historical Journal, 21, 1 (1978): 117-141.

________. The Evolution of National Insurance in Great Britain. London: Michael Joseph, 1966.

Gosden, P.H.J.H. Voluntary Associations in Nineteenth-Century Britain. London: B. T. Batsford, 1973.

Grigg, John. Lloyd George: The People's Champion. London: Eyre Methuen, 1978.

Hill, Charles and Woodcock, John. The National Health Service. London: Christopher Johnson, 1949.

Hill, A. Bradford. "The Doctor's Day and Pay." Journal of the Royal Statistical Society. Vol. 64, (1951): 1-34.

Honigsbaum, Frank. The Struggle for the Ministry of Health. Occasional Papers on Social Administration, No. 37. London: G. Bell and Sons, 1970.

Johnson, Paul. Land Fit for Heroes. Chicago: University of Chicago Press, 1968.

Lees, D. S. and Cooper, M. H. "Payment Per-Item-Of-Service: The Manchester and Salford Experience, 1913-28." Medical Care, 2 (July-September 1964): 151-156.

Levy, Herman. National Health Insurance. London: Cambridge University Press, 1944.

Marks, John. The Conference of Local Medical Committees and Its Executive: A Review of Sixty Years. London: British Medical Association, 1972.

________. The History and Development of Local Mecical Committees, Their Conference and Its Executive. Edinburgh: Unpublished Dissertation, 1974.

Morris, R. J. Cholera 1832. London: Croom Helm, 1976.

Little, Ernest Muirhead. History of the British Medical Association 1832-1932. London: British Medical Association, 1932.

Peterson, M. Jeanne. The Medical Profession in Mid-Victorian London. Berkeley: University of California Press, 1978.

Roberts, David. Victorian Origins of the British Welfare State. New Haven: Yale University Press, 1960.

Rosenberg, Charles E. The Cholera Years. University of Chicago Press, 1962.

Searle, G. R. The Quest for National Efficiency. Berkeley: University of California Press, 1971.

Shyrock, Richard Harrison. Medicine and Society in America 1660-1860. Ithaca: Cornell University Press, 1975.

Singer, Charles and Underdown, E. Ashworth. A Short History of Medicine. Oxford: Oxford University Press, 1962.

Smith, F. B. People's Health 1830-1910. London: Croom Helm, 1979.

Stevens, Rosemary. Medical Practice in Modern England, The Impact of Specialization and State Medicine. New Haven: Yale University Press, 1966.

Titmuss, Richard M. Problems of Social Policy. London: United Kingdom Civil Histories, 1950.

Vaughan, Paul. _The Doctors' Commons, A Short History of the British Medical Association_. London: Heinemann, 1959.

Woodroofe, Kathleen. "The Making of the Welfare State in England: A Summary of Its Origins and Development." Henry R. Winkler ed. _Twentieth Century Britain_. New York: New Viewpoints, 1976.

Woodward, John and Richards, David, ed. _Health Care and Popular Medicine in Nineteenth Century England_. London: Croom Helm, 1977.

Woodward, John. _To Do the Sick No Harm, A Study of the British Voluntary Hospital System to 1875_. London: Routledge & Kegan Paul, 1974.

INDEX